THE WORLD'S GREAT
CHESS GAMES

Other Books by Reuben Fine

BASIC CHESS ENDINGS
CHESS THE EASY WAY
THE IDEAS BEHIND THE CHESS OPENINGS
CHESS MARCHES ON!
THE WORLD'S A CHESSBOARD
PRACTICAL CHESS OPENINGS
THE MIDDLE GAME IN CHESS
THE TOURNAMENT AT AMSTERDAM 1936
THE ALEKHINE-EUWE MATCH 1937
MODERN CHESS OPENINGS 6TH EDITION
THE KASHDAN-RESHEVSKY MATCH 1942

With Fred Reinfeld

THE ALEKHINE-BOGOLJUBOW MATCH 1934
DR. LASKER'S CHESS CAREER

With Dr. Max Euwe

THE CHESS KEY

THE
WORLD'S GREAT
Chess Games

Edited by

REUBEN FINE

CROWN PUBLISHERS, INC.

NEW YORK

LIBRARY OF CONGRESS CATALOG CARD
NUMBER 51–12014

PRINTED IN THE UNITED STATES OF AMERICA
BY KINGSPORT PRESS, INC., KINGSPORT, TENN.

Contents

1.

The Game of Kings

CHESS was first played in India about the seventh or eighth century. For more than a thousand years it remained the pleasure of the elite, the "game of kings." The names and powers of the pieces, and the set-up of the board were originally symbols of fierce wars.

Little is known of the early development of chess; there are only scattered references here and there. We do know that it was always a game which aroused violent passions. One story has it that in India players sometimes became so fanatically absorbed that they gave up wives, businesses, everything else, just to play. Some records of the Middle Ages tell us of the clerics being chided by their superiors for forgetting the ways of God and losing themselves over the checkered board. Such addiction to chess is familiar to everybody who has ever come close to the game. Usually, in my experience, people become violently attached to chess for a few years and then give it up. But with many, chess is like a delicious drug which offers such heavenly delights that they can never tear themselves away from it completely.

Some time during the Middle Ages chess was brought to Europe, where for several centuries it remained an obscure pastime for a few. Perhaps it was the alteration of the rules which led to the beginning of greater popularization, for around the sixteenth century we find the changes taking place that led to the present rules. Yet even today there are many people who play according to a brand of special rules which they have picked up somewhere or other. As a matter of fact, when I learned how to play, I was taught the old Italian rule for castling: all the pieces except the King and the Rook have to be cleared off the last rank before the King can exchange squares with the Rook. Several amusing incidents come to mind of how many people play the game in a manner most decidedly not according to Hoyle. When I was in college, a professor asked me to play a few games with him. I drew the white pieces and opened with an advance of the Queen's Pawn. He protested violently, claiming that the only permissible opening move was the advance of the King's Pawn! Some years ago, I was playing in a tournament in Hollywood. A number of the movie stars came to watch the play, and once one invited me to a few games. After seven moves I found myself in check and interposed a Pawn. This was illegal, he claimed; the only legal way to meet a check was to move the King. I convinced him that interposition was permissible, and proceeded to win the game. His alibi was that I won because I used my rules—if we'd used his rules he would have won!

Modern chess really was born in the sixteenth century. The first great player of whom we have any note is Ruy Lopez. He not only was the strongest of his time, but he also laid down a pattern which many later masters were to follow: he wrote a book. The treatise is hardly worth much by modern standards. A sample can show how much chess has advanced since then. Here he analyzes the opening named after him:

1.	P–K4	P–K4
2.	Kt–KB3	Kt–QB3
3.	B–Kt5	B–B4

This is now known as the classical defense, no doubt revolutionary in its day.

4.	P–B3	P–Q3
5.	P–Q4	P x P
6.	P x P	B–Kt5ch
7.	Kt–B3	B–Q2
8.	B–Kt5	Kt–B3
9.	Q–Q3	B x Ktch ?
10.	P x B "with the better game."

Position after 10. P x B—"with the better game."

Ruy Lopez must have been aware of some of the major principles of development, but his combinative skill was hardly brilliant. Here is the most impressive example that I have been able to find:

BLACK: *Leonardo da Cutrie* (MADRID, 1575)

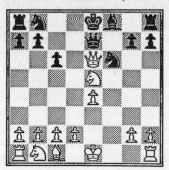

WHITE: Ruy Lopez

1. Q–B8ch   Q–Q1
2. Q x Qch   K x Q
3. Kt–B7ch and wins.

In the sixteenth century long division was so complicated that it was taught in the universities; today it comes in the fourth grade. The advance of chess has been almost as great.

Chess mastery has a way of settling in one or two countries. In the sixteenth and seventeenth centuries its greatest exponents were found in Spain and Italy. After Lopez, the most eminent figure in the chess world was the Italian, Giacchino Greco, who lived in the seventeenth century. His play already represents some improvement over Lopez, although it is hopelessly backwoodsish by modern standards. Here is a specimen combination from the collection which he began in 1619:

BLACK: *Unknown*

WHITE: Greco

1. B—K6ch !!   K x B
2. Q—K8ch   KKt—K2
3. P—Q5 mate

Philidor

In the eighteenth century chess supremacy began to leave Spain and Italy and emerge in France and England. The outstanding master of this period was the Frenchman François André Danican Philidor, who was universally regarded as the strongest player and greatest theoretician of his time, though the title of world champion was not yet in existence. He towers head and shoulders over his predecessors. He swept all opposition before him in his travels on the Continent and in England. Besides being a great player, he was the first to write a worthwhile book on the game. His *Analyse des Echecs*, first published in 1749, has gone through more editions and been more widely circulated than any other chess book. It is still often encountered in second-hand bookstores all over the world. Chess players are a hard lot to please—they won't buy a book unless they get something out of it! The success of Philidor's work shows that he had captured some of the basic principles of chess and been able to put them down in readable form. His analysis of the ending with Rook and Bishop against Rook, known as Philidor's Position, is still considered sound. Here, at last, was a man whose technical skill could for the first time be compared to some degree with that of the moderns, although he was still quite inferior by our standards.

Philidor also began the custom of blindfold exhibitions, in which the single player takes on a number of opponents without sight of the board or pieces. He could play three boards, which is of course trivial compared to the present world's record of forty-five. But three was considered such a stupendous achievement in his day that he had witnesses attest to it, and took an advertisement in the paper to record for posterity that it had actually been done. Two hundred years later Najdorf was greeted with the same incredulity in his forty-five board exhibition. Perhaps two hundred years from now, when the average master will routinely be playing a hundred boards blindfold, people will look at Najdorf's achievement with the same amused condescension that we look at Philidor's.

Besides his chess prowess, Philidor was also a musician of considerable note. He composed a number of operas, some of which are still performed. His bust adorns the Paris Opera. Rousseau's *Confessions* mentions Philidor many times with reference to music and chess.

Philidor was famous for his ability to handle the Pawns. He is reputed to have said that the "Pawn is the soul of the game." Here is a sample of his play:

CAPT. SMITH   PHILIDOR

King's Bishop's Opening
London, 1790

1. P—K4   P—K4
2. B—B4   Kt—KB3
3. P—Q3   P—B3

To occupy the center.

4. B—KKt5 ?   . . . .

White has little feeling for positional chess. Anything else is better!

4. . . . .   P—KR3
5. B x Kt   Q x B
6. Kt—QB3   P—QKt4
7. B—Kt3   P—QR4
8. P—QR3   B—B4
9. Kt—B3   P—Q3
10. Q—Q2   B—K3

11. B x B   P x B !

An excellent idea. This opens the KB file for the attack. Philidor's mastery of positional concepts is striking, though he neglects the safety of his King too much.

12. O—O   P—Kt4
13. P—R3   Kt—Q2

14. Kt—KR2   P—R4
15. P—KKt3   . . . .

White's play is impossibly bad throughout. He is playing move on move with no clear idea of the consequences.

15. . . . .   K—K2
16. K—Kt2   P—Q4
17. P—B3   Kt—B1
18. Kt—K2   Kt—Kt3
19. P—B3   QR—KKt1
20. P—Q4 ?   B—Kt3
21. QP x P   Q x P

22. Kt—Q4 ?   . . . .

Better was P x P first.

22. . . . .   K—Q2
23. QR—K1   P—KR5
24. Q—KB2   B—B2 ?

RP x P immediately was more precise.

25. Kt—K2   . . . .

Missing the obvious KP x P.

25. . . . .   RP x P
26. Q x P   Q x Qch
27. Kt x Q   Kt—B5ch
28. K—R1   R x P
29. R—KKt1   . . . .

29.	R x Ktch !
30. K x R	R—R1ch
31. Kt—R5	R x Ktch
32. K—Kt3	Kt—R6ch
33. K—Kt4	R—R5 mate

Not great chess, as yet, but a long stride forward in the development of general principles.

2.

From Philidor to Morphy

AFTER Philidor chess supremacy remained in the hands of the French for a long time. Philidor was succeeded by Deschapelles, who was also a noted whist player. And Deschapelles was followed by his pupil Labourdonnais. In those days chess matches were leisurely, almost informal affairs. There were no clocks to harry the contestants—each player could take as much time as he wanted to.

Labourdonnais' greatest achievement was his marathon contest against the English champion Alexander MacDonnell, which the Frenchman won by a ratio of three games to two. From this match dates the first immortal game of chess history.

LABOURDONNAIS

MACDONNELL

50th Match Game, London, 1834

Queen's Gambit Accepted

1. P–Q4   P–Q4
2. P–QB4   P x P
3. P–K4   . . . .

A move which is today considered inferior. The principles of center play were but half understood at that time.

3. . . . .   P–K4 !
4. P–Q5   P–KB4
5. Kt–QB3   Kt–KB3
6. B x P   B–B4

Black's position is freer.

7. Kt–B3   Q–K2

8. B–KKt5 ?   B x Pch !
9. K–B1   . . . .

For if 9. K x B, Q–B4ch.

9. . . . .   B–Kt3
10. Q–K2   P–B5
11. R–Q1   . . . .

Preparing to lose.

11. . . . .   B–Kt5
12. P–Q6   P x P
13. Kt–Q5   . . . .

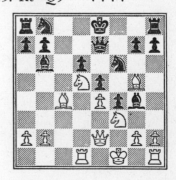

7

13.	Kt x Kt !!

The move White had over-looked.

14. B x Q	Kt—K6ch
15. K—K1	K x B

Black has two pieces and a powerful attack for the Queen. Subsequent analysis has never been able to demonstrate a really adequate defense.

16. Q—Q3	R—Q1
17. R—Q2	Kt—B3
18. P—QKt3	. . . .

P—QR3 was better, but 18. . . . . QR—B1 still retains the bind.

18.	B—QR4
19. P—QR3	QR—B1
20. R—Kt1	. . . .

White unsuccessfully struggles to free himself.

20.	P—QKt4
21. B x P	B x Kt
22. P x B	Kt—Q5
23. B—B4	Kt x Pch
24. K—B2	Kt x R(Q7)
25. R x Pch	K—B3
26. R—B7ch	K—Kt3
27. R—Kt7	Kt(Q7) x B
28. P x Kt	R x P
29. Q—Kt1	. . . .

It is curious how the Knight keeps the White Queen immobile.

29.	B—Kt3
30. K—B3	R—B6
31. Q—R2	Kt—B5 dis ch
32. K—Kt4	R—KKt1
33. R x B	P x R
34. K—R4	K—B3
35. Q—K2	R—Kt3
36. Q—R5	Kt—K6

White Resigns.

There is no defense against . . . Kt—Kt7ch followed by R—R6 mate.

MacDonnell was in turn on the receiving end of a brilliant combination against Captain Evans, inventor of the Gambit which dominated tournament chess for almost a century. Here is the position:

London, about 1820

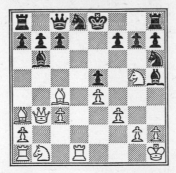

EVANS   MACDONNELL

1. R x Ktch !!   Q x R
2. Kt x BP !!   Q—R5

The prettiest part of the combination is, as so often, untold. If 2. . . . Kt x Kt; 3. B—Kt5ch !, P—B3; 4. Q—K6ch, Q—K2; 5. Q x Q mate, and if 2. . . . B x

Kt; 3. B x Bch, Kt x B; 4. Q—K6ch and mate next. But 2. . . . Q—B3 was much better than the text.

3. Q—Kt5ch   P—B3
4. Q x KPch   K—Q2
5. Q—K6ch   K—B2
6. B—Q6 mate

In France the leading player after Labourdonnais was the colorful Pierre Charles Fourné de St. Amant. St. Amant had a variety of talents apart from chess. For a while he worked as secretary to the governor of French Guiana—a position which he lost because he protested against the slave-trade. Later he tried his hand at the stage, and then he became a successful wine merchant. In the revolution of 1848 he was a captain in the National Guard and saved the Tuileries. In 1851 he was French consul in California.

St. Amant held sway until the Englishman Howard Staunton dethroned him in a series of memorable matches in 1843. As with so many other losers, at least he had the satisfaction of winning the most brilliant game.

ST. AMANT   STAUNTON
13th Match Game,
Paris, 1843
Queen's Gambit Declined

1. P—Q4   P—K3
2. P—QB4   P—Q4
3. P—K3   Kt—KB3

4. Kt—QB3   P—B4
5. Kt—B3   Kt—B3

Still a standard opening today.

6. P—QR3   . . . .

Not a very good move, but the intricacies of modern positional play were then *terra incognita*.

6.	B–K2
7. B–Q3	O–O
8. O–O	P–QKt3
9. P–QKt3	B–Kt2

10. BP x P	KP x P
11. B–Kt2	P x P
12. P x P	B–Q3

Both sides have lost time needlessly.

13. R–K1	P–KR3
14. R–QB1	R–B1
15. R–B2	R–B2
16. QR–K2	Q–B1
17. P–R3	Kt–Q1
18. Q–Q2	P–R3

Neither player has any definite plan in mind; both are jockeying for an opening.

19. P–QKt4	Kt–K3
20. B–B5	Kt–K5

Better was . . . B–B5.

21. Kt x Kt	P x Kt
22. P–Q5 !	. . . .

A move which was hailed by the French as a "Labourdonnais' Attack."

22.	P x Kt ?

The decisive error. B–B5 was essential.

23. R x Kt	Q–Q1

24. B–B6 !!	. . . .

The splendid point.

24.	P x B

25. R x B !	. . . .

Here it is reported that the spectators broke out into enthusiastic applause. If 25. . . . . Q x R; 26. Q x RP and mates.

25.	K–Kt2
26. R x Q	R x R

Nowadays one would resign here.

27. B–K4	P x P
28. Q–B4	R–B5
29. Q–Kt4ch	K–B1
30. Q–R5	K–K2
31. P–Q6ch	K x P
32. B x B	K–B2
33. B x RP	Black Resigns.

Howard Staunton

Howard Staunton was one of the most vital personalities in chess history. He burst upon the game at a relatively late age—about thirty. Born in 1810, his first interest was in the theater and, after a brief interlude as an actor, he became an eminent Shakespearean scholar, one of the leading authorities of his day. His annotations on Shakespeare's writings are still highly prized today.

It was not until 1840 that he came upon the chess scene. He defeated Popert, then the strongest player at the London club, and thereby immediately acquired considerable standing as a master. Because of his literary bent he began a magazine called the British Miscellany and Chess Player's Chronicle which ran for a number of years. It soon became evident that he was by far the strongest player in England, and he now devoted the major part of his time to the game. By temperament he was an extremely aggressive, vigorous man who loved nothing better than a good argument in print. In the course of his life, he engaged in countless violent attacks on his contemporaries. A good example is this passage from his journal:

"A Barrister, Temple.—Calls our attention to the ridiculous alterations of the Laws of Chess, by G. Walker, in his New Treatise on Chess, and asks, 'Is it possible that such absurdities are sanctioned by the London Chess Club?' The only sanction given to Walker's puerilities by the committee is to laugh at them. His books on chess are no authority except among the lowest class of players."

Beside endearing him to his enemies, these diatribes paradoxically enough earned him the admiration of a large part of the chess community who were not personally involved. And there was no question but that Staunton was doing great work for chess. He wrote, he played, he traveled all over, lecturing and giving simultaneous exhibitions. He was obviously a man of tremendous egotism. This is true of so many great chess masters that one is prone to wonder whether this quality is not inherent in the personal equipment needed for the game. His egotism found an outlet in his passions for the game, and he had a way of carrying people along with him.

It is of some psychological interest that despite the great violence he displayed in personal quarrels, his style was remarkably placid at the chess board. This contrast between the personality and the chess style is again not unusual among masters. All too often we see milquetoasts like Spielmann who pour their aggressions onto the chessboard, and choleric geniuses like Staunton whose passions almost vanish when they come to play.

Because of his style, Staunton's play is not very impressive to our eyes. Morphy described him as the author of a *Handbook* and some "devilish bad games." The best game of his that I have been able to find is from his match with St. Amant.

ST. AMANT   **STAUNTON**
5th Match Game, Paris, 1843
Sicilian Defense

1. P—K4   P—QB4
2. P—KB4   . . . .

Now obsolete, but then routine.

2. . . . .   P—K3
3. Kt—KB3   Kt—QB3
4. P—B3   P—Q4
5. P—K5   Q—Kt3

Labourdonnais used to play P—B3. I would prefer 5. . . . P—Q5.

6. B—Q3   B—Q2
7. B—B2   R—B1
8. O—O   Kt—R3
9. P—KR3   B—K2
10. K—R2   P—B4
11. P—R3   P—QR4

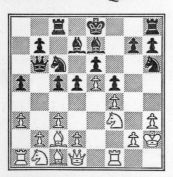

The typical close game of that period.

12. P—QR4   . . . .

If the subtleties of some of these moves escape the reader, he need not be too surprised; they escape me too.

12. . . . .   Kt—B2
13. P—Q4   P—R3
14. R—K1   . . . .

To prevent . . . P—Kt4.

14. . . . .   P—Kt3
15. Kt—R3   P x P
16. Kt x P   Kt x Kt
17. P x Kt   P—Kt4
18. Kt—Kt5   . . . .

St. Amant has no clear-cut plan.

18. . . . .   B x Kt
19. P x B   R—B5?
20. B—Q3!   R—QB1

For if 20. . . . R x P; 21. B—K3. Staunton's maneuver was a loss of time.

21. B—K2   P x P
22. R—B1   . . . .

Better was B x P.

22. . . . .   Kt—Kt4
23. B x P   Kt—K5
24. R—B1   R x R
25. Q x R   K—Q2
26. Q—K3   B—Kt4
27. B—Q3   R—KKt1
28. B x Kt   QP x B
29. B x B   P x B
30. Q—QKt3   P—Kt5

31. R—Q1? . . . .

Overly cautious. With R x P! he should have been able to draw anyhow.

31. . . . . P x P
32. Q x P Q—Q1

Here Staunton comments: "The latter portion of this game is conducted with remarkable caution and skill by both parties." Staunton, like many another master after him, was in the habit of praising his opponent when he won, thereby proving how good Staunton was. From time immemorial chessmasters have excelled at two things: chess and alibis.

33. P—Q5 K—B1

Not 33 . . . R—R1; 34. P x Pch.

34. Q—B3ch K—Kt1
35. P—Q6 P—B5
36. Q—B5 P—K6
37. Q—B2 Q—R5ch
38. K—Kt1 R—QB1

39. Q—K2 . . . .

Losing immediately, but there was no good defense.

39. . . . . R—R1

White Resigns.
It is recorded that this game lasted 9½ hours; today it would take between 4 and 5. The introduction of the chess clock has speeded up the game and made for better chess.

LONDON 1851 — CHESS TOURNAMENTS BEGIN

Chess had reached such universal popularity by the middle of the nineteenth century that the idea of a tournament to determine the relative strengths of masters in different countries came into being. It was the British, spurred on both by Staunton's prowess and aggressiveness, who took the initiative. In the year 1851 London had a "Great Exhibition of Art and Industry," and this also seemed a propitious occasion to hold a chess tournament. Invitations were extended to the leading players in the world but, for one reason or another, many were forced to decline. Still, it was a very strong contest. There was Kieseritzky from Paris, Szen and Loewenthal from Hungary, Anderssen and Mayet from Germany, Staunton, Bird, and a number of others from England—sixteen players in all.

The tournament was run by the knockout system which prevails today in tennis. This system allows too many accidental results in chess, and it has since been abandoned in favor of the round-robin method, where each player contests one game (sometimes two or more) with every other. In the third round Anderssen met and defeated Staunton by a score of 4–1. Anderssen was now the unofficial champion of the world; the title was not yet in existence.

Adolf Anderssen

Pure combinative chess reached its climax in Adolf Anderssen. He represents the spirit of sacrifice, free and unrestrained.

Anderssen's life bridges the chasm from the isolated, localized chess activity of the early nineteenth century to modern international tournament play. When he began, there were no tournaments, no clocks, virtually no chess magazines, not even clearly established rules; when he died, master chess, though still relatively young, had already begun its march forward to the place it occupies in modern society.

From the age of nine, when his father taught him the moves, chess was Anderssen's major interest. Breslau, where he was born in 1818, was one of the most flourishing centers in Germany, the most vital chess stimulant of the last century. The local worthies were no great masters, but they were tough competition. And visiting celebrities—Bledow, von der Lasa, Mayet, Loewenthal, among others—were frequent.

Anderssen was given every chance to develop his genius. For a while chess was so important that school was neglected, but that stage did not last long. Perhaps because his parents were poor, his only personal ambition, apart from chess, was to find a secure berth as a teacher, and biographical details are accordingly meager: tutor in a private family in Pomerania from 1847 to 1851, instructor in German and mathematics at a gymnasium in Breslau for the remainder of his life. He never married, though we are told that he could "give a gallant turn" to conversations with women. With the personal problem solved, all his energy could be applied to chess.

There is a curious contrast between his over-the-board brilliance and uninspired safety first attitude in everyday affairs. For a few brief months, in 1851, he toyed with the idea of chess as a profession, but there was too much uncertainty involved. His letters from tournaments consist almost entirely of chess chatter and a detailed enumeration of the "scandalous" prices in restaurants and hotels. We are reminded of Spielmann, whose main concern, apart from chess, was to accumulate enough money to buy limitless quantities of beer. The real lives of dazzlingly brilliant chess geniuses are sometimes hopelessly dull.

Curiously, Anderssen first became prominent as a problem composer. In 1842 a collection of his problems was published although he was scarcely known as a player at that time. Those were the days before international tournaments, and reputations were not easy to establish. Anderssen rose to fame by challenging and beating everybody and anybody he could lay his hands on. By 1846, when chess magazines were first issued in Germany, he was a contributing editor to the *Deutsche Schachzeitung* and one of the leading masters in the country; by 1851 he was recognized as the best.

Up to that time Germany had not yet produced any really great master. Since the days of Philidor, French and English players had dominated the chess world. The match between Staunton and St. Amant in 1844 was generally looked upon as one for the top honors, and Anderssen, in company with everybody else, thought of Staunton as the greatest alive.

Then came London 1851, the beginning of modern chess. The chief absentee was St. Amant, who refused to abandon the California gold rush for mere chess. The conditions do not look very palatable today. Everybody had to pay his own expenses. There was an entrance fee of five pounds. Players were classified by an unexplained method.

Despite all the handicaps, and a certain feeling of insecurity, Anderssen won first prize in splendid style. It was a sensational victory, and Anderssen was universally acclaimed as the world's leading master. Though the title was not in use, he undoubtedly was the first world champion in modern times.

From 1851 to his death in 1878, Anderssen played chess whenever and wherever he could get a chance. There were few tournaments (none at all from 1851 to 1857) but countless offhand games, formal and informal matches. Though he lost to his two great rivals, Morphy (in 1858) and Steinitz (in 1866), to the end of his days Anderssen remained one of the two or three best in the world. After 1851, first prizes at London 1862 and Baden-Baden 1870 (almost unique for a man of fifty-two) were the climaxes of his career.

Anderssen's untiring zeal and love for the game certainly did much to give Germany the preeminent chess role it had until 1914. Recognition came early and was most gratifying. In 1865, Breslau University awarded him an honorary doctorate—the only time in history the academic world has ever granted chess more than a perfunctory nod.

There is a natural tendency to compare Anderssen with the two men who outdistanced him, Morphy and Steinitz. Morphy beat him mercilessly for a very simple reason: Morphy understood the importance of the center, while Anderssen did not. Anderssen developed haphazardly, seized any attacking opportunity that offered at the earliest moment, and often succeeded brilliantly. But such tactics could not work against a solid position managed by a real master.

The difference between Morphy's attacks and Anderssen's is quite obvious: with Morphy the attack flowed out of the position, with Anderssen it was always an inspiration of the moment, not organically connected to what preceded it.

Anderssen himself did not fully appreciate why he had lost! After the match he wrote: "He who plays with Morphy must abandon all hope of catching him in a trap, no matter how cunningly laid, but must assume that it is so clear to Morphy that there can be no question of a false step." This opinion, which does not give any credit at all to Morphy's revolutionary treatment of the center in the opening, epitomizes Anderssen's style: sacrifice, attack, with reason if possible, but if not, sacrifice, attack.

In a comparison with Steinitz, Anderssen comes off somewhat better, chiefly because Steinitz had not yet reached full stature. Steinitz won by outcombining his renowned opponent; the positional ideas which are the foundation of present-day chess came somewhat later.

Anderssen's true greatness appears when we examine his predecessors and early contemporaries. By and large, chess even at its best in Labourdonnais, MacDonnell, St. Amant and Staunton, was, despite the frequency of gambits, boring, long-winded and full of blunders. Opening play was stodgy and shot through with incredible distortions; there were even some who seriously argued that odds of Pawn and move are an advantage because they allow Black to develop very quickly and attack along the open KB file. Into this arid waste Anderssen came with the force of a mountain torrent. His chess was fresh, lively, full of ideas, happy inspirations, novelties and surprises. Sacrifices, in season and out, were the main vehicle of his genius; few have ever demonstrated greater ingenuity in their conception and execution.

In a very real sense, Anderssen was the first modern master; certainly, with his decisive flair for combinations he did much to pave the way for modern chess.

His two most famous games have gone down in chess history as the "Evergreen" and the "Immortal." Here is the Immortal Game:

ANDERSSEN	KIESERITZKY
London, 1851	
King's Gambit	

1. P—K4	P—K4
2. P—KB4	P x P
3. B—B4	Q—R5ch

Nowadays . . . P—Q4 followed by quick development is preferred.

4. K—B1	P—QKt4
5. B x P	Kt—KB3
6. Kt—KB3	Q—R3
7. P—Q3	Kt—R4

8. Kt—R4 . . . .

Anderssen's feel for the attack comes to the fore. Other moves mean much less.

8.	Q—Kt4
9. Kt—B5	P—QB3
10. P—KKt4 !	Kt—B3
11. R—Kt1 !	P x B
12. P—KR4	Q—Kt3
13. P—R5	Q—Kt4
14. Q—B3	. . . .

Threatening B x P. The way in which the Black Queen has been bottled up is most ingenious.

14.	Kt—Kt1
15. B x P	Q—B3

16. Kt—B3	B—B4
17. Kt—Q5	Q x P

18. B—Q6 !!   B x R

The sacrifices are beautiful. If 18. . . . Q x Rch; 19. K—K2, Q x R; 20. Kt x Pch, K—Q1; 21. B—B7 mate!

19. P—K5 !!! . . . .

This magnificent quiet move is the key to the combination.

19.	Q x Rch
20. K—K2	Kt—QR3
21. Kt x Pch	K—Q1
22. Q—B6ch !!	Kt x Q
23. B—K7 mate	

Here is the conclusion of the Evergreen game:

BLACK: *Dufresne*

WHITE: *Anderssen*

1. QR–Q1   Q x Kt
2. R x Ktch   Kt x R
3. Q x Pch !!!   . . . .

The point.

3. . . . .   K x Q
4. B–KB5ch   K–K1
5. B–Q7ch   K–B1 (or Q1)
6. B x Kt mate

Anderssen's games are so chock full of brilliancies that a whole volume could be devoted to them. Here are a few which are a perennial source of delight:

3 Anderssen Brilliancies

Anderssen—TO PLAY

(Breslau 1863—offhand)

Rosanes

1. . . . .   B–K4 !
2. P–R4   Q–B8ch !!
3. Q x Q   B x Pch
4. B–K3   R x B
5. K–Kt1   R–K8 mate

Schallop

(Berlin, 1864)

Anderssen—TO PLAY

1. Q x Pch   Kt x Q
2. B x P mate

Zukertort

(Berlin, 1869)

Anderssen—TO PLAY

1. Q x P ch !   K x Q
2. P—B6ch   K—Kt1
3. B—R7ch !   K x B
4. R—R3ch   K—Kt1
5. R—R8 mate

3.

The Age of Morphy

Aftered Anderssen's victory at London in 1851 he was universally acclaimed as the world's leading player. Staunton tried to challenge him, but the negotiations failed, thereby setting another precedent for the future. Time and again the two greatest masters of an era have not been able to get together for a match, on one pretext or another. This was true of Morphy and Staunton, Steinitz and Tarrasch, Lasker and Pillsbury, Alekhine and Capablanca, and it is still true today of Botvinnik and his rivals. Defeat in an important chess match is such a blow to a master's ego that it is no surprise to see so many of them finding excuses for avoiding a contest.

Anderssen, however, was never averse to a chess match and, unlike Staunton, readily accepted Morphy's challenge to a match in Paris. Morphy's victory immediately placed him in the fore of the world's masters.

Paul Morphy

Morphy is unique. In little more than a year he became world champion by beating almost all his serious competitors—a feat which has never been equalled. More important, in a sense, is the fact that millions since have looked upon him as the greatest and most brilliant master of all time, the champion of champions.

Paul Charles Morphy was born in New Orleans June 22, 1837, of a Spanish-Irish father and a French Creole mother. Both his father and his uncle were enthusiastic chess players and at ten Paul was taught the moves. In two brief years he had improved so incredibly that he not only beat everybody in sight, but also defeated the well-known expert Loewenthal during a visit to New Orleans. Morphy is one of the three chess boy wonders who have become eminent in later life—the other two are Capablanca and Reshevsky.

School absorbed his attention until 1857, when he received a degree in law. Too young to practice in his native city, he devoted his time to travel and chess.

First stop was the American championship at New York, in 1857. There were sixteen competitors, mostly mediocrities, but one, Louis Paulsen, was among the strongest alive, Morphy won decisively.

Then in June, 1858, he went to England, where he announced his willingness to play a match with any first-class master. Money was no object, for his family was wealthy. Staunton was then English champion and one of the leading authorities on chess. Morphy's eagerness to meet Staunton, however, was matched only by the Englishman's desire to avoid a serious encounter, and a match could never be arranged. Morphy had to content himself with beating everybody else in sight, including his old antagonist Loewenthal. His superiority was so crushing that he gave Rev. Owen odds of Pawn and move and did not lose a single game.

From England Morphy went to Paris where he first swept Harrwitz out of the way and then in December, 1858, turned his attention to Anderssen, winner of the London, 1851 tournament. Again Morphy scored a crushing victory.

At twenty-one Morphy was undisputed champion of the world. Back in New York, he was wined and dined. To his fellow Americans he was the hero of the hour.

Here, inexplicably, the epic march to glory ends, and the tragedy begins. After the Anderssen victory, except for a minor match with Mongredien, Morphy withdrew completely from serious chess. Steinitz, Kolisch, Zukertort, Blackburne appeared while he was still young and healthy, but Morphy merely deepened his pathological aversion to the game which had made him immortal.

Unable to make a success of his law career, partly because of the disturbed condition of the South after the Civil War, partly because people thought of him primarily as the chess champion, he slowly lost his mind. Most of the remaining years of his life were spent quietly with his family in New Orleans, where he died in 1884.

That chess had something to do with his mild derangement seems probable, but the exact connection is hard to ascertain.

The most likely explanation of the role that chess played in his mental life is this: Morphy was troubled by a peculiar dilemma, which has bothered many other great masters. Eminence in chess was a useless achievement to most of the people around him. Worse, he was afraid that people thought of him as a kind of freak, or at best as a kind of unusual gambler who had learned all the tricks. That is why Morphy always insisted so strongly on his amateur status. Once when an admirer paid him a compliment by calling him the professional chess champion of the world, Morphy objected most earnestly on the grounds that his father had left him $136,472.23 and that he had never accepted a penny for any chess activities. (There is a rumor current that a girl refused him because she did not want to marry a mere chess player.) Then, Morphy's great goal in life, we have repeatedly been told, was to be a prominent lawyer and he found that prospective clients gaped at the chess genius, but could not take the lawyer seriously.

He must have reflected on how different the situation would have been if he had achieved equal prominence in some other field. Thus the twin delusions that chess was worthless, and that he could not do anything else, continually increased his isolation, and finally led to loss of balance.

While Morphy was still alive, a curious development occurred. It was obvious to all that he was the most successful master yet seen. But, not content with such faint praise, his glorifiers went on to urge that he was the most brilliant genius who had ever appeared. It was claimed that he had the most marvellous intuition any mortal was ever granted, that he won his games by combinations of incredible beauty, that he could have beaten any of his successors with ridiculous ease. In short, Morphy became to millions the most gifted, the most dazzling, in every respect the greatest chess master of all time.

But if we examine Morphy's record and games critically, we cannot justify such extravaganza. And we are compelled to speak of it as the Morphy myth.

Morphy's games fall into two categories. Of the 403 contained in Maroczy's book, only 55 are tournament or match games; the remainder are offhand simultaneous or odds games. Few of the 55 serious games—the only kind modern masters include in such collections—can by any stretch be called brilliant. He beat his major rivals because he had a clearer grasp of the essentials of position play. In fact, Morphy is the first who really appreciated the logical basis of chess. He could combine as well as anybody, but he also knew under what circumstances combinations were possible—and in that respect he was twenty years ahead of his time.

There is a curious paradox about Morphy's games. He was so far ahead of his rivals that it is hard to find really outstanding examples of his skill. Imagine Joe Louis at his prime in a country where his most dangerous competitor was 5' 6" and weighed 150 pounds. Morphy was in this same position: his real abilities were hardly able to be tested. His games were won with effortless ease. We do not see sustained masterpieces; rather flashes of genius. The titanic struggles of the kind we see today he could not produce because he lacked the opposition. Morphy himself must have sensed this when he offered anybody in the world Pawn and move.

Anderssen could attack brilliantly, but had an inadequate understanding of its positional basis. Morphy knew not only how to attack, but also when—and that is why he won. The tragedy is that when others, like Steinitz, who knew when, came along, Morphy refused to meet them.

Even if the myth has been destroyed, Morphy remains one of the giants of chess history. His meteoric career together with the freshness and originality of his games will always continue to inspire all who love chess.

In the New York Tournament of 1857, Morphy's chief rival was the absent-minded Paulsen, whom he defeated in one of his most brilliant efforts:

PAULSEN   MORPHY

New York, 1857
Four Knights' Game

1. P—K4	P—K4
2. Kt—KB3	Kt—QB3
3. Kt—B3	Kt—B3
4. B—Kt5	B—B4

Preparing to sacrifice a Pawn for quick development—a typical Morphy idea.

5. O—O	O—O
6. Kt x P	. . . .

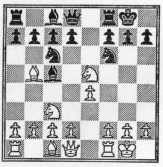

6. . . . .   R—K1

With 6. . . . Kt x Kt; 7. P—Q4, B—Q3 Black regains the Pawn with a satisfactory game, but Morphy has other intentions.

7. Kt x Kt	QP x Kt
8. B—B4	P—QKt4
9. B—K2	. . . .

If instead 9. B—Kt3, B—KKt5; 10. Q—K1, P—Kt5 and . . . R x P or . . . Kt x P is decisive.

9.	Kt x P
10. Kt x Kt	R x Kt
11. B—B3	R—K3

Morphy has regained the Pawn, but actually White has a little the better of it if he plays P—Q3, P—B3, P—Q4, etc.

12. P—B3 ?   . . . .

A positional blunder—typical of Morphy's opponents.

12. . . . .   Q—Q6

Naturally.

13. P—QKt4   . . . .

Now Paulsen must struggle to free his game.

13.	B—Kt3
14. P—QR4	P x P
15. Q x P	B—Q2
16. R—R2	QR—K1

Threatening Q x Rch and R—K8 mate.

17. Q—R6   . . . .

17. . . . .   Q x B !!

A decisive sacrifice.

18. P x Q   R—Kt3ch
19. K—R1   B—R6
20. R—Q1   . . . .

The only chance. If 20. R—Kt1, R x Rch and 21. . . . R—K8 followed by mate.

20. . . . .   B—Kt7ch

The text is stronger than . . . B x P 21. Q—B1.

21. K—Kt1   QB x P dis ch
22. K—B1   B—Kt7ch

A minor inaccuracy. Quicker was 22. . . . R—Kt7, threatening . . . R x BPch, e.g., 23. Q—Q3, R x Pch; 24. K—Kt1, R—Kt7 dbl ch; 25. K—R1 (or K—B1), R—Kt8 dbl ch and mate. But the text is also good enough.

23. K—Kt1   B—R6ch
24. K—R1   B x P
25. Q—B1   . . . .

The only way to prevent mate.

25. . . . .   B x Q
26. R x B   R—K7

27. R—R1   R—R3
28. P—Q4   B—K6

White Resigns
For if 29. B x B, R(R3) x Pch and 30. . . . . R(K7)—Kt7 mate.

Of the Morphy-Anderssen games none are very good by modern standards because Anderssen did not grasp the principles of development. Here is the best of the match:

MORPHY   ANDERSSEN

9th Match Game, Paris, 1858
Sicilian Defense

1. P—K4   P—QB4
2. P—Q4   P x P
3. Kt—KB3   Kt—QB3
4. Kt x P   P—K3
5. Kt—Kt5   P—Q3
6. B—KB4   P—K4 ?

Anderssen thinks nothing of weakening his Pawn structure. . . . Kt—K4 was sounder.

7. B—K3   . . . .

7. . . . .   P—B4 ?

Continuing a premature attack.

8. QKt–B3	P–B5?	14. B x Pch	K–Kt3
9. Kt–Q5!	P x B	15. Q–R5ch	K x Kt
10. Kt(Kt5)–B7ch	K–B2	16. P x P	Kt x Pch
11. Q–B3ch	Kt–B3	17. K–K2	Black Resigns.
12. B–B4	Kt–Q5?		

Loses quickly. The best hope was 12. . . . K–Kt3, and if 13. Q–Kt3ch, K–R3.

13. Kt x Kt dis ch   P–Q4

There is no defense. If 17. . . . Kt x R 18. Kt–K8ch, K–K2; 19. Q–B7 mate. Or if 17. . . . Q x Kt; 18. R–B1ch, K–K2; 19. R–B7ch, K–Q3; 20. R x Q, K x R; 21. R–QB1.

A perennial favorite among the Morphy gems is an offhand game played at the Paris opera which for sheer elegance and simplicity can scarcely be surpassed. The story goes that it was played during *The Marriage of Figaro*, and that the Paris editorials next day criticized the Duke of Braunschweig for being so sacrilegious as to play chess at the opera. The Duke sued—and lost!

MORPHY   DUKE OF BRAUN-
               SCHWEIG and
               COUNT ISOUARD

Paris, 1858
Philidor's Defense

1. P–K4	P–K4
2. Kt–KB3	P–Q3
3. P–Q4	B–Kt5?

A positional blunder. . . . Kt–Q2 or . . . Kt–KB3 was better.

4. P x P	B x Kt
5. Q x B	P x P
6. B–QB4	Kt–KB3?

Q–K2 first was necessary.

7. Q–QKt3	Q–K2
8. Kt–B3	. . . .

Spurning the Pawn, capture of which allows the exchange of Queens after 8. Q x P, Q–Kt5ch.

8.	P–B3
9. B–KKt5	P–QKt4

10. Kt x P!	P x Kt
11. B x Pch	QKt–Q2
12. O–O–O!	. . . .

12.	R–Q1
13. R x Kt!	R x R
14. R–Q1	Q–K3
15. B x Rch	Kt x B

9. K–R4　　　Kt–K6
10. Q–Kt1　　Kt–B4ch
11. K–Kt5　　Q–R4 mate

16. Q–Kt8ch !　　Kt x Q
17. R–Q8 mate

Here are a few more glorious Morphy brilliancies which helped to earn him his fame.

SCHULTEN　　　　MORPHY

New York, 1858

Morphy–TO PLAY

MARACHE　　　　MORPHY

New York, 1857

Morphy–TO PLAY

Marache

1. . . . .　　　Kt–KKt6 !
2. Q x Q　　　Kt(Q5)–K7 mate

This is reminiscent of the famous Lewitzky-Marshall sacrifice. Morphy was also one of the great blindfold masters: he pushed the record up to eight boards simultaneously, a routine enough feat today, but unheard of in his time. Here is the conclusion of a blindfold game from an eight-board display at Paris, 1858.

Schulten

1. . . . .　　　R x B !
2. Kt x R　　　Kt–Q5
3. Q–Kt1　　　B x Ktch
4. K–B2　　　Kt–Kt5ch
5. K–Kt1　　　Kt–B6ch !
6. P x Kt　　　Q–Q5ch
7. K–Kt2　　　Q–B7ch
8. K–R3　　　Q x BPch

Baucher

Morphy—TO PLAY

1. R—B3 B—Q2?
2. R—R3 P—R3

If 2. . . . B x Kt; 3. R x Pch, K x R; 4. Q—R5 mate.

3. Q—Q2 ! K—R2
4. Q x B B—Q3
5. R x Pch !! K x R
6. R—Q3 K—R4
7. Q—B7ch Black Resigns.

Henry Edward Bird

Of the men whom Morphy defeated, apart from Anderssen, about the only one worthy of mention is the Englishman, Henry Edward Bird. When he met Morphy, Bird was only twenty-eight and virtually at the beginning of his chess career, for he remained active for almost fifty years after this. Bird was what we would call today a "natural player." He cared little for theory, that is, what others thought, and went his own way. The attack was his happy hunting ground, and he often disregarded positional considerations to pursue it for all it was worth. Against the great masters this policy did not work, but against lesser lights he produced many a sparkling gem. Incidentally, Bird was an outstanding accountant and became an authority on railway finance; in 1866 he published a book entitled *An Analysis of Railways in the United Kingdom.* Perhaps the meticulousness and precision of his profession led him to adopt a style of play in which he could give his imagination free reign. In his old age he suffered from a disease otherwise unknown to chess masters, gout!

Here is a beautiful example of Bird's ability to conduct a sustained attack. This game rightly earned him a brilliancy prize.

BIRD   **MASON**

New York, 1876
French Defense

1. P—K4 P—K3
2. P—Q4 P—Q4
3. Kt—QB3 Kt—KB3
4. P x P . . . .

Today considered a dull drawing variation. But Bird liked open positions regardless of their theoretical evaluation.

4. . . . . P x P
5. Kt—B3 B—Q3
6. B—Q3 O—O
7. O—O P—KR3

To prevent B—KKt5.

8. R—K1	Kt—QB3
9. Kt—QKt5	B—QKt5
10. P—B3	. . . .

10.	B—R4

Avoiding complications. If 10.
. . . B—K2 11. B—KB4, P—
QR3; 12. Kt x P, Kt—KR4; 13.
B—K5 ! with good attacking
chances.

11. Kt—R3	B—KKt5
12. Kt—B2	Q—Q2
13. P—QKt4	B—Kt3
14. P—KR3	B—KR4
15. Kt—K3	KR—K1
16. P—Kt5 !	Kt—K2
17. P—Kt4	B—Kt3
18. Kt—K5	Q—B1
19. P—QR4	P—B3
20. P x P	P x P
21. B—R3	. . . .

Bird has built up a fine position,
but Black still has many defensive chances.

21.	Kt—K5 ?
22. Q—B2	Kt—Kt4 ?

This faulty maneuver has served
to make his position even worse.

23. B x Kt	R x B
24. B x B	P x B
25. Q x P !	Kt x Pch
26. K—R2	Kt—B5
27. Q—B5 !	. . . .

Better than 27. Q x BP, Q—B1,
and the attack passes to Black for
a while.

27.	Kt—K3

If instead 27. . . . Q x Q; 28.
Kt x Q, R(K2)—K1; 29. K—Kt3,
wins easily enough.

28. Kt—Kt2	Q—B2 ?

A poor move in a bad position,
but the only hope was 28. . . .
B—B2. Had he played that, however, this game would never have
been included in this collection.

29. P—R5	B x RP
30. R x B !	R—KB1

Not 30. . . . Q x R; 31. Kt x P.

31. R—R6 !! ?	. . . .

The Queen sacrifice is the real
point of the combination.

31.	R x Q
32. P x R	Kt—Q1 ??

Making Bird's life easy. After
32. . . . Kt—Kt4, threatening
. . . Kt—B6ch, the outcome is
most unclear.

33. Kt—KB4	Q—B1
34. Kt(B4)—Kt6	R—K1

35. Kt x P !!

This second sacrifice is correct in all variations. If 35. . . . R x R; 36. Kt(B6)—K7ch wins the Queen.

35.	Q—B2ch
36. Kt(B6)—K5	Q x P
37. R—K3	Q—Q7

Not 37. . . . Q x P; 38. Kt—B3 ! and wins.

| 38. K—Kt2 | Q x P |
| 39. P—B6 ! | P x P |

More or less forced.

| 40. R x BP | Kt—K3 |

41. R—KKt3	Kt—Kt4
42. Kt—Kt4	K—Kt2

43. Kt—B4 !! . . . .

Preventing . . . Q x R by Kt—R5ch.

43.	Q—K5ch
44. K—R2	Kt—R2
45. Kt—R5ch	K—R1
46. R x P	Q—B7
47. Kt(R5)—B6	R—K2
48. K—Kt2	P—Q5
49. Kt—K5 !	Q—B1

To prevent R—Kt8 mate. If 49. . . . R—KKt2; 50. Kt—B7ch !, R x Kt; 51. R—Kt8 mate.

| 50. Kt—Kt6ch | Black Resigns |

4.

The Age of Steinitz

Wilhelm Steinitz

AFTER the disappearance of Morphy from the international arena, Anderssen remained the strongest player until he was superseded by the man who was destined to revolutionize the course of chess history, Wilhelm Steinitz.

In more than one way Steinitz was a unique phenomenon in the chess world. He was the first to claim the title of world champion officially; he was the first who evolved any kind of theory which made sense. He elaborated the principles of position play which have since become the ABC of all chess knowledge. He was the first completely professional chess master who devoted his entire life to the game. And he was the first who showed that writing about chess can produce good literature.

Wilhelm Steinitz was born at Prague, Bohemia in 1836, the same year, curiously, as Morphy. We have little knowledge of what he did before he became a chess master, but by 1862, at the age of twenty-six, he had already made a name for himself in Austria and was sent as a representative of his native country to the London tournament of 1862. In this affair he did poorly, finishing sixth, but he found conditions sufficiently favorable in London to induce him to remain and make a living at chess. Evidently his main source of income for quite a while was offhand games at Simpson's Divan and various chess clubs; the more lucrative columns came later.

Until 1866 Steinitz was just another strong foreign master to the English; London was full of them. In that year a match was arranged between him and Anderssen, which Steinitz won by a score of 8 to 6. Immediately he began to look upon himself as the world champion, although at the time nothing was officially at stake, and for many years to come little was said in print about the title. But today we date Steinitz's reign from 1866, the year he beat Anderssen, to 1894, the year he lost to Lasker. To hold the title for twenty-eight years was remarkable indeed; to do it as Steinitz did even more so. For he actively sought out every one of his major rivals, and all who accepted were decisively trounced in individual match play.

Unlike his successors, Steinitz' fame did not rest chiefly on tournament play. There were several reasons for this, but the chief one was that active tournaments were few and far between. The modern master can easily play in three strong tournaments a year if he is so minded, but Steinitz could hardly find one every three or four years. And then his temperament made him more partial to match play. It was in individual encounters that he shone; up to the time he met Lasker he won every match he ever played. No doubt his personality accounts for this preference; Steinitz was a man who burned with the ambition to prove that he was the best in the world. He was always ready to accept any challenge, no matter who offered it. If a personal encounter was impossible, he went to great lengths to demonstrate his superiority. For example, for many years a fierce controversy raged about who was better, Morphy or Steinitz. In countless articles Steinitz never tired of proving over and over again how many blunders Morphy had been guilty of, how ignorant he was of the principles of position play, and so on.

In his match with Anderssen, Steinitz still adhered to the conventional gambit style of his day. But soon after he began to evolve a new approach to chess, which came to be known as the "modern" school, in contrast to the so-called classical school of Anderssen. In this approach Steinitz established the principles of position play, especially the supreme importance of the center, which had been almost completely neglected before his time.

Like many another world champion after him, Steinitz had many detractors whom he considered personal enemies, and vigorously attacked in print with such epithets as "inky ruffians" and "literary hooters." While some of the attacks on Steinitz were personal, occasioned by his stubborn pride and penchant for literary arguments, most of them came from people who glorified the "good old days," thereby setting a pattern which has remained ever since. By the time Steinitz was champion, chess was popularized. All the leading European newspapers had columns. Many chess magazines were founded; some, like the British Chess Magazine, are still being published. Most of the editors of these publications were second-rate masters who at once envied Steinitz' genius and failed to understand the really revolutionary significance of his theories. Since Steinitz' games, unlike those of his predecessors, needed an annotator to explain them to the public, the uninstructed reader found himself baffled by what Steinitz was doing, or turned away from his play with annoyance or boredom. The "critics," writing for such a public, could readily find agreement when they criticized his play or his ideas.

By 1871 Steinitz' enemies in London had reached the stage where they imported a foreign player, Zukertort, to dethrone him. This attempt was pathetically unsuccessful, for he ripped Zukertort by 7 to 1; nevertheless the arguments were so heated that for almost ten years Steinitz was virtually inactive as a player, confining himself to writing and journalism. In 1883, disheartened by what he called "literary hooting" in England, he sailed for the United States, where he remained with brief interruptions until his death in 1900.

Aside from his contributions as a player, Steinitz ranks among the great writers on the game. His journal (*The Chess International*) is one of the masterpieces of chess literature, and can still be read with profit by the young masters.

It was the position play which Steinitz developed in such magnificent detail which won him his victories. The second match with Zukertort (the first was in 1872), in 1886, is a case in point. Zukertort had a flair for combinative play which was certainly not inferior to Steinitz', but he took too many chances with his Pawn structure. In this game we have an example of how Steinitz outmaneuvered him by simple positional principles.

ZUKERTORT   STEINITZ

9th Match Game, New Orleans, 1886
Queen's Gambit Accepted

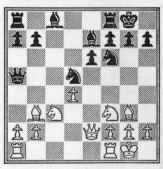

1. P—Q4	P—Q4
2. P—QB4	P—K3

The delayed acceptance of the gambit is not so good as the immediate 2. . . . P x P. But all this was uncharted territory in 1886.

3. Kt—QB3	Kt—KB3
4. Kt—B3	P x P
5. P—K3	P—B4
6. B x P	P x P
7. P x P	B—K2
8. O—O	O—O
9. Q—K2	QKt—Q2
10. B—Kt3	Kt—Kt3
11. B—KB4	Kt(Kt3)—Q4
12. B—Kt3	Q—R4

A variation which in one form or another was contested innumerable times between these two opponents. Black has his Rock of Gibraltar at Q4, solid unchallengeable control of the center, which Steinitz rightly maintained gave Black the better of the game from a theoretical point of view, though the tactical question always remains of how long this control can be maintained. White on the other hand must aim for a rather vague attack.

13. QR–B1	B–Q2	21.	R x B
14. Kt–K5	KR–Q1	22. P–QB4	R(Q4)–Q1
15. Q–B3?	. . . .	23. R–K3	. . . .

Typical of his positional confusion. If anything is to be done with such a position it must come via P–B4–B5, and B–KR4.

This belated attempt to attack brings on his final downfall.

15.	B–K1	23.	Q–Q3
16. KR–K1	QR–B1	24. R–Q1	P–B3
17. B–KR4	Kt x Kt	25. R–R3	P–KR3

Gives up the center for the two "hanging pawns." As usual, this steers the game into the endgame channels which Steinitz loved.

		26. Kt–Kt4	Q–B5
		27. Kt–K3	B–R5 !
18. P x Kt	Q–B2	28. R–B3	Q–Q3
19. Q–Q3	. . . .	29. R–Q2	B–B3
		30. R–Kt3	P–B4

With no clear-cut plan. 19. B–Kt3 was better.

		31. R–Kt6	B–K5
		32. Q–Kt3	. . . .
19.	Kt–Q4	32.	K–R2 !

While Steinitz is clear about his goals—exchange and head for the ending, when White's weak Pawns will be indefensible.

Simple and decisive. If now 33. R–Kt3, P–B5 wins.

		33. P–B5	R x P
20. B x B	Q x B	34. R x P	R–B8ch
		35. Kt–Q1	Q–B5
		36. Q–Kt2	R–Kt8
		37. Q–B3	R–QB1 !
		38. R x B	Q x R (K5)

White Resigns.

21. B x Kt ?? . . . .

No modern master of Zukertort's stature could conceivably make such a positional blunder.

Like Morphy, Steinitz realized that correct positional play, dry though it may first appear, frequently leads to the most beautiful combinative play. Here is a case in point, one which brings out Steinitz' unique gifts more than any other he ever played.

STEINITZ   TCHIGORIN

4th Match Game,
Havana, 1892
Ruy Lopez

1. P–K4	P–K4
2. Kt–KB3	Kt–QB3

3. B—Kt5 Kt—B3
4. P—Q3 . . . .

The Steinitz variation. The idea is to hold the center solid while preparing a flank attack.

4. . . . . P—Q3
5. P—B3 P—KKt3
6. QKt—Q2 B—Kt2
7. Kt—B1 O—O

Premature. Black does better to develop first, attempt a break in the center, and wait for White to clarify his plans.

8. B—QR4 Kt—Q2
9. Kt—K3 Kt—B4
10. B—B2 Kt—K3 ?

Pointless. Better was P—B4 immediately. Again we see here that while Steinitz has a clear-cut plan in mind, Tchigorin wavers.

11. P—KR4 ! . . . .

The purpose of White's maneuvers now becomes clear. With the center solidified an attack against the King's side is initiated.

11. . . . . Kt—K2
12. P—R5 P—Q4
13. RP x P BP x P

14. P x P Kt x P
15. Kt x Kt Q x Kt
16. B—Kt3 Q—B3
17. Q—K2 B—Q2
18. B—K3 . . . .

Threatening Kt—Kt5, for if in reply 18. . . . . Q x KtP; 19. O—O—O !

18. . . . . K—R1
19. O—O—O QR—K1
20. Q—B1 ! . . . .

Preparing P—Q4 and sundry things.

20. . . . . P—QR4

Useless, but not more so than other moves. The best try was . . . Kt—B5.

21. P—Q4 P x P
22. Kt x P . . . .

The point of his 20th move now becomes clear. If 22. . . . Kt x Kt; 23. R x Pch !!, K x R; 24. Q—R1ch and mates shortly.

22. . . . . B x Kt
23. R x B ! Kt x R

It was hopeless anyhow.

24. R x Pch K x R
25. Q—R1ch K—Kt2

26. B–R6ch	K–B3
27. Q–R4ch	K–K4
28. Q x Ktch	Black Resigns

One move before mate.

Steinitz could, of course, also produce many brilliancies in the classical style. Here is a game with a combination which ranks among the most profound ever made.

STEINITZ   VON BARDELEBEN

Hastings, 1895
Giuoco Piano

1. P–K4	P–K4
2. Kt–KB3	Kt–QB3
3. B–B4	B–B4
4. P–B3	Kt–B3
5. P–Q4	P x P
6. P x P	B–Kt5ch
7. Kt–B3	. . . .

A variation which lost Steinitz the championship to Lasker, but with which he stubbornly persisted.

7.	P–Q4

Lasker won several times with 7. . . . Kt x P; 8. O–O, B x Kt; 9. P x B, P–Q4. Correct is 8. . . . B x Kt; 9. P–Q5, with complications–theoretically equal.

8. P x P	KKt x P
9. O–O	B–K3
10. B–KKt5	B–K2
11. B x Kt	QB x B
12. Kt x B	Q x Kt
13. B x B	Kt x B ?

After this Black remains tied up. 13. . . . K x B ! and if 14. R–K1ch, K–B1 ! was preferable.

14. R–K1	P–KB3
15. Q–K2	Q–Q2
16. QR–B1	P–B3 ?

Allowing the combination. The best chance was 16. . . . K–B2; 17. Q x Ktch, Q x Q; 18. R x Qch, K x R; 19. R x Pch, and White still has the winning chances – but the end-game is difficult.

17. P–Q5 !!	P x P
18. Kt–Q4	K–B2
19. Kt–K6	KR–QB1
20. Q–Kt4 !	P–KKt3
21. Kt–Kt5ch	K–K1

22. R x Ktch !!!   K–B1

Now every White piece is en prise. If instead 22. . . . K x R;

23. R—Klch, K—Q3; 24. Q—
Kt4ch, K—B2; 25. Kt—K6ch,
K—Ktl, 26. Q—B4ch, and wins.

23. R—B7ch !   K—Ktl
24. R—Kt7ch !   K—R1

Note how the Rook cannot be
taken. If . . . K x R, the Queen
is captured with check, while if
. . . Q x R, the Rook is captured
with check.

25. R x Pch   Black Resigns

For if 25. . . . K—Ktl, White
has a conclusive win or a mate in
ten moves as Steinitz demon-
strated at the time: 25. . . . K—
Ktl; 26. R—Kt7ch, K—R1; 27.
Q—R4ch, K x R; 28. Q—R7ch,
K—Bl; 29. Q—R8ch, K—K2; 30.
Q—Kt7ch, K—Kl; 31. Q—Kt8ch,
K—K2; 32. Q—B7ch, K—Ql; 33.
Q—B8ch, Q—Kl; 34. Kt—B7ch,
K—Q2; 35. Q—Q6 mate.

Here are a few more flashes of
Steinitz' genius:

Mr. Rock

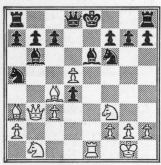

Steinitz—TO PLAY

London, 1863 (QR odds)

1. P x B !   Kt x Q
2. P x Pch   K—Q2
3. B—K6ch   K—B3
4. Kt—K5ch   K—Kt4
5. B—B4ch   K—R4
6. B—Kt4ch   K—R5
7. P x Kt mate

Zukertort

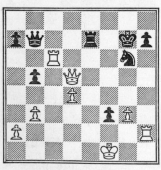

Steinitz—TO PLAY

Match: London, 1872

1. R x Pch   K x R
2. Q—R5ch   K—Ktl
3. R x Ktch   R—Kt2
4. R—KR6   K—Bl
5. R—R8ch   Black Resigns

For if 5. . . . K—K2; 6. Q—
K5ch, K—B2; 7. Q—K8ch, K—
B3; 8. R—R6ch, K—B4; 9. Q—
K5ch, K—Kt5; 10. Q—B4 mate.

Dr. Simonson

Steinitz—TO PLAY

New York, 1883 (simultaneous exhibition)

1. K—Q3 !!   Q—R4
2. P—Kt4ch   Q x P
3. Kt—K4ch and wins.

A. Mongredien

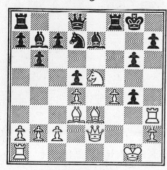

Steinitz—TO PLAY

London, 1862

1. R x P !!	Kt x Kt
2. BP x Kt	K x R
3. Q x P	KR—Kt1
4. Q—R5ch	K—Kt2
5. Q—R6ch	K—B2
6. Q—R7ch	K—K3
7. Q—R3ch	K—B2
8. R—B1ch	K—K1
9. Q—K6	R—Kt2
10. B—Kt5	Q—Q2
11. B x Pch	R x B
12. Q x Rch	K—Q1
13. R—B8ch	Q—K1
14. Q x Q mate	

Several of Steinitz' contemporaries deserve attention. Up to his time, the world champion had towered head and shoulders above all rivals; but from Steinitz on, it was to be *primus inter pares*. Men such as Zukertort and Anderssen repeatedly outdistanced Steinitz in tournaments and individual games. Henceforth much more must be said of the contenders for the world's title.

Ignatz Kolisch

Kolisch stands out in chess history for a most curious reason—he made a fortune! In 1868 he met one of the Rothschilds in Vienna, who was so taken by his combination of good manners and good chess that he started him in business, where Kolisch did remarkably well.

Kolisch was born in Hungary in 1837 and, as was then the custom, went to London as soon as he had achieved something of a reputation. In 1858 he had drawn a match with Anderssen; consequently he was already a player of some renown. In 1861 Kolisch challenged Morphy to a match, but it did not materialize because of Morphy's retirement from the game.

Although his career lasted only about ten years, Kolisch ranked among the great of his day. His outstanding achievement, apart from the drawn match with Anderssen, was first prize in the Paris Tournament of 1867, 1½ points ahead of Steinitz.

Kolisch's play was in the classical tradition. Here is a pretty game against a man who both won and lost many great games.

KOLISCH   ANDERSSEN
London, 1861
Evans Gambit

1.	P–K4	P–K4
2.	Kt–KB3	Kt–QB3
3.	B–B4	B–B4
4.	P–QKt4	B x P
5.	P–B3	B–R4
6.	P–Q4	P x P
7.	O–O	P x P

19. Kt x Pch !!   Kt x Kt

Dangerous for Black.

Or *19. . . . K–Kt2; 20. Kt x Kt, K x Kt; 21. Q–K6ch, Kt–Q3; 22. Kt–Q4ch, K–Kt3; 23. B x Kt, P x B; 24. Q x Pch, K–Kt2; 25. Q–B6ch, K–R2; 26. Q–R6 mate.*

8.	Q–Kt3	Q–B3
9.	P–K5	Q–Kt3
10.	Kt x P	P–QKt4

20. Q–K6ch   K–Q1
21. R–Q1ch   Kt–Q3
22. R x Ktch . . . .

To gain time.

An unnecessary brilliancy—22. B x Kt was quicker.

11.	Kt x P	R–Kt1
12.	Q–K3	KKt–K2
13.	Q–K2	Q–R4
14.	B–R3	B–Kt2
15.	QR–Q1	Kt–B4 ?
16.	R x P !!	K x R
17.	P–K6ch	K–B1
18.	P x P	B–R1

22. . . . .   P x R
23. Q x Pch   K–B1

24. B–K6ch   K–Kt2
25. B–Q5ch   Q x B

Forced, for if 25. . . . K–B1;
26. Q–K6ch, K–B2; 27. B–
Q6ch and mates shortly.

26. Q x Qch   K–R3
27. Q–B4ch   K–Kt2

28. Q–K4ch   Kt–B3
29. Kt–K5   K–R3
30. Q–B4ch   K–R2
31. B–B5ch   R–Kt3
32. B x Rch   B x B
33. Kt x Ktch B x Kt
34. Q x B   Black Resigns

Johannes Herrmann Zukertort

By far the greatest of Steinitz' rivals was Johannes Herrmann Zukertort. Born in Lublin, in 1842, in what was then Russian Poland, he was of mixed Prussian and Polish descent. He was a man of considerable attainments. At one time he was music critic of the leading Silesian journal; he was a foreign correspondent, linguist, military man, musician, chess master all rolled into one.

In 1871 he was brought to London to challenge Steinitz and remained there until his premature death in 1889. After he came to London, chess became the ruling passion of his life, and his one overwhelming ambition was to dethrone Steinitz. The two could not agree on terms for a return match until 1886, when it was financed in the United States. Zukertort lost—his spirit was so badly broken that he lived on only a short while.

The greatest triumph of Zukertort's career came at London in 1883, where he won first prize ahead of Steinitz and all the other leading masters of the day. His victory over Blackburne in this contest was described by Steinitz as "one of the most brilliant games on record."

ZUKERTORT   BLACKBURNE

London, 1883

Queen's Gambit Declined

1. P–QB4   . . . .

Like another eminent master of the attack, the American Frank Marshall, Zukertort preferred to commence with close openings.

1. . . . .   P–K3
2. P–K3   Kt–KB3

3. Kt–KB3   P–QKt3
4. B–K2   B–Kt2
5. O–O   P–Q4
6. P–Q4   B–Q3
7. Kt–B3   O–O
8. P–QKt3   QKt–Q2
9. B–Kt2   Q–K2?

Anti-positional—first . . . P–QR3 was essential. Such precautions, which are today routine in every club tournament, were still novel then.

10. Kt—QKt5	Kt—K5
11. Kt x B	P x Kt
12. Kt—Q2	QKt—B3
13. P—B3	Kt x Kt
14. Q x Kt	P x P

Again faulty.

15. B x P	P—Q4

To stop P—K4, but it does so only temporarily.

16. B—Q3	KR—B1
17. QR—K1	R—B2
18. P—K4	. . . .

Black has been completely outplayed.

18.	QR—B1
19. P—K5	Kt—K1
20. P—B4	P—Kt3
21. R—K3	. . . .

Threatening R—R3 followed by P—B5 and Q—R6.

21.	P—B4
22. P x P e.p.	Kt x P
23. P—B5	Kt—K5
24. B x Kt	P x B
25. P x KtP !!	R—B7
26. P x Pch	K—R1
27. P—Q5 dis ch	P—K4

28. Q—Kt4 !!	R(B1)—B4
29. R—B8ch	K x P
30. Q x Pch	K—Kt2
31. B x Pch	K x R
32. B—Kt7ch !!	. . . .

The final surprise. If 32. . . . . Q x B; 33. Q—K8 mate.

32.	K—Kt1
33. Q x Q	Black Resigns.

Like so many other up-and-coming masters of his day, Zukertort sat at the feet of the venerable Anderssen. The two are supposed to have played more than 6,000 games together. Here is one of the prettiest on record.

ZUKERTORT   ANDERSSEN

Berlin, 1865
Sicilian Defense

1. P—K4	P—QB4
2. Kt—KB3	P—K3
3. P—Q4	P x P
4. Kt x P	Kt—KB3
5. Kt—QB3	B—Kt5
6. B—Q3	. . . .

Weak by modern theory. P—K5 is considered best.

6.	Kt–B3
7. B–K3	P–Q4
8. P x P	Kt x P
9. O–O	Kt(Q4) x Kt ?

Both sides mishandle the opening. 9. . . . Kt x B was better, to be followed by the simple 10. . . . O–O.

10. P x Kt	B x P
11. Kt x Kt	P x Kt
12. R–Kt1	O–O ?
13. R–Kt3	B–R4

On the alternative 13. . . . B–B3; 14. B–B5 wins too, e.g., 14. . . . R–K1; 15. B x Pch K x B; 16. Q–R5ch, K–Kt1; 17. R–KR3.

14. B–QB5	R–K1

15. B x Pch !	K x B
16. R–R3ch	K–Kt1
17. Q–R5	P–B4
18. R–Q1 !	B–Q2
19. Q–R7ch	K–B2
20. R–KKt3	. . . .

20.	B–B6

Black is lost. If instead . . . R–KKt1; 21. Q–Kt6 mate.

21. Q–Kt6ch	K–Kt1
22. R x B(B3)	P–B5
23. R–KR3	R–K2
24. Q–R7ch	K–B2
25. Q–R5ch	K–Kt1
26. B x R	Q x B
27. Q–R8ch	K–B2
28. Q x R	Black Resigns.

Joseph Henry Blackburne

Blackburne, like Bird, was another of those natural geniuses whom England has so often produced. At eighteen he took part in one of Morphy's blindfold exhibitions. Within a month he was successfully playing ten blindfold games simultaneously, a figure which he later increased to sixteen. He utilized his native gift for the game by becoming a professional, and the remainder of his life was devoted to it.

Love for study did not fit in with Blackburne's outgoing personality; he remained a "natural player" with all the advantages and disadvantages of that style. Against inferior masters he could produce one brilliancy after another, but against Steinitz he came to grief because of his faulty positional play.

Blackburne was one of the historic figures of British chess, and stories about him are still going the rounds. One story has it that he was so enraged at Steinitz during one of their match games that he picked him up and almost threw him out of the window. His capacity for Scotch is said to have rivalled that of some other great masters. He strikes one as an uncomplicated soul who loved chess and exuberant living.

Blackburne's greatest success came at Berlin in 1881, where he finished first, ahead of Zukertort and every other leading master with the exception of Steinitz, who did not participate. Here is his most brilliant game in that event.

BLACKBURNE   SCHWARZ

Berlin, 1881
French Defense

1.	P–K4	P–K3
2.	P–Q4	P–Q4
3.	Kt–QB3	Kt–KB3
4.	P x P	P x P
5.	Kt–B3	B–Q3
6.	B–Q3	P–B3
7.	O–O	O–O
8.	Kt–K2	B–KKt5
9.	Kt–Kt3	Q–B2
10.	B–K3	QKt–Q2
11.	Q–Q2	KR–K1

16.	K–Kt2 !	B–Q3
17.	R–R1	Kt–B1
18.	R–R3	P–KKt3
19.	R(K1)–R1	QR–Q1
20.	B–KKt5	R–Q2
21.	P–QB4	. . . .

An unpromising opening variation for White.

12.	QR–K1	Kt–K5
13.	Q–B1	QB x Kt

Better 13. . . . . P–KB4

Steinitz writes: "White's design especially from the 21st move in combination with the brilliant finish, belongs to the finest efforts of chess genius in modern match play."

14.	P x B	Kt x Kt
15.	RP x Kt	B x P

21.	. . . .	P x P
22.	B x BP	P–KR4
23.	R–R4	P–Kt4
24.	B–Kt3	Kt–K3
25.	B–B6	Kt–B5ch

Playing for a draw: if 16. P x B, Q x Pch and perpetual check.

Loses, but there was no sufficient defense. If 25. . . . . B—K2; 26. B x Kt, P x B; 27. Q—Kt5 wins.

26. Q x Kt !!	B x Q
27. R x P	P x R
28. R x P	Black Resigns

Mate cannot be averted.

Even in his later years Blackburne was a competitor to be feared. Here is his beautiful win against the then world champion, Emanuel Lasker. Blackburne was fifty-seven years old at the time.

LASKER   BLACKBURNE

London, 1899
Ruy Lopez

1. P—K4	P—K4
2. Kt—KB3	Kt—QB3
3. B—Kt5	P—Q3
4. P—Q4	B—Q2
5. P—Q5	. . . .

An experiment.

5.	Kt—Kt1
6. B—Q3	B—K2
7. Kt—B3	Kt—KB3

8. Kt—K2	P—B3
9. P—B4	Kt—R3
10. Kt—Kt3	Kt—B4
11. B—B2	P—QKt4

Positionally poor, but he stakes everything on the attack.

12. P—Kt4	Kt—Kt2
13. QP x P	B x P
14. P x P	B x KtP
15. P—QR4	B—Q2

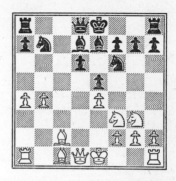

Certainly not a position in which anyone playing Black would expect to beat a Lasker.

16. O—O	P—Kt3
17. P—R3	P—KR4

Typically Blackburne.

18. B—K3	P—R4
19. P—Kt5	R—QB1
20. R—B1	Kt—B4
21. Kt—Q2	P—R5
22. Kt—K2	P—Kt4 !

The attack begins!

23. B x P	R—KKt1
24. B x P	B x RP
25. B—KKt3	B—K3

Black has strong Knights—and open files.

26. R—K1	Kt—Kt5 !
27. Kt—B1	B—Kt4 !
28. R—Kt1	R—KR1

A comparison of this position with the previous diagram shows how much progress Black has made. The immediate threat is Q—B3—R3.

| 29. Kt—B3 | . . . . |

So that if . . . Q—B3; 30. P—B3.

29.	B—KB5 !
30. Kt—Q5	Q—Kt4
31. P—B3	. . . .

31.	R—R8ch !!
32. K x R	B x B
33. Kt x B	. . . .

If 33. P x Kt, Q—R5ch and mate next.

33.	Kt—B7ch
34. K—Kt1	Kt x Q
35. Kt—B5	B x Kt(B4)
36. P x B	Q—Q7

The remainder is simple.

37. R(K1) x Kt	Q x B
38. QR—B1	Q x BP
39. Kt—Kt6	R—Q1
40. Kt—B4	Kt—Kt2
41. Kt—K3	Q—B5
42. K—B2	Q x RP
43. R—B7	Kt—B4
44. R—KR1	R—Q2
45. R—B8ch	K—K2
46. R(R1)—R8	Q—Q5

White Resigns

Michael Ivanovitch Tchigorin

The third of Steinitz' great rivals was the Russian, Michael Ivanovitch Tchigorin. As with so many other masters of his day, and contrary to the rule nowadays, Tchigorin developed late. Born in 1850, he did not come into prominence until 1880, when he beat Schiffers for the Russian Championship.

This question of the age at which a chess master reaches renown is of considerable interest. Before Lasker, with the exception of Morphy, most of the stars of the royal game were in their late twenties or early thirties before they became famous; some did not even learn the moves before twenty. In Lasker's time the masters made their mark in their early twenties. For the past thirty years, almost all the leading players have scored some notable victory before their twenty-first birthday. It must be the increasing popularity of chess and the growing emphasis on youthful achievement in all fields which accounts for this shift.

Tchigorin was not a professional chess player; he was a government official. But he devoted all of his leisure time to the game, founded the St. Petersburg Chess Club, and was the inspiration for Russian chess masters for twenty years. In recent times there has been a Tchigorin revival in Russia, where he has been hailed as the founder of the modern school.

Tchigorin's major successes were in the era of the gay nineties. In 1889 he tied for first at New York, in 1893 he drew a match with Tarrasch, in 1895 he finished second at Hastings. Against Steinitz and Lasker he did poorly; but for them, he had no superior in his heyday.

Tchigorin has gone down in history as a master of the "old" school, his play being full of dashing brilliancies. This is certainly true, but not completely. His love for the attack was proverbial, yet he also developed a number of highly positional defenses, of which Tchigorin's Defense in the Ruy Lopez and to the Queen's Gambit are the best known.

One of Tchigorin's outstanding victories was his second prize at Hastings, 1895, a tournament which assembled all the leading masters of the day for the first time. Tchigorin won his first three games, against Pillsbury, Lasker and Mason, but his play later became rather uneven. The first round game against the newcomer Pillsbury turned out to be an epic struggle. At that time nobody even dared to suspect that Pillsbury would finish first, much less give Tchigorin such a tussle. Here is the game, one in which the caliber of both attack and defense is sensational:

TCHIGORIN	PILLSBURY

Hastings, 1895

King's Gambit Declined

1.	P–K4	P–K4
2.	P–KB4	B–B4
3.	Kt–KB3	P–Q3
4.	B–B4	Kt–QB3
5.	Kt–B3	Kt–B3
6.	P–Q3	B–KKt5

. . . B–K3 is today considered better.

7.	P–KR3	B x Kt
8.	Q x B	Kt–Q5

9. Q—Kt3   . . . .

Quite willing to enter on complications.

9. . . . .   Kt x Pch ?

. . . P x P ! is the sharpest.

10. K—Q1   Kt x R
11. Q x KtP   K—Q2

All standard play at the time. If
11. . . . R—KB1 ? 12. P x P; P x
P; 13. R—B1, B—K2; 14. B—
KKt5 and wins.

12. P x P   P x P
13. R—B1   B—K2
14. Q x BP ?   . . . .

Lasker felt that 14. B—KKt5
was not only stronger, but probably decisive, e.g., 14. . . . R—
KKt1; 15. Q x BP, R x B; 16.
Q—K6ch, K—K1; 17. R x Kt,
R—Kt2; 18. Kt—Q5, Q—Q3; 19.
Kt x Pch, Q x Kt; 20. B—Kt5ch,
K—Q1; 21. R—B8ch, B x R; 22.
Q—K8 mate.

14. . . . .   K—B1
15. B—KKt5   R—KB1
16. Q—K6ch   K—Kt1
17. B—KR6   R—K1
18. Q x P   . . . .

White is a full Rook behind, yet
his attack is most potent.

18. . . . .   Kt—Q2
19. Q—KR5   Kt—Kt3

Lasker recommends instead 19.
. . . B—B1; 20. B—KKt5, B—
K2 with a draw as the best course
for both. But both want to win!

20. B—Q5   P—QR3
21. K—Q2   Kt x B

22. Kt x Kt   R—Kt1
23. P—KKt4   B—Kt5ch ?

Too ingenious. . . . B—B4 was
better.

24. Kt x B   Q—Q5
25. Kt—B2   Kt x Kt
26. K x Kt   R—Kt3

Time to take stock. White has
emerged from the complications
with two Pawns for the exchange
and a well-developed position.
He stands better.

27. B—Q2   R—Q3
28. R—B3   Q—R5ch
29. K—B1   Q x RP
30. B—B3   R—QB3
31. Q x P   P—Kt4
32. Q—K7   Q—Kt6
33. K—Q2   P—R4
34. R—B5 !   . . . .

Preventing . . . P—Kt5.

34. . . . .   K—Kt2
35. R—QB5   R(R1)—R3
36. P—Kt5   . . . .

The decisive advance begins.

36. . . . .   R x R
37. Q x R   R—QB3
38. Q—Q5   Q—R5

The ending is hopeless for Black after the exchange of Queens.

| 39. P–Kt6 | P–Kt5 |
| 40. P–Kt7 ! | . . . . |

Anyhow!

| 40. . . . . | P x Bch |
| 41. P x P | Q–R6 |

Black has no check.

42. P–Kt8 = Q	Q x Pch
43. K–K2	Q–B7ch
44. K–B3	Q–Q8ch
45. K–Kt3	Q–Kt8ch
46. K–R4	Q–B7ch
47. K–R5	Q–B6ch
48. Q–Kt4	Q–B3
49. Q(Kt4)–B5	Q–R3ch
50. K–Kt4	Black Resigns.

Tchigorin was also capable of superlative positional play. Here is a game which is so modern that it could have been played yesterday:

SCHLECHTER   TCHIGORIN
Cambridge Springs, 1904
Ruy Lopez

1. P–K4	P–K4
2. Kt–KB3	Kt–QB3
3. B–Kt5	P–QR3
4. B–R4	Kt–B3
5. O–O	B–K2
6. R–K1	P–QKt4
7. B–Kt3	P–Q3
8. P–B3	O–O

Nowadays . . . Kt–QR4 and . . . P–QB4 are more in vogue.

| 9. P–KR3 | B–K3 |

Safer is 9. . . . . Kt–QR4. Bronstein recently revived the text move against Botvinnik at Moscow, 1944; the game continued: 10. P–Q4, B x B; 11. Q x B, P x P; 12. Kt x P, Kt x Kt; 13. P x Kt, P–B4; 14. P x P, P x P; 15. P–K5, Kt–Q2; 16. P–QR4, with a slight advantage.

10. P–Q4	P x P
11. P x P	B x B
12. Q x B	Kt–QR4
13. Q–Q3	P–B4

Black has an endgame advantage in his Q-side Pawn majority, while White relies on his K-side attack.

14. Kt–B3	Kt–B3
15. B–Kt5	P–R3
16. B–R4	R–K1
17. QR–Q1	P–B5 !
18. Q–Kt1	Kt–QKt5
19. P–K5	Kt(B3)–Q4
20. B x B	Q x B
21. Kt x Kt	Kt x Kt
22. R–K4	. . . .

As Chernev points out, the roles are reversed, "and it is Schlechter who attempts a King-side attack —a maneuver doomed to failure according to Steinitz's teachings. Tchigorin, the bold resourceful fighter, shows that he can win a game scientifically, while Schlechter attempts to assume the discarded mantle of his adversary."

22.	Kt—B3
23. R—R4	P x P
24. P x P	Kt—Q2
25. R—K1	Kt—B4
26. R—Kt4	Kt—Q6
27. R—K3	Q—B4
28. Q—B2	. . . .

The Pawn cannot be held. If 28. R(Kt4)—K4, R—K3 followed by . . . QR—K1.

28.	Kt x KP
29. Kt x Kt	R x Kt
30. R(K3)—KKt3	P—Kt4
31. P—KR4	K—Kt2
32. P x P	P x P

Black now threatens . . . R—K8ch and . . . R—R1ch.

33. P—Kt4 !   . . . .

A last desperate try. If 33. . . . . P x P e.p. ??; 34. R x Pch, R x R; 35. Q x Q wins.

33.	R—K8ch
34. K—R2	R—R1ch
35. R—R3	R x Rch
36. K x R	Q—K4
37. P—Kt3	P—B3
38. Q—Q2	Q—K7
39. Q—K7ch	K—Kt3

White Resigns.

5.

The Age of Lasker

CHESS became a professional enterprise in the age of Lasker. Before him there were some notable exceptions who devoted most of their time to the game; after him the number was legion. Lasker himself remained a professional most of his life; although he tried other things he always came back to chess.

Lasker's reign began in 1894, the year he defeated Steinitz, and lasted until 1921, the year he lost to Capablanca. In this period, the first twenty years of which were peaceful, the institution of the chess tournament was really developed. Now there were half a dozen international tournaments every year and innumerable local ones. Chess clubs sprang up in all the leading cities of the world. A thriving literature came into being, which has reached the point where it dwarfs the literature on all other games, both in quantity and quality. Chess became a vigorous international language—the period was a veritable Renaissance.

Steinitz hailed from Central Europe, and from his time on, chess supremacy passed to the German-speaking peoples and neighboring regions. The English, who had had so many eminent masters in the nineteenth century, could not produce a single man of Blackburne's stature in the twentieth. The only one who showed great promise, C. H. Alexander, was discouraged by the poor future that lay in store. Still the English retained their interest in the game and arranged many contests, including the first great tournament of modern times, Hastings, 1895. In France there were no chess masters of renown, and interest in the game itself had dwindled. In America there were many new clubs and much activity, but in spite of Morphy, Pillsbury and Marshall, there were few masters of any consequence. Latin America was an unknown quantity until Capablanca burst upon the chess scene.

Emanuel Lasker

Of chessdom's immortals, Emanuel Lasker was by far the most versatile. His chess career was the most outstanding of all time; he made significant contributions to mathematics and philosophy; he wrote the best books available on the technique of games; and the list of his "minor" achievements, such as a book on unemployment and the invention of a forerunner of the tank, is almost endless.

What he did in chess is truly staggering. His exploits may be summed up in one sentence: For thirty years Lasker was the superman of the chess world. Marco exultantly spoke of him as "Lasker the unique"; Tartakower wonderingly called him "a piece of chess history."

His record is easy to recapitulate, for he played relatively little. But when he did play it was phenomenal.

Born in Berlinchen, near Berlin, on December 24, 1868, the son of Polish Jews, Emanuel learned the moves from his almost equally gifted brother Berthold at about the age of ten. While at the University of Berlin he picked up odd sums of money playing chess and cards at the cafés. In 1890 came an offer to go to England as a chess professional. Lasker snapped at the opportunity. In two years his game had so improved that he could trounce England's leading masters, including the brilliant Blackburne.

World Champion Steinitz was then living in New York. Lasker was glad of the chance to go to the New World in 1892. The tale was simple and brief: he came, he played, he won. In 1894 he defeated "Old Man" Steinitz for the title with almost ridiculous ease. At the age of twenty-six Lasker was the acknowledged king of chess.

From that time until his loss to Capablanca in 1921, Lasker scored a series of incredible victories. Any ordinary mortal would be happy to place third at Hastings, 1895, tie for second at Cambridge Springs, 1904, tie for first at St. Petersburg, 1909, draw in a match against Schlechter, 1910—but for Lasker these were the most serious "setbacks" of his career. On all other occasions, in all other tournaments and matches, he was first, first . . . more than first, one would have to say in some cases. At London in 1899 he outstripped the field by 4½ points; at St. Petersburg in 1914 he scored 7 points out of 8 against Capablanca, Alekhine, Marshall and Tarrasch.

Whether Lasker should have lost to Capablanca in 1921 is a moot point which it is fruitless to discuss. The older generation must always give way to a younger group. The old masters are dethroned because they continue to play when their powers are waning. Morphy-Anderssen, Steinitz-Lasker, Lasker-Capablanca, Capablanca and Alekhine against the modern group—all are incidents in the tragic tale of the decline of a chess champion's empire.

Even after Capablanca had won the championship, it took him fifteen years and four tries to come ahead of Lasker in tournament play. Lasker's sensational comeback at New York in 1924, where he outdistanced the players of both the older and younger generation, is unparalleled. Most chess masters are unable to stand the physical strain of a tournament at fifty; to win first prize against the flower of the world's talent at fifty-five, as did Lasker, is an exploit that probably never will be duplicated.

In 1925 Lasker retired from active competition. In 1935, at the age of sixty-seven, he played through nineteen gruelling rounds at Moscow and finished, without loss of a game, only half a point behind Flohr and Botvinnik, ahead of Capablanca. The papers rightly called it a biological miracle.

The last few years of his life, which ended in January, 1941, were spent in exile in New York. Never did a word of bitterness or reproach cross his lips. His intellectual honesty and alertness were an inspiration never to be forgotten.

"Lasker occasionally loses a game, but he never loses his head," said the penetrating critic Tarrasch. Every great chess master must necessarily be gifted with an immense amount of innate chess ability; I have a feeling that the masters differ but little in this respect. What accounts for variations in achievement is a psychological factor—the attitude towards the game. Does the man want victory at chess more than anything else in life? That is the case with Alekhine and Reshevsky. Is he convinced that he has but to think about a chess position to generate marvellous moves? That was true of Capablanca. Is he a mathematician who believes that profound study can always find the solution? That held for Tarrasch, and it holds for Euwe.

None of these things held for Lasker. The distinguishing characteristic of his mastery was an intuitive understanding of the human element. He looked upon the chess pieces as actors who, subject to certain conditions, were to be moved about by two playwrights. To him, chess was a dramatic conflict, a struggle between two human beings who agree upon certain rules. What really counted was the finished product, in which both competitors shared. That is why Lasker "never lost his head."

Lasker's dramatic insight helped to solve many a perplexing problem. Victory did not elate him unduly; defeat did not depress him disproportionately. He could make a mistake—and he made many mistakes—and smile, for he well knew that perfection is not granted to mortal man.

Lasker's games, ideas, books and personality are a priceless heritage. In the conventional sense, he has founded no school. But in reality all chess players are his pupils. His games are an inexhaustible source of enjoyment and instruction. What they lack in superficial polish (for he was little addicted to brilliancies, though more than enough are to be found in his play) they make up in freshness and profundity. To me, many of his games are bottomless wells—I have been through them a dozen times and each time I have unearthed new ideas in them which I had not seen before.

Of all the unplayed matches in chess history, none are more regrettable than Rubinstein-Lasker and Pillsbury-Lasker. Pillsbury and Lasker met a number of times in tournaments, and produced immortal chess on almost every occasion. Here is one of Lasker's wins in the Quadrangular Tournament at St. Petersburg, 1895–6, one of his outstanding combinative efforts.

PILLSBURY   LASKER

St. Petersburg, 1895–6
Queen's Gambit Declined

1. P–Q4   P–Q4
2. P–QB4   P–K3
3. Kt–QB3   Kt–KB3
4. Kt–B3   P–B4
5. B–Kt5   BP x P
6. Q x P   Kt–B3

After this game Pillsbury subjected this variation to careful analysis and came to the conclusion that 7. B x Kt gives White the better game. He saved his "find" for eight years until he had a chance to play it against Lasker at Cambridge Springs in 1904.

7. Q–R4   B–K2
8. O–O–O   . . . .

Risky, but typical Pillsbury.

8. . . . .   Q–R4
9. P–K3   B–Q2
10. K–Kt1   . . . .

To safeguard the RP and free the Knight.

10. . . . .   P–KR3 !

Forcing a decision.

11. P x P   P x P
12. Kt–Q4   O–O !

Lasker always played logically regardless of the consequences. The sacrifice 13. B x P, P x B; 14. Q x P, fails against 14. . . . . Kt–K4 !

13. B x Kt   B x B
14. Q–R5   Kt x Kt
15. P x Kt   B–K3
16. P–B4   QR–B1

Black's superior development begins to create threats.

17. P–B5   R x Kt !!
18. P x B   . . . .

If instead 18. P x R, Q x P with a crushing attack that forces White to give back the material gained.

18. . . . . R—QR6 !!!

The real point to the combination.

19. P x Pch . . . .

The sacrifice is sound in all variations. If 19. P x R, Q—Kt3ch; 20. K—R1, B x Pch; 21. R x B, Q x Rch; 22. K—Kt1, P x P; 23. B—K2, Q—K5ch; 24. K any, R—B7 and wins.

19. . . . . R x P
20. P x R Q—Kt3ch
21. B—Kt5 . . . .

Practically forced, for if 21. K—R1, B x Pch; and if 21. K—B2, R—B2ch.

21. . . . . Q x Bch
22. K—R1 R—B2

Threatening . . . R—B8ch ! and . . . B x Pch with mate to follow.

23. R—Q2 R—B5
24. R(R1)—Q1 R—B6
25. Q—B5 Q—B5 !
26. K—Kt2 . . . .

There was no defense. If 26. K—Kt1, R x P; 27. Q—B2, R—B6; 28. Q—Kt2, P—QKt4 wins.

26. . . . . R x P !
27. Q—K6ch K—R2
28. K x R . . . .

If Q—B5ch, simply . . . K—R1.

28. . . . . Q—B6ch
White Resigns.

Black mates in four: 29. K—R4, P—Kt4ch; 30. K x P, Q—B5ch; 31. K—R5, B—Q1 mate.

Of all the threats to Lasker's supremacy, none was more serious than the youthful Capablanca, who became famous when he beat Marshall in a match in 1909 and won first prize at San Sebastian in 1911. Negotiations for a match between Lasker and Capablanca proved fruitless. It was not until 1914 that these two met in a tournament, at St. Petersburg. Capa led for quite a while, but he was finally overtaken by Lasker in a magnificent end spurt. The game in which Lasker defeated Capa is one of the landmarks of chess history; it was played in an atmosphere charged with suspense.

LASKER CAPABLANCA
St. Petersburg, 1914
Ruy Lopez

1. P—K4 P—K4
2. Kt—KB3 Kt—QB3
3. B—Kt5 P—QR3
4. B x Kt . . . .

In one of the most crucial games of his life, Lasker chooses this inocuous—but psychologically potent—variation; he had to win in order to gain first prize and overhaul Capa, who led by ½ point.

4.	QP x B
5. P—Q4	P x P
6. Q x P	Q x Q
7. Kt x Q	B—Q3

B—Q2, in order to facilitate Q-side castling, is more accurate.

| 8. Kt—QB3 | Kt—K2 |
| 9. O—O ! | . . . . |

Beginning a war of nerves. Lasker knew that Capa and Alekhine had prepared a thorough analysis against the objectively better, but stereotyped 9. O—O—O.

9. . . . .   O—O

Imitation is the sincerest form of flattery. It is fatuous to point out that O—O—O is stronger and more usual. What is significant is that this inaccuracy revealed that Capablanca has not mastered the psychological tension. In spite of his superb intuition, he fears a prepared variation.

| 10. P—B4 | R—K1 |
| 11. Kt—Kt3 | P—B3 ? |

Correct is 11. . . . B—K3 !, e.g., 12. P—B5, B x Kt; 13. RP x B, B—K4; 14. B—B4, Kt—B1; or 11. . . . B—K3; 12. P—K5, B—QKt5; 13. Kt—K4, B—KB4; or 11. . . . B—K3; 12. B—K3, B x Kt !; 13. RP x B, Kt—

Q4 ! with complete equality in any case.

12. P—B5 !   . . . .

Lasker chooses a move which turned out to be Alekhine's undoing in their individual encounter. Capa never expected this striking tactical stroke, after which it is difficult to see a straight road to equality for Black.

12. . . . .   P—QKt3

Correct is 12. . . . B—Q2; 13. B—B4, B x B; 14. R x B, P—QKt3 !; 15. P—KKt4, Kt—B1; and Black's counterplay against the White KP reduces White's plus to a minimum.

13. B—B4   B—Kt2

The alternative 13. . . . B x B; 14. R x B, P—B4; 15. R—Q1, B—Kt2; 16. R—B2, QR—Q1; 17. R x R, R x R; 18. R—Q2, R x R; 19. Kt x R, leaves White with a slight edge. (Lasker)

14. B x B !!   P x B

Lasker now has worked out a

complete winning method, which
is simplicity itself: he will tie
Black's pieces to the defense of
the QP (that was impossible before the Pawns were undoubled)
and build up his K-side attack via
P–KKt4–5. He also hopes to
plant a Knight on K6.

15. Kt–Q4   QR–Q1
16. Kt–K6   R–Q2
17. QR–Q1   Kt–B1

Patiently waiting, but . . . P–
Q4 would have freed his game a
bit.

18. R–B2   P–QKt4

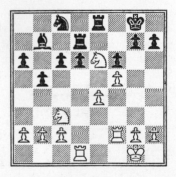

. . . R x Kt would be equivalent to an admission of defeat,
but would have created not in-
considerable technical difficulties. Black is now choked to
death.

19. R(B2)–Q2   R(Q2)–K2
20. P–QKt4   K–B2
21. P–QR3   B–R1

If 21. . . . Kt–Kt3; 22. R x P,
Kt–B5; 23. R–Q7, threatening
the murderous Kt–Q8ch.

22. K–B2   R–R2
23. P–Kt4   P–R3
24. R–Q3   P–QR4
25. P–KR4   P x P
26. P x P   R(R2)–K2
27. K–B3   R–Kt1
28. K–B4   P–Kt3

Else P–Kt5 would soon be
crushing.

29. R–Kt3   P–Kt4ch
30. K–B3 !   . . . .

Not 30. P x P ?, RP x Pch; 31.
K–B3, R–R1 with some counterplay.

30. . . . . .   Kt–Kt3
31. P x P   . . . .

Not 31. R x P, Kt–B5; 32. R–
Q4 ?, Kt–K4ch followed by
P x P with good prospects.

31. . . . .   RP x P
32. R–R3   R–Q2

The sacrifice of the exchange
would have prolonged the game.

33. K–Kt3   K–K1
34. QR–KR1   B–Kt2

Or . . . Kt–B5; 35. R–R8
wins a piece. Black is helpless.

35. P—K5 !! . . . .

Not the only, but certainly the most artistic winning continuation.

35. . . . . **QP x P**

Good defensive moves are conspicuous by their absence: on 35. . . . P—Q4; 36. P x P, K—B2; 37. Kt—B5 is murderous; while if 35. . . . BP x P; 36. Kt—K4, Kt—Q4; 37. R—R7 !; B—B1; 38. R—R8 wins a piece to begin with.

36. Kt—K4	Kt—Q4
37. Kt(K6)—B5	B—B1
38. Kt x R	B x Kt
39. R—R7	R—B1

To free the Knight.

40. R—R1	K—Q1
41. R—R8ch	B—B1
42. Kt—B5	Black Resigns.

After the New York Tournament of 1924, where he again won first prize, Lasker retired from active chess because he felt that the organization of the game was inimical to his best efforts as an artist. More than one master has had that feeling, though what Lasker was protesting against was really some suspicious financial dealings in the New York Tournament. He remained in retirement until 1934. The next year, at Moscow in 1935, he astonished the chess world by finishing third without the loss of a game. In his first round game against Kan we still catch a glimpse of the old Lasker.

KAN	LASKER

Moscow, 1935
Queen's Gambit Declined

1. P—Q4	P—Q4
2. P—QB4	P—QB3
3. P x P	P x P
4. Kt—QB3	Kt—QB3
5. Kt—B3	Kt—B3
6. B—B4	B—B4

As always, Lasker is satisfied with simple openings.

7. Q—Kt3 ? . . . .

A faulty idea.

7.	Kt—QR4
8. Q—R4ch	B—Q2
9. Q—B2	R—B1
10. P—K3	P—QKt4 !
11. P—QR3	P—K3
12. B—Q3	B—K2

Black has captured the initiative.

13. Kt—K5	Kt—B5
14. Q—K2	O—O
15. O—O	B—K1
16. QR—B1	Kt—Q2 !
17. Kt x Kt(B4)	KtP x Kt
18. B—Kt1	P—B4
19. P—B3	Kt—Kt3
20. B—B2	. . . .

Preparing P—Kt3.

20.	B—Q3
21. B x B	Q x B
22. KR—Q1	B—Q2
23. Q—Q2	B—B3

Maneuvering for time.

24. R—K1	R(B1)—Q1
25. R—K2	R—Q2
26. R(B1)—K1	P—Kt3
27. R—Q1	R—Kt1
28. Q—K1	R(Q2)—QKt2
29. R(Q1)—Q2	Kt—Q2
30. B—Kt1	P—K4!

At last.

31. Q—Kt3   Q—K3?

A mistake; correct was 31. . . .
Q—B3!

32. P—K4!   KP x P!?

Complications were always Lasker's forte.

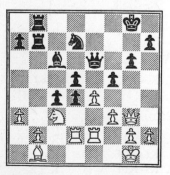

33. P x BP?   . . . .

Kan blunders also. The right way was 33. P x QP!, Q—B3; 34. P x B, P x Kt; 35. R x Kt, R x P; 36. R x R, R x R; 37. Q—K1!, with an easy win. From now on Lasker regains his composure and finishes in wonderful style.

33.	Q—B3
34. R—K6	P x Kt!!

This is what Kan must have overlooked.

35. R x Q	P x R
36. R x Pch	. . . .

The only chance. If 36. B—B2, Kt x R.

36.	P x R
37. Q x Pch	K—B1
38. Q—Q6ch	K—K1
39. B—B2	. . . .

Threatening P—B6 as well as Q x B.

39.	R—Kt3!
40. P—B6	K—Q1
41. P—B7	K—B1
42. P—B8 = Qch	Kt x Q
43. Q x Ktch	K—Kt2
44. Q—B6	K—R3!

Preparing . . . B—R5.

45. Q—Q6   R—K1

Preferable to 45. . . . B—R5; 46. Q x P.

46. P—KR4	R—K8ch
47. K—R2	R—QB8
48. B—B5	. . . .

The last gasp.

| 48. . . . . | P—Q8 = Q |
| 49. B—B8ch | K—R4 |

White Resigns.

For if 50. Q—B5ch, K—R5!
and he is checkless.

Here are a few more examples of
Lasker's skill:

Bauer

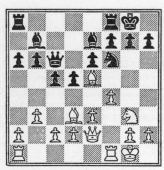

Lasker—TO PLAY

Amsterdam, 1889

1. Kt—R5	Kt x Kt
2. B x Pch !	K x B
3. Q x Ktch	K—Kt1
4. B x P !	K x B
5. Q—Kt4ch	K—R2
6. R—B3	P—K4
7. R—R3ch	Q—R3
8. R x Qch	K x R
9. Q—Q7 and wins.	

Edward Lasker

Emanuel Lasker—TO PLAY AND
DRAW

New York, 1924

| 1. Kt—Kt2 | R—Q7 |
| 2. K—B3 ! | R—Q1 |

Not . . . R x Kt; 3. P—Kt7,
R—B7ch !; 4. K x R, P—Kt7—
draw.

3. K—K4	K—Q3
4. K—Q4	R—QB1
5. P—Kt7	K—K3
6. P—Kt8 = Qch	R x Q
7. K—B4	R—Kt6
8. Kt—R4	K—B4
9. K—Kt4	K x P

Drawn.

Lasker—TO PLAY

Steinitz

Match, 1896–7

1. . . . . R–KKt1 !!
White Resigns.

ZUGZWANG!!

1. The Bishop cannot move because of R–Kt7ch.
2. The Queen must remain at Q2 to defend the Bishop and the mate.
3. P–B6 allows . . . R x B.
4. K–Kt1 loses the Bishop.
5. If the Rook moves to any place except KKt1, . . . Q x BP wins.

The only move which remains is 2. R–KKt1, which loses quickly after: 2. . . . R x B ! 3. Q x R, Q–Q3ch; 4. R–Kt3, P x Rch; 5. Q x P, B–K1; 6. P–R4, Q x Qch; 7. K x Q, P – Kt4 !

Lasker—TO PLAY

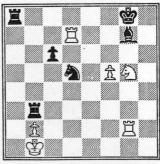

Alekhine

St. Petersburg, 1914

1. . . . . R–Q6 !!
2. R x Kt . . . .

Forced. White cannot meet the double threat of . . . Kt–B6ch or . . . R–Q8ch followed by Kt–K6ch. If 2. K–B1, R–R8ch; 3. K–B2, Kt–Kt5 mate.

2. . . . . R x R and wins.

Lasker—TO PLAY

London, 1914

Amateur

The arch-wizard saves a lost game!

1. . . . .   R—B6ch
2. K—Kt4 ??   . . . .

2. K—B2, R—B7ch; 3. K—K3, R—B6ch; 4. K—Q2, would have won.

2. . . . .   R—B5ch
3. K—Kt5   R—KR5 !!
4. K x R   P—Kt4ch !! and
                  wins.

Black plays K—Kt2 next, and Queens his Pawns first.

Siegbert Tarrasch

Tarrasch considered himself the strongest player in the world when Lasker came upon the scene; many who thought that Steinitz was passé agreed with him. In fact, when talk of a match between Lasker and Tarrasch first arose in 1895, Tarrasch declined, claiming that Lasker had yet to prove himself a great player! The long awaited match did not take place until 1908, when Tarrasch was no longer in his prime.

When Tarrasch died in 1934, Euwe wrote an appreciation for the *Magyar Sakkvilag*, the gist of which was: "He played many great games, he won many first prizes, he wrote many great books." We can add that Tarrasch was another of the select handful of geniuses who were of world championship caliber but did not secure the title because of an unkind fate.

Breslau, where he was born on March 5, 1862, had long been an important chess center, Anderssen above all was its pride, but Zukertort had lived there too, and many a minor master. Tarrasch liked to think that he had continued the splendid German tradition which had reached its high water mark in Anderssen. Ironically, Tarrasch and Lasker, both Jews, were the last really great German masters.

In an autobiographical sketch, Tarrasch tells us nothing about his parents, but he does reveal, apologetically, that he was born with a club foot. Compensation for this physical handicap goes far to explain much of his character. As a boy he felt the urge to be at the top of his class all the time. Every bad mark—such as finishing second or third best—made him feel guilty; in later years he felt compelled to justify every bad move and every lost game.

An obviously gifted student, he completed his medical course at twenty-three. The rest of his life was divided between medical practice, abandoned only in old age, and chess, his real love.

At fifteen he learned the chess moves and, as usual with great masters, progress was rapid. For several years nothing mattered but chess. It seemed that every chess master goes through a period in his adolescence when the sixty-four squares are more important than bread and butter. In Tarrasch's case, the total absorption in chess ended with a love affair. After that came university years with the customary rounds of wine, women and song, though chess was by no means neglected. In 1885, when he obtained his degree, he was already a full-fledged master, and made an extraordinary debut in the German Chess Association tournament by dividing second prize with a number of the world's best.

After the initial plunge, Tarrasch's career falls into three parts. In the first, from 1885 to 1894, after some hesitation he won almost everything in sight. After his victory at Manchester in 1890, he justly complained because the Germans merely referred to him as the champion of Germany; the English, on the other hand, placed him second to Steinitz, champion of the world, and proposed a match between the two. Certainly Tarrasch in 1890 was, if second at all, second only to Steinitz. It is a pity—a tragedy for Tarrasch—that he declined the invitation of the Havana Chess Club to meet Steinitz there in the winter of 1890–91. Had he accepted, he might well have won the title which he afterwards coveted so vainly and so bitterly. The great opportunity knocked but once for Tarrasch, and he missed it. Very soon Lasker appeared, and Lasker was always Tarrasch's superior.

By 1894 the big four were Lasker, Steinitz, Tchigorin and Tarrasch, and as yet there appeared to be little to choose among them. The next year Pillsbury joined the chosen few.

The second period of Tarrasch's life, from 1894 to 1908, is dominated by his rivalry with Lasker. All others had to bow, as he demonstrated most convincingly at Vienna in 1898 and Ostend in 1907 (where he had himself awarded the title of tournament champion of the world); even the younger generation could be kept off, as Marshall learned in 1905. But Lasker was immovable. And when the match finally came, in 1908, Tarrasch did not have a chance. Some great masters have discovered to their sorrow that there is one who is greater, and have twisted it into tragedy.

From 1908 to his death in 1934, Tarrasch continued to play an active role in the chess world. But there were new stars in the firmament, new names on everybody's lips, especially after the first world war. His main influence then was exerted through his writings.

In chess literature Tarrasch occupies a unique position. *Praeceptor Germaniae* he was called when his articles and books first became known; later it was *praeceptor mundi*. And he undoubtedly was the teacher of the world. For more than a generation—roughly 1895 to 1925—he was the leading authority on chess. What Tarrasch said was law.

Yet, curiously, though he formulated the principles which dominated chess until they were shattered by the hypermoderns, all his works except the last were annotated tournament or match books.

Dreihundert Schachpartien is his masterpiece—a collection of 300 of his games, with detailed notes and a running autobiographical sketch, first published in 1894. It is, indeed, one of the monuments of our game—up to the 1920's it was the best chess book ever written. The subtitle is "An unsystematic manual of chess for experienced players," and in the midst of his excellent notes he manages to intersperse all the basic principles which almost everybody tacitly accepted until 1914 and against which the generation of the hypermoderns rose in angry and somewhat uncritical revolt.

Morphy laid the basis for combination play by his demonstration of the value of development; Steinitz founded position play with his theory of the center. But it remained for Tarrasch to unite the two in one complete system (Morphy and Steinitz are really complementary). The pillars of this system are so familiar nowadays that it is hard to realize how bad master chess was before they were pointed out. Such everyday concepts as development, center, the two Bishops, Pawn structure, attacking procedure, etc. were a complete mystery to all but a few before the days of Steinitz and Tarrasch.

By 1914 anybody who read books understood the principles of the open game, and they understood them either directly or indirectly because of Tarrasch's untiring efforts.

But unfortunately Tarrasch did not realize, at least in his writings, the limitations of his theory. "A cramped position bears the germs of loss," he pontificated, forgetting why and under what circumstances. The hypermoderns could reply with uncounted cases where cramped positions won instead of losing, but with an equally mistaken emphasis at the other extreme. The quarrel went on for many years, and Tarrasch did not help any by his assumption of infallibility. In most of his books the dogmatic air is so evident that we often feel they should have been entitled: "Thus Spake Tarraschustra."

Because he was the dean of the chess world for thirty years Tarrasch's vices and virtues have been magnified out of all proportion. True, he was often petty, domineering, and vain; true, he frequently indulged his vindictive sense of humor with malice towards some—his club foot tells

part of the story. To the generation which came after him his major fault
was that he was uninspiring. He could criticize them, but he could not
help them to build. As a result they built without him and against him,
neglecting his real contributions.

Yet there is another side to the picture, as indeed there must be to explain his enormous influence. As a practicing grandmaster he was for thirty
years one of the best three or four. But more important—throughout he
preached the cause of chess. Tarrasch believed in chess, with a fiery conviction which too few of his colleagues have shared. He felt that chess is a
significant pursuit, that it is our right and duty to spread its practice, that
ability and improvement are ample reward for the time spent in serious
study.

As his most fitting epitaph, we cannot do better than quote the famous
sentence from his *The Game of Chess*: "Chess, like music, like love, has
the power to make men happy."

Though his gospel was the attack, Tarrasch produced many defensive masterpieces. The following is one of his greatest, a battle
royal from start to finish.

TCHIGORIN   TARRASCH
4th Match Game,
St. Petersburg, 1893
French Defense

1. P—K4   P—K3
2. Q—K2   P—QB4
3. P—KKt3   Kt—QB3
4. Kt—KB3   . . . .

P—KB4 is preferred nowadays.
But Tchigorin's plan is to provoke . . . P—K4 and then break
with P—KB4—amazingly mod-
ern!

4. . . . .   B—K2

. . . P—KKt3, to control Q5, is
more logical; but Tarrasch just
develops normally, and has con-

fidence in the powers of his position.

5. B—Kt2   P—Q4
6. P—Q3   Kt—B3
7. O—O   O—O
8. Kt—B3   P—QR3 !

Starting his Q-side counterattack.

9. B—Kt5   P—R3
10. B—B4   P—QKt4
11. KR—K1   P—Q5

A courageous decision, even
though it is a confession that he
has been outmaneuvered. The
alternative . . . B—Kt2; 12. P x
P, P x P; 13. Kt—KR4 !, R—K1;
14. Kt—B5, B—KB1; 15. Q—Q2,
R x Rch; 16. R x R, B—B1 is tol-
erable, but 12. P—K5 ! creates a
cramped position for Black where
it would take a longer time to develop his counterattack.

12. Kt—Q1   Kt—Q2
13. K—R1 !   R—K1
14. R—KKt1   . . . .

P—K5 was worth a thought.

14.	. . . .	P—K4
15.	B—Q2	Kt—B1
16.	Kt—K1	Kt—K3
17.	P—KB4	B—Kt2
18.	P—B5	Kt—Kt4

The problem for White—as Tchigorin most certainly realized —is how to advance his K-side Pawns most effectively. Tarrasch tosses it off with a dogmatic shrug by recommending simply P—KR4, Kt—KB3, Q—B2, P—KKt4, etc., when White's attack "could hardly have been stopped." Tchigorin should have chosen that method, but there is far more life in Black's position than Tarrasch is willing to admit. E.g., 19. P—KR4, Kt—KR2; 20. Kt—KB3, R—QB1; 21. Q—B2, P—B5; 22. P—KKt4, P x P; 23. P x P, P—B3; 24. Q—Kt3, Kt—Kt5 with considerable counterplay.

19.	Kt—B2	R—QB1
20.	Q—R5	Kt—KR2 !
21.	Kt—B3	P—B5

Every move counts.

22. B—KB1   . . . .

As Ben Franklin would have said, a clumsy woman can cramp anybody's style. White's Queen at R5 is out of play and prevents the direct Pawn advance. E.g., on 22. Kt—Kt4, B—B1 ! holds everything.

22. . . . .   P x P

First blood!

23.	P x P	Kt—Kt4 !
24.	B x Kt	B x B
25.	Kt—Kt4	. . . .

Threatening P—KR4

25. . . . .   K—B1 !!!

A stroke of genius. The King cannot be defended well where he is, so he is moved out of the way.

26.	B—K2	B—B3
27.	P—KR4	Q—Q3
28.	Kt(B3)—R2	. . . .

28. . . . .   Kt—K2 !!

Another magnificent idea. The Kt retreats to Kt1 to hold back the enemy BP. If now 29. Kt x B, Q x Kt; 30. Kt—Kt4 ?, Q x BP!

29. QR—KB1 . . . .

Not 29. Kt x RP, P x Kt; 30. Q x RPch, K—Kt1; 31. QR—KB1, R—B3 ! and Black is safe.

29. . . . .   Kt—Kt1 !
30. B—Q1   R—B2
31. B—Kt3   R(K1)—B1
32. Kt—B2   B—Q1 !

Creating more delay, since 33. P—KKt4 ?? allows Kt—B3 winning the Queen.

33. Q—K2   P—QR4
34. Kt—B3   P—R5
35. B—Q1   B—QB3 !

Of this move Tarrasch writes: "The beginning of a fine maneuver which makes it possible for the Rooks to penetrate to the seventh rank." We fully agree.

36. P—KKt4   P—B3
37. Kt—R3   B—K1
38. Q—R2   B—B2
39. P—R3   B—Kt6
40. Kt—B2   B x B
41. Kt x B   R—B7
42. Q—Kt3   . . . .

Better was R—B2, but he is intent on the attack. And it seems that Black finally is unable to prevent P—Kt5. Another crisis is at hand.

42. . . . .   P—Kt5 !
43. P x P   Q—R3 !!

The point.

44. Kt—B2   R x P
45. P—KKt5   . . . .

At last!

45. . . . .   RP x P
46. P x P   R(B1)—B7
47. Kt—Kt4   Q—Q3
48. P x P ?   . . . .

48. Q—R3 ! would have won: e.g., . . . Q—B2; 49. Q—R8 !, Q—B2; 50. R—R1 !!, R x P; 51. P x P, P x P; 52. Kt—R4 !, R(Kt5)—Kt7 (otherwise Kt—R6); 53. R x P and Black is helpless against the countless openings on all sides.

In over-the-board-play, however, it was extremely difficult to realize that the text, which wins the Black Queen, could be adequately countered by the advance of the QRP.

48. . . . .   B x P
49. Q—R3   P—R6 !!

Another stroke of genius: the only defense is to ignore White's attack! On 49. . . . . Q—B2; 50. Q—R8, transposing into some of the above variations is too strong.

50. Kt x B   Q x Kt
51. R—Kt6   . . . .

Once more Tarrasch appears to be on the brink of disaster.

51. . . . .   P—R7 !!!

And once more he escapes, this time permanently.

52. R x Qch ?   . . . .

Tarrasch's suggestion 52. Kt—Kt5 would have drawn: 52. . . . K—K2 (forced, since he cannot afford to give up the Queen for a Knight); 53. R x Q, P x R; 54. Q—R7ch, K—Q3; 55. Kt—B7ch, K—B3; 56. Q x Kt ! R—Kt8 !, and now 57. Kt x Pch !, P x Kt; 58. Q—Q5ch is the clearest—the remarkable feature is that White with Q and Kt for a R can lose quite easily if he tries too hard to win.

52. . . . .   P x R
53. R—Q1   . . . .

Q—Kt3 or R—KKt1 are no better.

53. . . . .   R—Kt8
54. Q—B1   R(B7)—QKt7
55. Kt—Q2   R x R
56. Q x R   R x Kt !
57. Q—QB1   R x P
58. K—Kt2   R—QB6
59. Q—QR1   R—B7ch
60. K—B3   P—Q6
61. Q—Q1   . . . .

Or 61. K—K3, P—Q7; 62. K—K2, R—B8.

61. . . . .   R—QKt7
62. Q—R4   P—Q7

To be followed by . . . R—Kt8. White Resigns. An epic struggle.

Tarrasch always developed a logical formation. Here is a classic example from one of his great tournament victories:

TARRASCH   MARCO
Vienna, 1898
Petroff's Defense

1. P—K4   P—K4
2. Kt—KB3   Kt—KB3
3. Kt x P   P—Q3
4. Kt—KB3   Kt x P
.5. P—Q4   B—K2
6. B—Q3   Kt—KB3
7. O—O   O—O
8. P—KR3   B—K3
9. P—B4 !   . . . .

The restricting maneuvers have begun.

9. . . . .   P—B3
10. Kt—Kt5 !   Kt—R3

Black cannot develop normally.

11. Kt—QB3   Kt—B2
12. P—B4   P—KR3
13. Kt—B3   Q—B1

14. Q—B2   R—Kt1
15. P—KB5   B—Q2

16. B—B4   P—QKt4
17. P—QKt3   P—B4 !?

Sacrificing a Pawn to free himself.

18. P—Q5 !   . . . .

With 18. P x BP, QP x P; 19. P x P he wins a Pawn, but keeping Black cramped is by far more important.

18. . . . .   P—Kt5
19. Kt—K2   P—QR4
20. P—Kt4   Kt—R2
21. P—KR4   . . . .

Intending P—Kt5.

21. . . . .   Q—Q1
22. B—Kt3   P—R5
23. K—R1   R—R1
24. QR—K1 !   . . . .

Exchanges must be avoided.

24. . . . .   Kt—K1
25. Kt—B4   B—KB3

26. Kt—K6 !!   . . . .

In such positions some sacrifice is bound to prove decisive. If in reply 26. . . . P x Kt; 27. BP x P, B—B1; 28. B x Ktch wins.

26. . . . .   P x P
27. P x P   Q—Kt3

Hoping for a stalemate.

28. Kt x R   K x Kt
29. P—Kt5 !   . . . .

Anyhow.

29. . . . .   P x P
30. P x P   Kt x P

31. Q—KR2 !   K—Kt1
32. Kt x Kt   B x Kt
33. P—B6 !   P—Kt3
34. B x KtP !   Black Resigns.

For if 34. . . . P x B; 35. P—B7ch.

Tarrasch was noted for his handling of the two Bishops. Here is a striking illustration from one of his later tournaments:

SPIELMANN   TARRASCH
San Sebastian, 1912
Ruy Lopez

1. P—K4   P—K4
2. Kt—KB3   Kt—QB3
3. B—Kt5   P—QR3
4. B—R4   Kt—B3

5. O–O	Kt x P
6. P–Q4	P–QKt4
7. B–Kt3	P–Q4
8. P–QR4	. . . .

Now out of date, partly as a result of this game.

8.	Kt x QP !
9. Kt x Kt	P x Kt
10. Kt–B3 !?	. . . .

| 10. . . . . | Kt x Kt ! |

The simplest.

| 11. P x Kt | P–QB4 ! |

The primary purpose is to closet the White Bishop.

| 12. RP x P | B–K2 |
| 13. Q–B3 ? | . . . . |

Tarrasch recommends 13. BP x P, P–B5; 14. B–R4, O–O; 15. P x P, R x P; 16. P–QB3.

13.	B–K3
14. R x P	O–O !
15. P x P	P–B5
16. B–R2	. . . .

If B–R4, Q–Q2 ! wins a piece!

16.	R x R
17. P x R	Q–R4
18. B–Kt1	P–B6 !

Now the Bishop is completely immobilized.

19. Q–Kt3	R–B1
20. P–B4	B–KB4
21. R–K1	B–B3
22. K–R1	P–R3

Not . . . Q x P ? at once because of 23. Q x P !, and if . . . R x Q; 24. R–K8 mate.

| 23. P–R3 | R–Kt1 |
| 24. B–K3 | Q x P |

The threat is . . . Q–R8.

25. R–Q1	Q–R8
26. Q–K1	B–K5
27. K–R2	B–K2
28. Q–B1	P–B4

As a result of the last ten moves, both of White's Bishops are desolate behind a wall of Pawns.

29. R–K1	B–R5
30. P–Kt3	B–K2
31. B–B2	B–Q3
32. R–B1	K–R2

White is reduced to marking time; Black prepares the breakthrough at his leisure.

33. R–K1	R–Kt3
34. R–B1	B–R6
35. R–K1	Q–Kt7
36. Q–K2	R–Kt5
37. R–Kt1	R–Kt3
38. R–K1	Q–Kt4 !
39. Q–R5	. . . .

If 39. Q–Q1, P–Kt4 does the trick.

39. . . . . .   Q x B !!
40. R x Q   R x R
41. P – Kt4   B – B8 !!

White Resigns. A remarkable finish. If 42. K – Kt3, P – Kt3 !; 43. Q – R4, B x Pch !; 44. K x B, P – Kt4ch.

Here are some brilliant excerpts from Tarrasch's games:

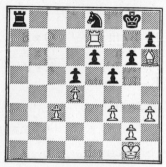

Reti

Tarrasch – TO PLAY

Vienna, 1922

1. K – R2 !   Kt – Q3
2. R – Kt7ch   K – R1
3. R – Q7 !   Kt – Kt4
4. K – Kt3   Kt x BP
5. K – B4   Kt – Kt4
6. K – K5   R – K1
7. K – B6   Back Resigns – an amazing position!

Walbrodt

Tarrasch – TO PLAY

Hastings, 1895

1. R x P !!   Kt x P
2. Kt x Kt !   R x Ktch
3. P x R   R x Pch
4. K – B1 !   R x Q
5. R – Kt4 !!!   Black Resigns.

Tarrasch—TO PLAY

Nuremberg, 1892

Harmonist

1. . . . .   B—Kt4

White Resigns.

If 35. B—Q3, R x R wins a piece. If 35. R—K1, P—Q4; 36. B moves, B x Ktch; 37. Q x B, R x Rch, etc.

Allies

Naples, 1914

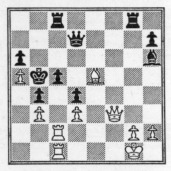

Tarrasch—TO PLAY

1. B—B7 !!!	Q x B
2. R x Pch	Q x R
3. Q—Kt7ch	K x P
4. R—R1 mate.	

Magnificent!

Tarrasch—TO PLAY

St. Petersburg, 1914

Nimzovitch

1.	Kt x Kt
2. Kt x Kt	P—Q5
3. P x P	B x Pch !
4. K x B	Q—R5ch
5. K—Kt1	B x P
6. P—B3	KR—K1
7. Kt—K4	Q—R8ch
8. K—B2	B x R
9. P—Q5	P—B4
10. Q—B3	Q—Kt7ch
11. K—K3	R x Ktch
12. P x R	P—B5ch
13. K x P	R—B1ch
14. K—K5	Q—R7ch
15. K—K6	R—K1ch
16. K—Q7	B—Kt4 mate.

Harry Nelson Pillsbury

Harry Nelson Pillsbury was one of the vital forces in chess history. Despite a tragically brief career, he became one of the monumental figures in the game, a towering and distinctive personality.

The Boston near which he was born on December 5, 1872, was just beginning to cede its cultural preeminence to New York; Pillsbury's development reflected the change. There is no record of exactly how he became interested in chess, but we do know that he learned the moves at the age of sixteen. His early surroundings were those of a typical middle-class American family. Evidently chess genius can occur in any environment.

At first Pillsbury's progress was unusual, but none too startling. He moved to Boston, became a confirmed denizen of all the chess clubs, met the strongest players and improved rapidly. By 1892 he was the best in Boston and—more important—had discovered his place in life. Earlier thoughts of a commercial career were discarded; all his time was devoted to chess, checkers and whist, with chess gradually crowding out the other two.

In 1893 his professional career was already started; successes against the Germans Walbrodt and Schottlaender, then on a visit to Boston, were an auspicious beginning. 1894 saw him in New York where, as always, the best American and foreign talent was concentrated. World champion Lasker and ex-champion Steinitz, who was Pillsbury's ideal, were there, as well as Hodges, Showalter, Delmar, Albin and others less well known. In the tournaments of the next two years, Pillsbury ranked about on a par with the top American masters, all of whom, however, were far inferior to Lasker and Steinitz.

Then, in 1895, came the turning point. The Hastings Chess Club of Hastings, England, organized the most important international tournament held up to that time, with every one of the great masters of the period, and many who were to become great later, present. Lasker, Steinitz, Tarrasch and Tchigorin were the favorites. Pillsbury had as yet done nothing to warrant blind faith; yet, to everybody's amazement, he captured first prize. It was the most sensational event since Morphy's triumphal tour.

After Hastings, it was clear that the world's five leading grandmasters (though the term was not then in common use) were Lasker, Steinitz, Tchigorin, Tarrasch and Pillsbury, with little to choose among them. It was not until St. Petersburg, at the end of 1895, and Nuremburg, in the summer of 1896, that Lasker demonstrated his superiority over the other four.

In succeeding tournaments, Pillsbury was always a high prize winner, but he could never repeat his performance at Hastings. Down to Paris,

1900, he was always second or third; after that, lesser lights managed to pass him by with increasing frequency. Poor health was most obviously the reason. At Cambridge Springs, in 1904, he was little more than a shadow; two years later he died.

In the five years, from 1895 to 1900, when Pillsbury was at the height of his powers, he was certainly the equal of anyone. Against Lasker he always did well in individual encounters; so well, indeed, that the chances would have been even if a match had been arranged between the two in that period. Pillsbury was not so well rounded as Lasker, but there are some respects in which he was greater. Pillsbury's stature in history is that of a world champion; he never had a chance to play for the title because of the way in which chess was organized.

His games reveal a tempestuous genius whose disappointments failed to produce sufficient subtlety. An incredible combinative gift was his great strength; impatience, especially in inferior positions, was his weakness. In a sense his chess and his career fall into similar patterns. He begins with the violence of a tornado; often the resistance is swept away in a blaze of brilliance—there he is at his grandest. But at other times the going is much more strenuous; then, where sheer force will not do, he frequently collapses. For Pillsbury it was always all or nothing.

His genius is expressed in the originality and bold sweep of his attacking ideas. Both the Queen's Gambit and the Ruy Lopez, the two major defensive weapons of the modern master, first became popular, chiefly because of the treatment which Pillsbury gave them. In middle games, where direct methods were applicable, he was incomparable. But where maneuvering—tacking to take advantage of the winds—was needed, he was less successful. In many endgames he did not feel at home. By and large, however, his collection of games is one of the finest; the only reason why some others are better is that Pillsbury's covered too short a time.

Pillsbury was one of the few great masters who were satisfied with the choice of chess as a profession. In exhibitions and tournaments he enjoyed himself immensely without any of the soul-torturing which has bothered others. Because he was such a marvellous entertainer, he was always a welcome guest. His blindfold powers and miraculous memory were a delight to behold. For quality of performance, his blindfold display against twenty-two participants in the *Hauptturnier* (just below master class) at Hannover, 1902, is still unequalled. One of his favorite displays was to conduct a number of chess and checker games (he ranked among the twenty best checker experts in the United States) blindfold and play whist at the same time. To make it easier, he would sometimes ask somebody in the audience to give him a list of thirty words which he repeated backwards when he was all through. His exhibitions were so impressive that the memories which they left are still vivid today, despite a lapse of forty years. As an exhibitor, Pillsbury has never had a peer.

The first successes of a new star always have a dramatic quality. It is as though a living picture were unfolding, depicting the change of the old order to the new. And when these initial triumphs are scored by defeating favorites, as in Pillsbury's case, artistic chess of the highest rank is produced.

In the first two rounds of the Hastings tournament in 1895, Pillsbury was paired with two of the greatest, Tchigorin and Tarrasch. Against Tchigorin he showed his mettle in a long, involved King's Gambit Declined, where he avoided a safe draw in order to retain some winning chances, disregarding the risks involved and finally lost. Sometimes a young master who begins with a defeat changes his style, fearful that he will collapse completely. But Pillsbury was not depressed by losses. With limitless confidence in his own powers, he adopted exactly the same tactics—all out to win—against Tarrasch. The result is superb. Here is the game, which Chernev, incidentally, considers the second greatest of all time.

PILLSBURY	TARRASCH

Hastings, 1895
Queen's Gambit Declined

1. P–Q4	P–Q4
2. P–QB4	P–K3
3. Kt–QB3	Kt–KB3
4. B–Kt5	. . . .

Relatively new at the time; B–B4 was then more usual.

4.	B–K2
5. Kt–B3	QKt–Q2
6. R–B1	O–O
7. P–K3	P–QKt3
8. P x P	P x P
9. B–Q3	B–Kt2
10. O–O	P–B4
11. R–K1	. . . .

A waste of time.

11.	P–B5
12. B–Kt1	P–QR3

13. Kt–K5 !	. . . .

The innovation which put the Q's Gambit on the chess master's map.

13.	P–Kt4
14. P–B4	R–K1
15. Q–B3	Kt–B1
16. Kt–K2 !	Kt–K5
17. B x B	R x B
18. B x Kt	P x B
19. Q–Kt3 !	P–B3

Otherwise P–B5–B6.

20. Kt–Kt4   K–R1
21. P–B5 !   . . . .

Again we are apt to miss the originality of Pillsbury's moves. But in 1895 only a select handful of great masters grasped the correct principles of position play.

21. . . . .   Q–Q2

Better was an immediate Q-side advance.

22. R–B1 !   R–Q1

More hesitation . . .

23. R–B4   Q–Q3

. . . still unable to take his bearings . . .

24. Q–R4 !   . . . .

Threatening Kt–B2, Kt–Kt3, etc.

24. . . . .   R(Q1)–K1
25. Kt–B3 ?   . . . .

Correct is 25. Kt–B2, and if B–Q4; 26. P–KKt4, P–R3; 27. Q–Kt3, P–Kt5; 28. P–KR4, Kt–R2; 29. Kt–R3, R–QB1 – White has the initiative, Black the counterplay. After the text move, however, Black gets the better of it.

25. . . . .   B–Q4
26. Kt–B2   Q–B3
27. R–B1   P–Kt5
28. Kt–K2   Q–R5

Or 28. . . . P–B6; 29. P–QKt3.

29. Kt–Kt4 !   Kt–Q2

Not . . . Q x P ??; 30. Kt x P ! and wins.

30. R(B4)–B2 !   K–Kt1

If 30. . . . Q x P; 31. Kt–B4, B–B2; 32. Kt–Kt6ch, B x Kt; 33. P x B, P–R3; 34. Kt x RP !!, P x Kt; 35. Q x RPch, K–Kt1; 36. R–B5 ! wins.

31. Kt–B1   P–B6
32. P–QKt3   Q–B3
33. P–KR3   P–QR4
34. Kt–R2   P–R5
35. P–Kt4   P x P
36. P x P   R–R1 ?

36. . . . P–R3 maintains the advantage. E.g., 37. Q–Kt3, Kt–B1 !; 38. P–R4, Kt–R2, and White must regroup for the advance.

37. P–Kt5 !

From here to the end Pillsbury's play is perfection.

37. . . . .   R–R6
38. Kt–Kt4   . . . .

38. . . . .   B x P

Allowing a beautiful conclusion.

39. R—KKt2 ! K—R1
40. P x P   P x P

40. . . . Kt x P; 41. Kt—K5 is
no improvement.

41. Kt x B   R x Kt
42. Kt—R6 !   R—Kt2
43. R x R !   K x R
44. Q—Kt3ch !! K x Kt

44. . . . K—B1; 45. Q—Kt8ch
costs a piece.

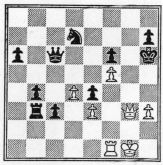

45. K—R1 !!!   . . . .

The enchanting key. Black is
helpless against the threatened
R—KKt1.

45. . . . .   Q—Q4
46. R—KKt1   Q x BP

. . . The remainder is more to
be pitied than criticized.

47. Q—R4ch   Q—R4
48. Q—B4ch   Q—Kt4
49. R x Q   P x R
50. Q—Q6ch   K—R4
51. Q x Kt   P—B7
52. Q x P mate.

A splendid battle.

Following are two startling wins
against Emanuel Lasker—two of
the finest games of Pillsbury's
short-lived career.

PILLSBURY   LASKER
Nuremberg, 1896
French Defense
(Best Played Game Prize)

1. P—K4   P—K3
2. P—Q4   P—Q4
3. Kt—QB3   Kt—KB3
4. P—K5   KKt—Q2
5. P—B4   P—QB4
6. P x P   Kt—QB3
7. P—QR3   Kt x BP
8. P—QKt4   Kt—Q2
9. B—Q3   P—QR4

Amazingly modern.

10. P—Kt5   QKt—Kt1
11. Kt—B3   Kt—B4
12. B—K3   QKt—Q2
13. O—O   P—KKt3
14. Kt—K2   B—K2
15. Q—K1   Kt—Kt3
16. KKt—Q4   B—Q2
17. Q—B2   Kt(3)—R5
18. QR—Kt1   P—R4

Not . . . O—O; 19. P—Kt4.

19. P—Kt6 !   Kt x B
20. P x Kt   B x P

Now comes the rock crusher . . .

21. P–B5 !!	KtP x P
22. Kt–B4	P–R5
23. R–R1	....

23. Kt x BP, P x Kt; 24. Kt x P leads to a vicious attack.

23.	B–K2
24. R x Kt !	B x R

25. Kt(B4) x KP !   ....

The point!

25.	P x Kt
26. Kt x KP	....

26.	B–Q2

There was no defense. E.g., if 26. ... Q–B1; 27. Q x BP, Q–B3; 28. B–Kt5, Q x Pch; 29. P–Q4, Q–Kt5; 30. Q–B7ch, K–Q2; 31. B x B, Q x B; 32. Kt–B5ch, K–Q1; 33. Kt x Pch, K–Q2; 34. Kt–B5ch, K–Q1; 35. Q x Pch, K–B2; 36. Q–Kt7ch, followed by Q x Rch and wins.

27. Kt x Q	R x Kt

The rest is anticlimactic.

28. B–B5	R–QB1
29. B x B	K x B

30. Q–K3	R–B3
31. Q–Kt5ch	K–B2
32. R–B1	R x Rch
33. Q x R	R–QB1
34. Q–K1	P–R6
35. P x P	R–Kt1ch
36. K–B2	P–R5
37. Q–Kt4	R–Kt3
38. K–B3	P–R6
39. Q x P	R x P
40. Q–B5	R–K3
41. Q–B7	K–K2
42. K–B4	P–Kt3
43. P–R4	R–QB3
44. Q–Kt8	B–K1
45. K x P	R–R3
46. Q–B7ch	K–B1
47. Q–Q8	P–Kt4
48. P–K6	R–R2
49. K–K5	P–Kt5
50. Q–Q6ch	Black Resigns.

Pillsbury had waited eight years for the revenge that was now his. It proved to be the last flickering of his genius, and the final encounter. . . .

PILLSBURY   LASKER

Cambridge Springs, 1904
Queen's Gambit Declined

1. P–Q4	P–Q4
2. P–QB4	P–K3
3. Kt–QB3	Kt–KB3
4. Kt–B3	P–B4
5. B–Kt5	BP x P
6. Q x P	Kt–B3

Better was . . . B–K2 followed by Kt–B3.

7. B x Kt !   ....

The "find" which Pillsbury had saved for eight years, ever since Lasker beat him at St. Petersburg, 1895–6. For the game, see the section on Lasker.

7. . . . .   P x B

If 7. . . . Kt x Q; 8. B x Q, Kt–B7ch; 9. K–Q2, K x B !; 10. K x Kt, P x P; 11. R–Qlch.

8. Q–R4   P x P

If . . . P–Q5; 9. O–O–O, P–K4; 10. P–K3, B–QB4; 11. P x P, P x P; 12. Kt–Q5 !

9. R–Q1   B–Q2
10. P–K3   Kt–K4

Loss of time. Better was B–K2.

11. Kt x Kt   P x Kt
12. Q x BP   Q–Kt3
13. B–K2 !   Q x KtP

Lasker wrongly accepts the challenge. Better was simply . . . B–B3.

14. O–O   R–B1
15. Q–Q3   R–B2

Still B–B3 was preferable.

16. Kt–K4   B–K2

17. Kt–Q6ch   K–B1

Not . . . B x Kt; 18. Q x B, Q–B6; 19. B–Kt5 ! winning immediately.

18. Kt–B4   Q–Kt4

19. P–B4 !!   . . . .

A splendid conception. White just wants to get at the King.

19. . . . .   P x P ?

Lasker stumbles in a bad position. P–K5 was essential–good or bad–for Black must keep the KB file closed.

20. Q–Q4   P–B3

Or . . . R–Kt1 ?; 21. Q x BP.

21. Q x BP   Q–QB4
22. Kt–K5   B–K1
23. Kt–Kt4   P–B4
24. Q–R6ch   . . . .

24. . . . .   K–B2
25. B–B4 !   R–B3
26. R x Pch !   Q x R
27. R–KB1   . . . .

Black gets two Rooks for the Queen, but his position is too open.

27.	Q x Rch
28. K x Q	B – Q2
29. Q – R5ch !	. . . .

Better than Kt – K5ch.

| 29. . . . . | K – Kt1 |
| 30. Kt – K5 | Black Resigns. |

Here are some more glimpses of Pillsbury at his best.

Gunsberg

Pillsbury – TO PLAY

Hastings, 1895

The endgame which clinched first prize for Pillsbury!

| 1. P x P ! | Kt x P |

Not . . . P x Kt; 2. P – K7, K x P; 3. P – B7.

2. Kt x Kt	K x Kt
3. P – K4 !!	P x P
4. P – Q5ch	K – Q3
5. K – K3	P – Kt5
6. K x P	P – R5
7. K – Q4	P – R4
8. P x P	P – R6
9. K – B4	P – B4
10. P – R6	P – B5
11. P – R7	Black Resigns.

Tarrasch

Pillsbury – TO PLAY

Vienna, 1898 – second game of the tie match

1. Q x Pch !	P x Q
2. B x Q	B x B
3. B – B6 !	B – Q3
4. B x Pch	K – R1
5. B x R and wins easily.	

Lasker   London, 1899

1.	Q–R6 !!	Q x Kt
2.	B x P	R–K2
3.	B x R	B x B
4.	R x P	Q x BPch
5.	R(1)–Kt2	Q–Q8ch

Drawn!

Pillsbury—TO PLAY

Judd   St. Louis, 1899

1.	Q–Q3ch !	K x Kt
2.	P–B4ch	K–R3
3.	Q–R3ch	K–Kt3
4.	P–B5ch	P x P
5.	KR x P !	R–R1
6.	Q–Kt4ch	K–R2
7.	KR x P	Black Resigns.

Pillsbury—TO PLAY

Akiba Rubinstein

Akiba Rubinstein is the great endgame artist of chess history. There are many remarkable achievements by other masters, but by and large, for accuracy, profundity and sheer beauty, Rubinstein's endgames have never been equalled.

At an early age, chess became the sense of existence for him. Born in Stawiski, in Russian Poland, on December 12, 1882, he was brought up in the strict classical Hebrew tradition, slated to study, meditate, perhaps add some new subtleties to the complexities of the Talmud. The form of his life indeed remained true to the pattern set up, completely divorced from everyday cares, dedicated in toto to an all-devouring discipline. But instead of the Holy Books, chess soon came to fill his mind day and night. At the age of sixteen he learned the moves—the relatively late date was probably a handicap. With typical Talmudic contempt for mundane considerations, he plunged into the game, immediately. He had found his metier and was never to leave it again.

As is always the case with chess geniuses, improvement was rapid. He had not been playing for more than four or five years when he won a match from Salwe, a true coffee-house champion, but a first-class expert nonetheless. Then to Barmen, in 1905, where he was officially awarded the title of master, according to the well-ordered German scheme.

Lasker was then champion; Tarrasch and the other members of the older guard—Maroczy, Burn, Janowski—were dominant. Of the younger generation only Marshall had broken into the ranks. But no sooner had Rubinstein earned the right to take part in international tournaments than he began his march to the top. At Ostend, 1905, third; Ostend, 1906, second. Then came the greatest victories of all—first at Carlsbad, 1907, with everybody there except Lasker, the win from Marshall in the equivalent of a match at Lodz in 1908, finally tie with Lasker for first at St. Petersburg, 1909. To cap it all, he won their individual encounter, an immortal masterpiece. Rubinstein was freely spoken of as the next champion.

Had Rubinstein played a match with Lasker in 1910, instead of Schlechter, he might well have realized the ambition of his life. But the poor Jewish boy from a Polish ghetto had little backing in his own country, and none in any other. No clubs or individuals—as with Alekhine —were so enthused by his genius that they offered to support him. There was nothing to do but continue until a lucky break came along. Instead, fate produced Capablanca.

After San Sebastian, 1911, when the Cuban star nosed him out, Rubinstein was still always near the top of the world's masters, but he never again regained the esteem he had enjoyed in 1909. True, in 1912, he scored no less than five first prizes in international tournaments. But neither Capa nor Lasker took part in any of them—and they were his only superiors. Then the serious setback at St. Petersburg in 1914, where he could not even make the finals, the war, four years of non-productive starvation, and Rubinstein was no longer one of the select handful of world championship candidates. Before his retirement in 1932, he gathered in countless first prizes, played numbers of great games, but the Lasker-Capablanca-Alekhine trio, not to mention Reti, Nimzovitch and many others, always outshone him.

Slowly a tragic persecution complex engulfed his mind. After 1932 serious chess was impossible, though he did play odd games with intimate friends. In 1940, when the Boches invaded Belgium, Rubinstein, in

Antwerp, was thought to be one of their victims. We know now, however, that Rubinstein is living with his family in Antwerp and doing some analysis on the openings. His son, a fair chess player, has recently visited this country.

We are filled with a sense of the tragic when we review Rubinstein's career. Here is a man who might have been champion (though Lasker was certainly a greater master) but was never given the chance. More important, in so many of his games, we are carried away by their classic perfection, and feel impelled to say: Better chess cannot be played by mortal man. And yet first prizes, later even third and fourth prizes, escaped him all too often. The tragedy of Rubinstein arose because he played too much beautiful chess and too little winning chess.

The difference between winning and beautiful chess is appreciated only when we look at the game in the right light, when we compare it with other occupations, serious and recreative. And that Rubinstein was unable to do. His incredibly intense absorption in chess, to the exclusion of all else, reveals that he was driven by a burning ambition which could not be realized precisely because it was so all-consuming. Paradoxically, to give the best that he has, the chess master must step to one side in order to see himself and the game in the proper perspective.

Personally, Rubinstein was the simplest of souls. Silence was his rule. Even in chess he said little. When the famous Swedish *Laerobok* was being written right after the last war, the sponsor, Colijn, heard that Rubinstein had a copy of the German *Handbuch*, with various marginal comments. Colijn bought the book for a fantastic price, about $1,000, but Rubinstein's "notes" did not cover two pages when they were put together. During the 1928 Bad Kissingen tournament Tartakower wittily remarked one day that he had just sent his one millionth telegram, while Rubinstein had just uttered his tenth word in two weeks.

All his passion, all his love, were given over to chess. And his games are things of beauty that will last forever. Rubinstein variations have enriched countless openings, most notable being the refutation of the Tarrasch defense, and the aggressive reply which virtually killed the Four Knights as a tournament weapon.

The middle game was Rubinstein's Achilles' heel. Naturally he could conduct both attack and defense creditably. What he lacked was the will to admit complications. Even in the opening, most of his innovations are methods of simplification. His genius was rectilineal, so to speak—suspense, uncertainty, were intolerable. He always played the board, never the opponent, which added to the objective value of his games, but made it so much harder for him to be successful. Curiously, in most of his greater games the Rook and Bishop—straight line pieces—stand out.

Knights are rarely seen; Queens, made for combined operations, are likewise infrequent.

In the endgame he is supreme. Here he could execute a set plan with little hindrance. And it is here, above all, that he provides us with an inexhaustible galaxy of masterpieces. In Rook and Pawn endings especially, he is beyond compare. To cite but one example, we need only recall his game with Mattison, at Carlsbad, in 1929, which his colleagues called black magic.

While we have emphasized the finales, it must not be supposed that Rubinstein could not play all-round great chess. Quite the contrary. We are enchanted by Rubinstein's play because of its objectivity, its clarity, and its precision. On the whole, in fact, his games are second only to Alekhine's.

Rubinstein's masterpieces are the priceless legacy of an unhappy genius. His immortal win against Rotlewi is one of the most famous games of all time. It was a harbinger of his brilliant future. The game follows.

ROTLEWI   RUBINSTEIN
Lodz, 1907
Queen's Gambit Declined

1. P–Q4	P–Q4
2. Kt–KB3	P–K3
3. P–K3	P–QB4
4. P–B4	Kt–QB3
5. Kt–B3	Kt–B3
6. QP x P?	. . . .

A positional error. 6. B–Q3 is good enough for equality.

6.	B x P
7. P–QR3	P–QR3
8. P–QKt4	B–Q3

If 9. P x P, P x P; 10. Kt x P?, Kt x Kt; 11. Q x Kt, B x Pch.

9. B–Kt2	O–O
10. Q–Q2?	. . . .

Sadly neglecting his development. 10. P x P, P x P; 11. B–K2 should have been played.

10.	Q–K2!
11. B–Q3?	. . . .

Confused by the complications, he makes a second error. 11. P x P, P x P; 12. B–K2 was not too bad.

11.	P x P!
12. B x P	P–QKt4
13. B–Q3	R–Q1
14. Q–K2	B–Kt2
15. O–O	Kt–K4
16. Kt x Kt	B x Kt
17. P–B4	. . . .

White is oblivious of the dangers; the chess world must be grateful to him.

17.	B–B2
18. P–K4?	QR–B1
19. P–K5	B–Kt3ch
20. K–R1	Kt–Kt5!

The fun begins.

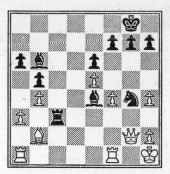

21. B–K4   Q–R5
22. P–Kt3   . . . .

If P–R3, B x B; 23. Kt x B, Kt–K6 wins.

Now comes the final gem—

25. . . . .   R–R6 !!!!

White Resigns.

It was indeed unfortunate that no match could ever be arranged between Lasker and Rubinstein. In the first encounter between them, the younger man produced a masterpiece.

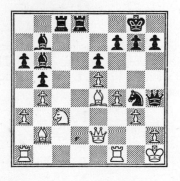

22. . . . .   R x Kt !!

A stunning sacrifice, and a prelude to many more.

23. P x Q   R–Q7 !!!
24. Q x R   B x Bch
25. Q–Kt2   . . . .

RUBINSTEIN   LASKER

St. Petersburg, 1909
Queen's Gambit Declined

1. P–Q4   P–Q4
2. Kt–KB3   Kt–KB3
3. P–B4   P–K3
4. B–Kt5   P–B4 ?
5. P x QP   KP x P
6. Kt–B3   P x P
7. Kt x P   Kt–B3
8. P–K3   B–K2

Lasker has played the opening poorly, and has a definite inferiority.

9. B–Kt5   B–Q2
10. B x KKt?   . . . .

Needlessly complicating matters. Better was simply B–K2.

10. . . . .   B x B
11. Kt x P   B x Kt
12. P x B   Q–Kt4
13. B x Kt   B x B
14. Kt–K3   O–O–O?

Correct was . . . B x P; 15. R–KKt1, Q–R4ch with equality, for if 16. Q–Q2, Q x Qch; 17. K x Q, B–K5; 18. R x P?, B–Kt3!

15. O–O   KR–K1
16. R–B1!   R x Kt
17. R x Bch   P x R

18. Q–B1!!   R x P
19. P x R   R–Q2
20. Q x Pch   K–Q1
21. R–B4!   . . . .

Threatening Q–R8ch and R–K4ch.

21. . . . .   P–B4
22. Q–B5   Q–K2
23. Q x Qch   K x Q
24. R x P   R–Q8ch
25. K–B2   R–Q7ch
26. K–B3   R x QKtP
27. R–QR5   R–Kt2

Now we are treated with a masterful Rubinstein endgame.

28. R–R6   . . . .

First restriction . . .

28. . . . .   K–B1
29. P–K4   . . . .

Then advance . . .

29. . . . .   R–QB2
30. P–KR4   K–B2
31. P–Kt4   K–B1
32. K–B4   . . . .

Finally invasion.

32.	K–K2
33. P–R5	P–R3
34. K–B5	K B2
35. P–K5	R–Kt2
36. R–Q6	. . . .

Threatening R–Q7ch !, R x R; 37. P–K6ch, K–K2; 38. P x R, K x P; 39. K–Kt6.

36.	K–K2
37. R–R6	K–B2
38. R–Q6	. . . .

Slowly but surely.

38.	K–B1
39. R–QB6	K–B2
40. P–R3 !	Black Resigns.

Black is in "zugzwang." If the King moves, K–Kt6 is decisive. And if 40. . . . R–K2; 41. P–K6ch, K–Ktl; 42. K–Kt6.

The war brought about a marked change in Rubinstein's personality. He became very withdrawn and uncommunicative. Curiously, this was paralleled by an increasing aggressiveness in his chess style. It was no longer the prudent Rubinstein of old. And his results showed it. Yet on many occasions he could still turn out things of beauty. Here is an elegant win over a future world champion.

EUWE   **RUBINSTEIN**

The Hague, 1921
Sicilian Defense

1. P–K4	P–QB4
2. Kt–KB3	Kt–KB3

3. P–K5	Kt–Q4
4. P–Q4	. . . . ,

Not the best, as the game shows. Kt–B3 is preferable.

4.	P x P
5. Q x P	P–K3
6. P–B4	Kt–QB3
7. Q–Q1	KKt–K2

Aiming at the KP.

8. B–Q2	Kt–Kt3
9. Q–K2	. . . .

9. B–B3, Q–B2 leads back to the game by transposition.

9.	Q–B2
10. B–B3	P–QKt3
11. P–KR4	. . . .

To get some kind of development.

11.	P–Q3 !
12. P x P	B x P
13. QKt–Q2	. . . .

13. B x P, R–KKtl; 14. B–B3, Kt–B5 is no improvement.

13.	Kt–B5
14. Q–K3	B–B4

15. Q—K4	P—B4
16. Q—B2	. . . .

| 16. . . . . | O—O ! |

Black is splendidly developed. Some combination is bound to appear.

17. P—KKt3	Kt—Kt3
18. P—R5	Kt(Kt3)—K4
19. Kt x Kt	Kt x Kt
20. P—QKt4	. . . .

Hoping for . . . B—K2; 21. B—Kt2.

| 20. . . . . | B x Pch ! |

Gruenfeld

Rubinstein—TO PLAY

The logical result of a perfect preparation.

21. K x B	Kt—Kt5ch
22. K—K2	Q x KtP
23. B—Q4	B—Kt2
24. R—R3	Q—Q3
25. Q—B3	P—K4
26. B—Kt1	P—B5

White is helpless against the avalanche.

27. P—B5	Q—R3
28. K—K1	P—K5
29. R—R4	Q—Kt4
30. Q—KR3	Kt—K6 !
31. B x Kt3	P x B
32. B—B4ch	K—R1
33. Kt—B1	Q—B3 !

White Resigns

It was in games such as these that Rubinstein came as close to achieving perfection as any mortal.

Here are some more examples of Rubinstein's wizardry:

Semmering, 1926

1. B x P	R(Q5) x B
2. R x R	R x R
3. R x Pch	K—R4
4. P—B3	Black Resigns.

Nimzovitch

Rubinstein—TO PLAY

Berlin, 1928

1.	Kt x QP !	R x Kt
2.	Q — K8ch	Kt — B1
3.	R — K7	P — KKt3
4.	Q — B7ch	K — R1
5.	R — K8	R — Q1
6.	Q x BPch	K — Kt1
7.	Q — K6ch	K — Kt2
8.	P — B6ch	Black Resigns.

Rubinstein—TO PLAY

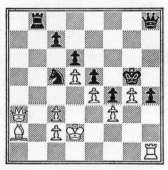

Wolf

Teplitz-Schonau, 1922

1.	. . . .	R — QR1
2.	Q — Kt2	P — R6 !
3.	B — B4	Q — R5
4.	B — K2	Q — B7 !!
5.	R x P	Q — K6ch
6.	K — K1	Kt — R5

White Resigns.

Hromadka

Rubinstein—TO PLAY

Mahrisch-Ostrau, 1923

1.	P — KKt3	Kt x RP
2.	R x P	Q — Q3
3.	Q — Kt6 !!	R — Q2
4.	B — B5	R x R
5.	B x Q	R — B7ch
6.	Q x R !	Kt x Q
6.	B — B5 !	Black Resigns.

The Knight is lost.

Marshall   Lodz, 1908

1. R x Kt !	K x R
2. Q–B4ch	K–K2
3. Q–B7ch	K–Q1
4. Kt–K6ch	Black Resigns.

Rubinstein—TO PLAY

Maroczy   Gothenburg, 1920

1. B–R4 !!   Black Resigns.

For if 1. . . . Kt x B; 2. Q–
K7 !

Rubinstein—TO PLAY

Frank James Marshall

Five years after Pillsbury stormed the chess world at Hastings in 1895, another American, Frank Marshall, made his international debut at Paris in 1900. While he finished only fourth, it soon became abundantly clear that America had added a new star to the chess firmament. Pillsbury died a few years later, and for almost thirty years Marshall was the outstanding American master and the leading U. S. representative in international play.

Marshall was born in New York in 1877. When he was eight years old his family moved to Montreal. Here young Frank learned the game from his father and, as he says in his autobiography, "As a child I had an unusual aptitude for chess. I took to it naturally, like a duck to water." Soon he was participating in the Montreal Chess Clubs. At sixteen he got his first big chance in a simultaneous exhibition against Steinitz. Although Frank lost the game, Steinitz predicted a brilliant future for him if he continued to play chess. Of this Marshall writes: "If I continued to play chess? Nothing could have stopped me. There was nothing else I wanted to do. Chess began to absorb my whole life. My head was full of it, from morning to night—and in my dreams as well. Gradually, it crowded out every other interest. I knew that I was going to devote my life to chess."

Chess did become his great devotion. After a few years he was second only to Pillsbury in America. In international play he made his mark in a number of tournaments; his greatest success was first prize at Cambridge Springs in 1904, ahead of Pillsbury and Lasker. Pillsbury died soon afterwards, and until the early thirties Marshall was the acknowledged king of American chess; he retired undefeated in 1936. In those years he played in every tournament that he could gain access to. Shortly before he died in 1944, a story in Life magazine described him as a "preoccupied old gentleman who looks like a Shakespearean actor, smokes strong cigars incessantly and takes a chess board to bed with him so he can record any plays he may think up." He admitted to being preoccupied, and added that since the age of ten not a day had gone by in which he had not played at least one game of chess.

I first visited the Marshall Chess Club in the spring of 1929, to play in a high school team match. Towards the end of the evening, a dignified gentleman with an old-fashioned lavaliere tie came in, and followed the games with keen interest. Afterwards he joined in the post-mortems, and showed us moves that we had never dreamed of. I was amazed to discover that the friendly kibitzer was the great Marshall.

Frank was like that—simple, democratic, full of encouragement and good cheer, glad to analyze any position that looked promising and more that did not. A whole generation of masters grew up around his cheerful twinkle and powerful cigars. He was an ideal man to create inspiration and real team spirit.

In personality Frank was anything but the stereotyped version of a chess master. He liked everything that pertained to good living. He could sit and recount stories of his chess exploits by the hour, especially after he had partaken of a little stimulation. Most of his stories told of how he could have won this or that tournament. One I remember very well. In one European tournament, he was scheduled to play Marco the next day. The night before, Marco came to see him, and said, "Frank, I don't feel well." "What's the matter?" "Stomach." "Here—take this," and Marco was given a drink, which Frank shared. But Marco was still sick, so they had a few more. "The next day he beat me like a child," Frank woefully concluded.

Marshall was what we call a "natural" player—his bent was for the attack. The tradition he followed was that of Anderssen and Blackburne, rather than Steinitz and Lasker. Because he was so willing to take chances, even against the greatest, he never quite managed to reach the world championship class, though he was always a high prize winner and a feared opponent. Positional subtleties meant little to Frank; he cared for the acrobatics of the pieces. I was often amazed by his incredible ingenuity in the most sterile positions; where others tried to compromise he took bold chances—and was usually justified. It was with good reason that European writers liked to refer to him as "der geniale findigreiche Amerikaner"—the gifted American who was so rich in resourcefulness. I have never met anyone, not even Alekhine, who had a keener eye for the purely combinative side of chess.

Here is a beautiful game from his early days, which Frank himself described as a "real Fourth of July fireworks show from beginning to end."

MARSHALL	TCHIGORIN

Ostend, 1905
Dutch Defense

1. P–Q4	P–KB4

Provoking the gambit, but Marshall needs little provocation!

2. P–K4	P x P
3. Kt–QB3	Kt–KB3
4. B–KKt5	P–B3
5. B x Kt	. . . .

Nowadays we prefer P–B3, which confers a more lasting attack.

| 5. . . . . | KP x B |
| 6. Kt x P | Q–Kt3 |

Unnecessary complications.

7. R–Kt1	P–Q4
8. Kt–Kt3	B–K3
9. B–Q3	Kt–Q2
10. Q–K2	K–B2
11. Kt–B3	R–K1
12. O–O	B–Q3

| 13. P–B3 | Kt–B1 |
| 14. Kt–R4 | B–KB4 |

| 15. Kt(R4) x B !! | R x Q |
| 16. Kt x Bch | K–K3 |

To trap the Knight.

| 17. Kt–B8 | Q–B2 |
| 18. B x R | K–B2 |

The point is that after . . . Q x Kt; 19. B–Kt4ch wins the Queen.

Marshall gives the pretty alternative 18. . . . P–KKt3; 19. KR–K1 !, P–KB4; 20. B–B3 dis ch, K—B3; 21. Kt—K7, Kt—K3; 22. B x P and wins.

It is still not clear how White can extricate his Knight . . .

19. Kt—B5 !!   . . . .

The real key.

19. . . . .   Kt—K3
20. Kt(B5)—Q6ch   K—Kt3
21. B—Q3ch   K—R4

Hoping to obtain the two Knights for his Rook.

22. QR—K1   Kt—B5
23. R—K7   Q—R4
24. B—Kt1   . . . .

B—B2 is a bit quicker.

24. . . . . .   P—KKt3
25. P—KKt3   . . . .

Preparing the mate.

25. . . . . .   Kt—R6ch
26. K—Kt2   Kt—Kt4
27. B—Q3   R x Kt
28. Kt x R   Q—Q1
29. P—KR4 !   Q x Kt

Or . . . Kt—B2; 30. R x Kt, Q x Kt; 31. R x Pch, K—Kt5; 32. P—B3 mate.

30. P x Kt   Black Resigns.

Frank won innumerable brilliancy prizes in the course of his career. The fact that the following game won only second prize aroused a storm of protest from its many admirers.

MARSHALL   BOGOLJUBOW
New York, 1924
Queen's Gambit Declined

1. P—Q4   Kt—KB3
2. Kt—KB3   P—K3
3. B—Kt5   P—Q4
4. P—K3   QKt—Q2
5. P—B4   P—B3
6. P x P   . . . .

To avoid the Cambridge Springs Defense (6. Kt—B3, Q—R4).

6 . . .   KP x P
7. Kt—B3   Q—R4 ?

A time-waster in this position.

8. B—Q3   Kt—K5
9. Q—B2   Kt x B
10. Kt x Kt   P—KR3
11. Kt—B3   B—K2
12. O—O   O—O

13. P–QR3   Q–Q1

A necessary retreat.

14. QR–K1   P–QR4

Another loss of time. B–Q3 was better.

15. Q–K2 !   Kt–B3 ?

Again B–Q3 was preferable.

16. Kt–K5   B–Q3
17. P–B4   P–B4
18. B–Kt1   B–Q2
19. Q–QB2   B–B3

To play . . . Kt–K5.

20. P x P !   B x P
21. K–R1   . . . .

Not 21. . . . Kt–K5 ? for 22. Kt x Kt costs him a piece.

21. . . . .   R–K1

22. P–K4 !!   . . . .

The most profound move of the game. If in reply 22. . . . P x P; 23. Kt x B, P x Kt; 24. Kt x P, Kt x Kt; 25. R x Kt, R x R; 26. Q x R, P–Kt3; 27. P–B5 wins.

22. . . . .   B–Q5
23. Kt x B   P x Kt

24. P–K5   Kt–Kt5
25. Q–R7ch   K–B1
26. P–KKt3   . . . .

The game is still not easy. If 26. Q–R8ch, K–K2; 27. Q x KtP, R–KKt1, with a strong counterattack.

26. . . . .   Q–Kt3
27. B–B5 !!   . . . .

The beauty of this game lies in moves such as these; the point will soon be clear.

27. . . . .   Kt–B7ch
28. R x Kt !   B x R
29. Q–R8ch   K–K2
30. Q x KtP   K–Q1

If instead 30. . . . B x R, Black is mated: 31. Q–B6ch, K–B1; 32. Q x RPch !, K–Kt1 (or 32. . . . K–K2; 33. Q–Q6 mate); 33. B–R7ch, K–R1; 34. B–Kt6ch, K–Kt1; 35. Q–R7ch and mate next.

31. Q–B6ch   R–K2
32. P–K6 !   B–Q5

33. P x P !!   B x Q
34. P–B8=Qch   K–B2

35. R x Rch   B x R
36. Q x R   K—Q3
37. Q—R8 !   Q—Q1
38. Q—K5ch, and White announced mate in five.

The finish would have been: 38. ... K—B4; 39. Kt—R4ch, K—B5; 40. Q—B3ch, K—Kt4; 41. B—Q3ch, K x Kt; 42. Q—B2 mate.

For some reason, Marshall always played beautifully against Nimzovitch. "I can beat him like a child," Frank used to say. Here is a game which won him a first brilliancy prize.

NIMZOVITCH   MARSHALL

Bad Kissingen, 1928
Queen's Indian Defense

1. P—Q4   Kt—KB3
2. P—QB4   P—QKt3
3. Kt—QB3   ....

P—B3 is strong.

3. ....   B—Kt2
4. B—Kt5   ....

A rather illogical move, not what one would expect from a Nimzovitch.

4. ....   P—K3
5. Q—B2   P—KR3
6. B—R4   B—K2
7. P—K4   ....

Marshall was trying to provoke this move.

7. ....   O—O
8. P—K5   ....

If 8. B—Q3, Kt—B3 ! is too strong.

8. ....   Kt—Q4 !

The mixing has begun!

9. B—Kt3   ....

Marshall recommends B x B instead.

9. ....   Kt—Kt5
10. Q—Kt3   P—Q4 !

Frank is in his element.

11. P x P e.p.   KB x P
12. O—O—O   ....

Risky, but what else was there?

12. ....   QKt—B3
13. B x B   Q x B
14. P—QR3   ....

Invites an elegant refutation, but there was no good defense.

14. ....   Kt x P !
15. R x Kt   ....

Or 15. Q x Kt, P—QB4; 16. Q—R4, B—B3; 17. Q—R6, Q—B5ch; 18. K—Kt1, Q x P wins.

15. ....   Q x R
16. P x Kt   Q x KBP
17. Q—Q1   KR—Q1

18. Q—K2	Q—B5ch
19. K—B2	P—QR4 !

A surprising maneuver!

20. P x P	R x P
21. Kt—B3	R—R8
22. K—Kt3	. . . .

Apparently the King has reached an asylum.

22.	P—QKt4 !!
23. Q—K5	. . . .

If 23. P x P, B—Q4; and if 23.

Kt x P, B—K5 followed by . . . P—QB3.

23.	P x Pch
24. K—Kt4	Q—B8
25. Kt—QKt5	. . . .

25. . . . .   P—B4ch !

With problem-like precision. If 26. Q x P, Q x Pch; 27. K x P, R—Q4ch.
White Resigns.

Here are some more snapshots of Marshall at his sacrificial best.

Marshall—TO PLAY

Janowsky

Match, 1912

1.	Q x Kt
2. P x B	Kt—B3 !
3. B—Kt2	Kt x KtP !!
4. B x Pch	K—R1
5. P x Q	B—R6ch
6. K—Kt1	Kt x Q
7. B x Kt	R—K7
8. R—QB1	QR—K1
9. B—B3	R(K1)—K6
10. B—Kt4	R x P(B6)
11. B—Q1	R—B3

White Resigns.

Rubinstein

Marshall—TO PLAY

Marshall—TO PLAY

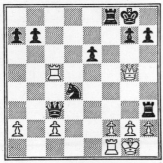

Levitsky

Burn

Marshall—TO PLAY

Moscow, 1925

1. P—QKt3 !   Q x KtP
2. Kt(B3)—Q2   Q—R7
3. Kt—QB3   Black Resigns.

Breslau, 1912

1. . . . . .   Q—KKt6 !!!
White Resigns.

The spectators were so thrilled with this magnificent play that they showered the board with gold pieces.

Ostend, 1907

The game where Burn never had a chance to light his pipe!

1. R x Kt !   P x R
2. B x Pch !   K x B
3. Kt—Kt5ch   K—Kt3
4. QKt—B3   P—K4
5. Kt—R4ch   K—B3
6. Kt—R7ch   K—K2
7. Kt—B5ch   K—K3
8. Kt x Bch   K—K2
9. Kt—B5ch   K—K3
10. P—Q5ch   K x Kt
11. Q x Pch   K—K5
12. O—O—O   Black Resigns.

Kupchik

Chicago, 1926

Marshall—TO PLAY

1. R x P ! and wins.
For if . . . K x R; 2. Q—Kt3ch,
any 3. Kt check wins the Queen.

Burn

Ostend, 1905

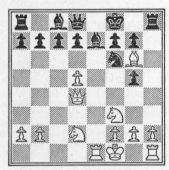

Marshall—TO PLAY

1. Kt—K5 !	P x B
2. Kt x KtPch	K—B2
3. R x Bch	K x Kt
4. Q—Q3ch	K—R3
5. P—KR4 !	P—Kt5
6. P—R5	Kt x P
7. Q—B5	P—KKt3
8. R x Ktch	P x R
9. Q—B6 mate.	

Karl Schlechter

Of all Lasker's rivals, the one who came closest to dethroning him was the Viennese Karl Schlechter. In their match in 1910, Schlechter was leading by one point at the end of nine games; the match was a ten-game affair. In the last game Schlechter had an easy draw, which he disdained, and thereby threw away his chance for the title, since Lasker won and retained his title in the event of a draw match!

Schlechter was born in Vienna in 1874, and lived there all his life, until his death from starvation in 1918. He became a chess master at an early age and devoted his entire life to the pursuit of the game. In all my peregrinations, I have never heard a single personal story about Schlechter —good, bad, or indifferent. Apart from drawn matches with Lasker and Tarrasch, his greatest achievement was first prize at Hamburg, 1910.

It was in his play against the great Lasker at Cambridge Springs, 1904, that Schlechter shone. Here is the game which netted him the first brilliancy prize.

SCHLECHTER   LASKER

Cambridge Springs, 1904
Queen's Gambit Declined

1. P–Q4	P–Q4
2. P–QB4	P–K3
3. Kt–QB3	Kt–KB3
4. B–Kt5	B–K2
5. P–K3	O–O
6. Kt–B3	P–QKt3

An antique defense which has been virtually abandoned.

7. B–Q3	B–Kt2
8. P x P	P x P
9. Kt–K5	P–B4
10. R–QB1	Kt–B3
11. O–O	Kt x Kt
12. P x Kt	Kt–K1
13. B–KB4	. . . .

Banking on his K-side attack.

13.	P–B4

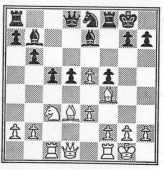

14. Q–B2 !	P–KKt4
15. B–Kt3	P–KB5 ?

Schlechter hoped to provoke this.

16. B x Pch	K–R1
17. Q–Kt6	. . . .

Threatening Q–R6.

17.	Kt–B3
18. P x Kt	R x P
19. Q–R5	K–Kt2
20. Q x Pch	K x B
21. B x P	R–Kt3
22. Q–R5ch	K–Kt2

With two Pawns ahead, White wins easily.

23. KR–Q1	P–Q5
24. B–Kt3	R–Kt4
25. B–K5ch !	K–Kt1

Not . . . B–B3; 26. Q x Rch.

26. Q–R8ch	K–B2
27. Q–R7ch	K–K3
28. B–Kt3	P x Kt
29. R x Q	P x P
30. R(Q8)–Q1	P x R=Q
31. R x Q	R–Q1
32. P–B4	R(Kt4)–Q4
33. P–K4 !	R–Q8ch
34. R x R	R x Rch
35. K–B2	R–Q5

36. P—B5ch   K—Q2
37. P—K5   Black Resigns.

Although Schlechter was chiefly a pacific positional player, he could produce many dashing sacrifices. Here is the conclusion of a game which won him a first brilliancy prize.

SCHLECHTER   SALWE

St. Petersburg, 1909
Ruy Lopez

1. P—K4, P—K4; 2. Kt—KB3, Kt—QB3; 3. B—Kt5, P—QR3; 4. B—R4, Kt—B3; 5. O—O, B—K2; 6. R—K1, P—QKt4; 7. B—Kt3, P—Q3; 8. P—B3, Kt—QR4; 9. B—B2, P—B4; 10. P—Q3, Kt—B3; 11. QKt—Q2, O—O; 12. Kt—B1, Q—B2; 13. B—Kt5, Kt—K1; 14. Kt—K3, B x B; 15. Kt x B, Kt—K2; 16. P—QR4, R—Kt1; 17. P x P, P x P; 18. Q—Q2, P—R3; 19. Kt—B3, B—K3; 20. P—Q4, Kt—KB3; 21. R—R6, R—R1.

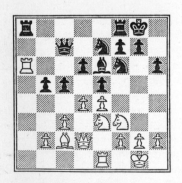

22. P x P !?   R x R ?

Correct is . . . Kt x P !

23. P x Kt   P x P
24. Kt—Q5   B x Kt
25. P x B   K—Kt2
26. Kt—R4   R—K1
27. P—R3   . . . .

To ward off mate threats.

27. . . . .   Q—Q1
28. R—K3   Kt—Kt3
29. Kt—B5ch   K—B1

30. R—K6 !!.   . . . .

An elegant finale.

30. . . . .   R x R

. . . P x R; 31. Q x Pch leads to mate.

31. P x R   P—Q4
32. Q x Pch   K—K1
33. P x Pch   K x P
34. Q—R7ch   K—K3
35. Q x Kt   . . . .

Finis. The rest exists because chess masters are human.

35. . . . .   R—R7
36. P—QKt4 !   P x P
37. Kt—Q4ch   K—Q2
38. B—B5ch   Black Resigns.

Schlechter was also famous in his day as a problem composer. Here is one of his prettiest themes.

White to Play and Mate in Three

The solution is 1. P—QKt4 !, with the main variation running: 1. . . . . K—B5; 2. Q—B3ch, K—Q4; 3. Q—B5 mate.

David Janowsky

Janowsky managed to get enough backing to play three matches with Lasker, although he really offered rather weak opposition. Born in Poland, he emigrated to France when he was still young, and soon became one of the "regulars" of the chess tournaments. His play was bold and dashing, which earned him many brilliancy prizes, but also many zeroes when the sacrifices failed.

Jan, as he was affectionately nicknamed in his later years in New York, was one of the most colorful figures of his time. He was an inveterate gambler, and would usually manage to lose his chess earnings at the roulette table. On many occasions chess tournaments have been promoted by gambling casinos, and Jan was frequently torn between his two loves. Once, the story goes, he foresaw what would happen, and gave a friend his money for safekeeping, with the solemn promise that it would not be turned over until he had left the gambling resort. By the middle of the tournament Janowsky could hold out no longer, and demanded his money back. The friend refused, and Jan was so enraged that he sued him!

In his New York days Jan became famous as a master of alibis as well as of chess. The radiator was too hot, or too cold, the windows were open too far or too little—there was always something which spoiled his play. Finally a tournament committee went to great lengths to make sure that everything was perfect. At this Jan was more furious than ever. "You have deliberately deprived me of any conceivable alibi," he stormed; "how can I possibly do my best?"

Janowsky's forte was his attacking ability. Here is one of his most famous games.

JANOWSKY   SCHALLOP

Nuremberg, 1896

Queen's Gambit Accepted

1. P—Q4	P—Q4
2. P—QB4	P x P
3. Kt—KB3	P—QB4
4. P—K3	P x P
5. P x P	B—Kt5 ?

Premature.

6. B x P	P—K3
7. Q—R4ch !	Kt—B3
8. Kt—K5 !	Q x P
9. Kt x Kt	Q—K5ch
10. B—K3	P x Kt

Not . . . Q x Kt; 11. B—Kt5.

11. Kt—B3	Q x P

12. B—Q5 !!	KP x B
13. Q x Pch	K—Q1

14. Q x Rch	K—Q2
15. Q—Kt7ch	K—K3
16. Q—B6ch	B—Q3
17. B—B4	Black Resigns.

If he captures both Rooks he is mated: 17. . . . Q x Rch; 18. K—Q2, Q x R; 19. Q x Bch, K—B4; 20. Q—K5ch, K—Kt3; 21. Q—Kt5 mate.

Here is the startling finish from a game which won him the brilliancy prize at Marienbad, 1925.

Saemisch

Janowsky—TO PLAY

1. Q—R6 !!!   Black Resigns.

For if 1. . . . P x Q; 2. R—Kt3 mate. The best try is 1. . . . P—B3, but then 2. R—Kt3, B x B; 3. Q—R7ch, K—B2; 4. R x Pch wins hands down.

Gcza Maroczy

Hungary has long been the birthplace of many a chess master, and Maroczy was its leading light in the early years of this century. Born in 1870, he first rose to prominence at the minor tournament in Hastings, 1895. Until 1908 he played regularly in international contests and was invariably a high prize winner. After that, he retired and devoted himself to his engineering profession.

When I first met him in the 1930's, he was the genial *Altmeister*, who came to chess tournaments for the fun of it, and cared little whether he won or lost. He was really too fond of simple living; "ambition should be made of sterner stuff." When he refereed the Euwe-Alekhine world championship match in 1937, he brought along some paprika from his native land, and ate it with every meal. With such contentment, why work hard at chess?

Maroczy was a solid master of the positional school. On occasion though, he could produce some hard-fought tactical battles. Here is one of his best.

JANOWSKY	MAROCZY

Munich, 1900
Albin Counter Gambit

1. P–Q4	P–Q4
2. P–QB4	P–K4
3. P x KP	P–Q5

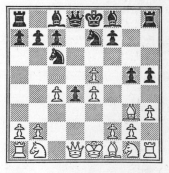

Today considered unsound, but championed by Weaver Adams.

4. P–K4 ? . . . .

Weak. 4. Kt–KB3 is the refutation; with straight development, White eventually gives back the Pawn and should get the better of it.

4.	Kt–QB3
5. B–B4	KKt–K2
6. B–Kt3	P–KR4
7. P–KR3	P–KKt4 !

White's position is uncomfortable.

8. P–KR4	P–Kt5
9. Kt–Q2	Kt–Kt3
10. P–B4	B–K2
11. B–Q3	Kt x RP !
12. Q–K2	Kt–Kt3
13. P–K6 !	. . . .

So that if . . . B x P ? 14. P–B5; and if . . . P x P; 14. P–K5.

13.	P–R5 !

Rising to the occasion.

14. Q x P	B x P
15. P–B5	B–QB1
16. B–R2	Kt(Kt3)–K4
17. Q–K2	Kt x Bch
18. Q x Kt	Kt–Kt5
19. Q–Kt3	P–QR4 !

Janowsky does not stand much of a chance against the 2 Bishops (known as the 2 rabbis when he had them).

20. Kt–R3	P–R5
21. Q–Q1	Kt–Q6ch
22. K–B1	Kt x P
23. Q–Kt4	R–QR3 !
24. Kt–B4	K–B1 !
25. Kt–Q5	R–QB3
26. B–K5	R–Kt1
27. Q–R5	B–Kt4

28. Kt–B3	Kt x P !
29. P–B6	. . . .

A last hope.

29.	Kt–K6ch !
30. Kt x Kt	B x Kt

Neither side has castled, yet Black's King is much safer.

31. R–Q1	B–Kt5
32. Q x P	B x Kt
33. P x B	R–B7
34. B x QP !	. . . .

34.	Q–R1 !!!

A magnificent finish. There is no defense against the threat of Q–R3ch.

35. R–Q3   Q–R3
White Resigns.

Maroczy's most famous production is an endgame which has the appearance of a problem. After 33 moves of hopelessly dull maneuvering, the following position was reached:

Marco-Maroczy, Vienna, 1899

Maroczy—TO PLAY

Marco

1.	K–Q3 !!

Black has a forced win!

2. K–K2	K–B2
3. K–B2	K–Kt3

White is reduced to passivity.

4. K–K2	P–R4

First the Pawn goes to R5.

5. K–B2	P–R5
6. K–K2	K–B2
7. K–B2	. . . .

Note that neither White Knight can move. If 7. Kt–Q3, Kt–B7 wins.

7.	K–Q3
8. K–K2	K–K2
9. K–B2	K–B2
10. K–K2	K–Kt2
11. K–B2	K–R2
12. P–Kt3	K–R3
13. K–K2	P–KB4
14. P x P	P x P

The White Knights are still bound by the Pawns. Black meanwhile prepares to bring his King into the fray.

15. K–B2	K–R4
16. K–K2	P–B5
17. P x P	P x P
18. K–B2	K–Kt4
19. K–K2	K–R5
20. K–B2	K–R6 !
21. Kt–Q3	. . . .

The only chance.

21.	Kt–B7
22. Kt x Pch	K–R5
23. Kt–Q3	. . . .

If 23. Kt–Kt6ch, K–Kt4; 24. Kt–K5, Kt(B7) x P; 25. Kt (Kt1) x Kt, Kt x Kt; 26. Kt x P, Kt–B5, and the Pawn queens.

23.	Kt(B7) x RP
24. Kt x Kt	Kt x Kt
25. Kt–B1	Kt–Kt8
26. Kt–R2	K–R6
27. K–K3	K–Kt6
28. P–KB4	K–Kt5

Again White is in zugzwang and must sacrifice material.

29. P—B5	K x P
30. K—Q3	K—B5
31. Kt—B1	K—B6
32. K—B2	Kt—R6ch
33. K—Q3	K—B7
34. K—Q2	Kt—B5ch
35. K—Q1	K—K6
36. K—B2	P—R6 !
37. Kt—R2	Kt—Kt7
38. Kt—B1	. . . .

38.	Kt—Q6 !!

The final blow. If 39. Kt x Kt, P—R7 is decisive; and if 39. Kt—R2, K—K7.

39. Kt—Kt3	Kt—K8ch
40. K—Q1	K—Q6 !
41. K x Kt	K x P
42. Kt—R1	K x QP !

A double finesse. 42. . . . . K—Kt7 ? only draws after 43. K—Q2 !, K x Kt; 44. K—B1.

43. Kt—B2ch	K—B6

The second finesse. If 44. Kt x P, K—Kt7 ! and the Knight is stuck.

44. K—Q1	P—R7
45. K—B1	P—Q5
46. Kt—R1	P—Q6
47. Kt—B2	P—B4 !

White Resigns.

Rudolf Charousek

At times in the history of the game there have been outstanding talents who did not reach the heights for which they were evidently destined because of premature death. Such a one was Rudolf Charousek. Playing over his early games is like reading Keats's poetry: you cannot help feeling a grievous, oppressive sense of loss, of promise unfulfilled. Born near Prague in 1873, he had become a finished master at twenty-three. At Nuremberg in 1896, his first masters' tournament, he did not even manage to win a prize, but he beat Lasker, Janowsky and Blackburne in their individual encounters. In his brief career, he had impressed everyone; tributes poured in from everywhere at the memorial ceremonies. Here is his most famous victory.

CHAROUSEK   TCHIGORIN

Budapest, 1896
King's Gambit

1. P—K4	P—K4
2. P—KB4	P x P
3. B—B4	Kt—QB3
4. P—Q4	Kt—B3
5. P—K5	P—Q4
6. B—Kt3	B—Kt5
7. Q—Q3	Kt—KR4

The kind of position Charousek loved.

8. Kt–KR3   Kt–Kt5
9. Q–QB3   Kt–R3
10. O–O   B–K7?

A needless waste of time.

11. B–R4ch !   . . . .

11. . . . .   P–B3
12. B x Pch !   P x B

13. Q x Pch   K–K2
14. Kt x P   Kt x Kt
15. B x Kt   P–R3

The Rook cannot be taken. If
15. . . . B x R; 16. B–Kt5ch,
P–B3; 17. P x Pch, K–B2; 18.
Kt–Q2, B–K7; 19. P x P, B x P;
20. B x Q, KR x B; 21. R–K1 and
wins.

16. Kt–B3   B–B5
17. P–K6 !   R–B1
18. B–B7 !!   . . . .

The point.

18. . . . .   P x P
19. B x Qch   R x B
20. Q–Kt7ch   R–Q2
21. R–B7ch   K x R
22. Q x Rch   B–K2
23. R–K1   R–K1
24. P–QKt3   K–B1
25. P x B   Black Resigns.

Milan Vidmar

Vidmar was another of the rising young stars who withdrew from chess to devote himself to another profession. He became an electrical engineer and later professor of theoretical physics, rising to the position of one of the world's leading authorities in this field. After the first World War, Vidmar was appointed rector of the University in his native Yugoslavia. He is one of the few chess masters who has found a successor in his own family; his son Milan Jr. is a chess master and one of the top ten Yugoslav players.

No particular traits distinguished Vidmar's chess style: he is an eclectic. Here is one of his finest wins.

RUBINSTEIN   VIDMAR

Berlin, 1918

Budapest Defense

1. P–Q4   Kt–KB3
2. P–QB4   P–K4

3. P x P   Kt–Kt5
4. B–B4   Kt–QB3
5. Kt–KB3   B–Kt5ch
6. Kt–B3   Q–K2
7. Q–Q5   B x Ktch
8. P x B   Q–R6

9. R–B1   P–B3

10. P x P   . . . .

If *10.* P–K6, P x P; *11.* Q–R5ch, P–Kt3; *12.* Q x Kt, P–K4, regaining the piece with a splendid position.

10. . . . .   Kt x P(B3)
11. Q–Q2   P–Q3
12. Kt–Q4   O–O
13. P–K3 ?   . . . .

The fatal error. P–B3 and P–K4 give White a comfortable position, though Black retains the pressure for a long time.

13. . . . .   Kt x Kt
14. BP x Kt   Kt–K5
15. Q–B2   Q–R4ch
16. K–K2   . . . .

16. . . . .   R x B !

Naturally.

17. P x R   B–B4
18. Q–Kt2   R–K1
19. K–B3   Kt–Q7ch

To gain time. The alternative . . . P–QR4; 20. P–R3, P–R5 also wins.

20. K–Kt3   Kt–K5ch
21. K–R4   . . . .

Or *21.* K–B3, when Black continues with . . . P–R4 as above.

21. . . . .   R–K3
22. B–K2   R–R3ch
23. B–R5   R x Bch !
24. K x R   B–Kt3 dbl ch

and Black mates next move.

Dr. Ossip Bernstein

Among Lasker's younger contemporaries, none in his day was considered more promising than the Russian, Ossip Bernstein. Born in 1882, he became prominent at a rather early age when he made an excellent stand in a match against Winawer at Warsaw in 1901. In the Russian Championship of 1903 he led for a long time, but fell back at the last moment and was overtaken by Tchigorin. His first international success came at Barmen in 1905, where he finished in a tie for fourth. After that he was a consistent prize winner in international play. After the war he emigrated to France, where he settled down to a law practice and retired from professional chess.

Bernstein was a highly imaginative player; a number of standard opening variations stem from him. Here is one of his outstanding victories.

BERNSTEIN   JANOWSKY

Barmen, 1905

Albin's Counter Gambit

1. P–Q4	P–Q4
2. P–QB4	P–K4

This gambit is considered unsound, but little was then known about it.

3. P x KP	P–Q5
4. Kt–KB3	Kt–QB3
5. QKt–Q2	. . . .

The strongest move.

5.	P–B3

Making a real gambit out of it. With 5. . . . KKt–K2 Black eventually regains his Pawn, but he gets the worst of it anyhow.

6. P x P	Q x P
7. Kt–Kt3	. . . .

P–KKt3 at once is preferable.

7.	B–Kt5 !
8. P–QR3	. . . .

To prevent the check.

8.	P–KR3
9. P–Kt3	O–O–O
10. B–Kt2	P–Q6 !

To expose oneself to such an attack against Janowsky took courage in those days!

11. O–O !	Kt–K4
12. B–B4	Kt–Kt3
13. B–K3	Kt–K4
14. B–B4	. . . .

Stronger is 14. QKt–Q2.

14.	Kt x Ktch ?

Janowsky only worsens his game in his anxiety to avoid the draw.

15. P x Kt	B–R4
16. Q–K1 !	B–B2
17. Q–R5 !	. . . .

This marauding maneuver unleashes White's attack.

17. . . .	Q–QKt3
18. Q–B3	Kt–B3
19. B–K3	Q–R3
20. Kt–Q2	P–KKt4

A typical Janowsky motif—bold sacrifice to get an attack.

21. P–QKt4 !   . . . .

Bernstein is not to be distracted from his plan. 21. B x P, B–Kt2 would be less favorable.

21.	B–Kt2
22. P–Kt5	Q–K3

If instead 22. . . . Q–R5; 23. Q–Kt4 ! forces the exchange and opens the R-file.

23. Q–R5 !   . . . .

Now White's attack breaks through.

23.	Kt–Q2
24. Q x RP !	. . . .

The exchange is of little importance.

24.	B x R
25. P–B4 !	QR–Kt1
26. Q x Pch	K–Q1
27. R x B	P x P
28. B x P	Q–QKt3
29. Q–R8ch	K–K2
30. R–K1ch	B–K3
31. Q–K4	Kt–B4
32. Q–K5	. . . .

Threatening both B–Kt5ch and B–K3. Janowsky finds himself being defeated by a man with his own style!

32.	Kt–Q2
33. P–B5 !	Kt x Q
34. P x Q	Kt–Q2
35. B–Q5	R–Kt3
36. B x P	K–B2
37. R x B !	. . . .

The coup de grace.

37.	R x R
38. P–QR4	. . . .

A curious position: there is absolutely nothing to be done against the advance of the Q-side Pawns.

38.	K–K2
39. B x R	K x B
40. P–R5	K–Q4
41. P–R6	R–QB1
42. P–Kt7 !	R x B
43. P–R7	R x P
44. P–R8 = Q	Kt–B4
45. K–Kt2	K–Q5
46. Kt–Kt3ch !	Kt x Kt
47. Q x R	P–Q7
48. Q–Q7ch	K–B6
49. P–Kt6	Kt–Q5
50. Q–Kt4	K–Q6
51. P–Kt7	Kt–K7
52. Q–B3ch	Black Resigns.

6.

The Age of Capablanca

IT WAS in the age of Capablanca that the last great revolution in chess thinking, the so-called hypermodern school, took place. Capa himself had nothing to do with this revolution; he grasped its essence, took what was good and discarded what was bad in it. But the other masters were more deeply concerned with it, and in the 1920's chess critics in their theoretical writings talked of little else. Since that time chess theory has remained fundamentally unchanged, nor is it likely to change in the future. What we see instead of new schools is an increasing refinement of technique, especially in the openings and endgame. Lasker used to say that, when he was young, common sense principles were sufficient for him in the openings, but by the time he was an old man no master could dispense with a precise knowledge of thousands of crucial variations. Even in amateur play more and more reliance is being placed on the "books."

Chess literature came to flourish as never before in this period. By the time of the Capablanca-Alekhine match in 1927, every important newspaper in the world carried full-length accounts of it. Chess had really become a universal language, and a number of chess masters took advantage of it to make a tour of the world. The number of professional masters increased enormously, especially in Europe. Chess had definitely arrived.

José Raoul Capablanca

In the constellation Caissa there has never been a more brilliant star than Capablanca. For a full quarter of a century he was the most renowned chess master alive. Millions who barely knew the moves had heard of the name and fame of the Cuban genius. To many devotees he was the perfect chessplayer, the chess machine, the only human being who had ever fully mastered all the intricacies of the royal game.

José Raoul Capablanca y Graupera was born in Havana, November 19, 1888, of a distinguished family. He learned the moves at the tender age of five by watching his father play. The boy was obviously so unusual that his family allowed him to go to the chess club and match wits with Cuba's best there. In a few years he could beat almost everybody in sight. When he was tweve years old a match was arranged with Corzo, national champion and an experienced expert. Incredibly, Capa won. It was the first of a long series of unbelievable exploits.

In 1904 he was sent to school in New York. Emanuel Lasker was there, as well as Frank Marshall and a host of lesser celebrities. They were still far above Capa's head, but his progress was speedy. In rapid-transit (ten seconds per move) particularly, it was not too long before he was tops.

Then, in 1909, came his first really serious trial, the match with Marshall. To all but a few staunch admirers of the "unknown" Cuban, the outcome was a foregone conclusion. What happened is best told in Capa's own words:

"No difficulty was experienced in arranging the match. Marshall was disposed to play in this case where he naturally discounted his victory. How far he was wrong the result proved. I beat him eight to one with fourteen draws thrown in between. I can safely say that no player ever performed such a feat, as it was my first encounter against a master, and such a master—one of the first ten in the whole world. The most surprising feature of all was the fact that I played without having ever opened a book to study the openings."

Two years later, at San Sebastian in 1911, Capa met and overcame the best that the old world had to offer. With every outstanding grandmaster present except Lasker, he finished first. Lasker, Capa and Rubinstein (who unexpectedly weakened and dropped out of the running in 1914) were the superclass of the chess world.

Capa was anxious to arrange a match with Lasker but the war prevented its realization for a full seven years. In 1921, Lasker agreed to play in Cuba. Unfortunately, Lasker was in inexplicably bad form. Several times he lost by outright blunders; after fourteen games, discouraged by repeated failure to hold his remorseless opponent, he resigned. That age had not really dulled his powers was shown at Maehrisch-Ostrau in 1923 and above all at New York in 1924. There has therefore been a great deal of speculation about whether Lasker at his best would have lost to Capa at his best. Any answer is a guess. This much is certain: Capablanca played remarkable chess all the way through and fully deserved both the victory and the world's championship.

As champion, Capa scored two first prizes, one second and one third in four tournaments of outstanding importance. The climax came at New York in 1927, where he outclassed the field completely. The chess world was convinced that he had no equal.

Then came the greatest disappointment of his life, the match with Alekhine in 1927. Alekhine was full of fire and had devoted years to the study of the latest opening wrinkles, did not neglect the minutest detail, even in his sleeping habits, to prepare for his supreme chance.

Capa, obviously expecting to bowl his rival over, as in the past, paid no attention to either his physical or psychological condition. The first game was a shock: in an even position, Capa made an outright blunder and heroic resistance merely prolonged the agony. While some lost ground was regained later, the realization that he was in for the most gruelling battle of his life had unnerved Capa; after three months of suspense he was dethroned.

After the loss of his title, Capa continued to appear at fairly regular intervals. By and large, his results for the period 1928–1939 were just as good as Alekhine's though Capa's victories at Nottingham and Moscow in 1936 are not as imposing qualitatively as Alekhine's at San Remo, 1930 and Bled, 1931. It must not be forgotten, however, that Alekhine's two greatest triumphs were scored against a fading generation of older men, while Capa was faced by a bunch of ambitious youngsters.

Capa's gift for chess was phenomenal. As Reti puts it, chess was his mother tongue. Combinations, position-play, middle game or endgame— in all he was supreme. Above all one must marvel at his intuitive grasp of the essentials of any situation that arose.

His speed in play was incredible in the earlier years. What others could not discover in a month's study he saw at a glance. Everything came to him as naturally as walking; effort, exertion, study were for him superfluous.

In many respects he was Fortune's darling. His countrymen—mirabile dictu—valued his genius and an appointment to the Cuban Foreign Office in 1911 freed him of financial cares for the rest of his life. Handsome, suave, an accomplished linguist, he was immensely popular all over the world.

Yet, for all the favors showered on Capa, he was often dissatisfied with his own achievements and we too, despite the rich heritage of his magnificent games, cannot avoid the feeling that he did not unfold his potentialities to the fullest degree. Why?

In the quest for the age-old illusion of immortality, man has set up three gradations in chess. The lowest is world's champion, next is the greatest champion of all time, and highest is the perfect chessplayer, the unique genius who never makes a mistake, the chess machine.

Capa was champion. Had he taken his miraculous flair for the game as a starting point and exerted himself to progress beyond it, instead of avoiding everything that could not be acquired effortlessly, he might well have become the most successful master of all time. But his crowning error—and it is this which imparted an unmistakable note of tragedy in his life—was the notion that he could play perfect chess, that he, Capa, was the instrument God had chosen to express His will on the chessboard, that he, Capa, was the chess machine, selected as the only man who ever knew all the answers, the only chess master who could never go wrong. These are but idle dreams, it may be protested, which could never have exerted any real influence. Nevertheless, they are the sole rational explanation of the many puzzling features in Capa's career. As early as 1920, before the title was definitely his, he felt impelled to write in *My Chess Career* (an admirable reflection of his personality):

"There have been times in my life when I came very near thinking that I could not lose even a single game of chess. Then I would be beaten, and the lost game would bring me back from dreamland to earth."

As far as style goes, there were three Capablancas. The first was the boy who, like every aspiring youngster, thought of brilliancies, attack at all cost. Then came the budding grandmaster, who tempered his combinative urge with sound position play and ingenious endings. Finally we see the mature champion, distinguished chiefly for his clock-like precision in the exploitation of small advantages, his dislike of complication and his addiction to clarity above all. It is this last Capa whom the chess world knows best; this is the style which gained him the sobriquet of "chess machine." Yet the other two were always there, as he had occasion to show time and again.

The need for clarity above all became more and more of a passion with Capablanca as time went on. For he could handle complications as well as anybody and better than most, but they required thought and effort; they were hard, yes, subject to the whims of chance now and then. Clear positions presented no problems; others might gape and wonder and try in vain to analyze how he did it—what really mattered was that to Capa they were as easy as breathing.

Yet Capa obviously felt that he could do better, that he could attack and sacrifice as well as he could play the ending. What restrained him was the lack of ambition more than anything else, for though his "dreamland" where he would never lose a game was a mirage, by comparison with it anything else seemed futile. It was this internal tension which slowed the lightning artist down to a snail's pace in later years, and which accounted for the unbelievable outright blunders on the part of a man to whom chess combinations were as natural as talking.

His games always retained a flavor of their own. In the defense he was almost unparalleled; where others let the attack come on and then parried it, he smelled the threats, so to speak, while they were still no more than the gleam in the other fellow's eye and so, before his opponent could really get an offensive started, his position was smashed.

In the openings he relied on his intuition to the very last; no midnight oil for him, regardless of the benefits it conferred on others. Instead of familiarizing himself with the latest theory before going to a tournament, he would draw his first four or five games, even against mediocre opponents and then, when he had absorbed all the novelties by watching the others produce them, he would really get started. The extra point or two he nonchalantly conceded in the early rounds were often regretted later.

When pressed, he could attack like a lion, but he never went out of his way to create positions where an attack was to the point. The ending was Capa's supreme forte; he tells us that some friends gave him a book on the endings when he was a boy; he liked them and read the book, the only one he ever looked at. His fondness for the endings remained; it is here that the passion for clarity is most frequently reflected.

Capablanca is and will always remain one of the really imposing figures in chess history. With his amazing intuition, his lightning vision, his keen mastery of the essentials, his numberless virtually faultless achievements, his name will be known and revered as long as chess is played.

No doubt there was a good psychological reason why he grew more and more fond of defensive play as he grew older. Perhaps he had to show that nobody was superior to him rather than to develop himself further. Here is the greatest defensive effort of his career, one of the immortal games.

CAPABLANCA   MARSHALL

New York, 1918

Ruy Lopez

1. P—K4   P—K4
2. Kt—KB3   Kt—QB3

Marshall avoids his favorite Petroff, which might have led Capa to suspect that he was in for a prepared variation.

3. B—Kt5   P—QR3
4. B—R4   Kt—B3
5. O—O   B—K2
6. R—K1   P—QKt4
7. B—Kt3   O—O
8. P—B3   P—Q4!

The Marshall Variation.

9. P x P   Kt x P
10. Kt x P   Kt x Kt
11. R x Kt   . . . .

The question is: Is Black's attack worth a Pawn? Subsequent analysis over the years has suggested various improvements for both sides, but neither the soundness nor the unsoundness of Marshall's sacrifice has ever been conclusively demonstrated.

11. . . . . .   Kt—B3

As a result of this game, . . .
P—B3 is played nowadays.

12. R—K1   . . . .

Slightly more accurate is P—Q4,
B—Q3; 13. R—K2.

12. . . . .   B—Q3
13. P—KR3   Kt—Kt5 !
14. Q—B3 !   . . . .

14. P x Kt ? would have led to
disaster after 14. . . . Q—R5.

14. . . . .   Q—R5
15. P—Q4 !   . . . .

Intuitive and absolutely correct.
The tempting R—K8 ? fails
against 15. . . . B—Kt2 !

15. . . . .   Kt x P !
16. R—K2 !   . . . .

This is why the Rook would
have done better to go to K2 immediately. 16. Q x Kt ? fails
against . . . B—R7ch ! 17. K—
B1, B—Kt6; 18. Q x Pch, R x
Qch !

16. . . . .   B—Kt5

The best chance. If 16. Kt—Kt5;
17. Kt—Q2 followed by Kt—B1
and Black's attack is dissipated.

17. P x B   B—R7ch
18. K—B1   B—Kt6

An alternative was 18. . . .
Kt—R8; 19. B—K3, Kt—Kt6ch;
20. K—K1, Kt x R dis ch; 21. K x
Kt, QR—K1; 22. Kt—Q2, winning.

19. R x Kt   Q—R8ch
20. K—K2   B x R

There is no good continuation
for Black. If 20. . . . . Q x B; 21.
R—B1, Q x Pch; 22. Kt—Q2 is
decisive.

21. B—Q2   B—R5
22. Q—R3 !   QR—K1ch
23. K—Q3   Q—B8ch
24. K—B2   B—B7

Still hoping.

25. Q—B3   Q—Kt8

The game still does not look
easy for White. True, he has two
pieces for a Rook, but his Rook
and Knight are immobilized and
it is not clear how he will develop
them. Capa finds a way.

26. B—Q5 !   P—B4
27. P x P   B x P
28. P—Kt4   B—Q3
29. P—R4 !   . . . .

Incredibly ingenious; the Rook
enters the game via the Rook file.

29. . . . .   P—QR4

Fishing for what might come up.

30. P x KtP   P x P
31. R – R6   P x P

32. Kt x P   . . . .

Suddenly White is fully developed, with a strong attack to boot.

32. . . . .   B – Kt5
33. P – Kt6   B x Kt
34. B x B   P – R3
35. P – Kt7   R – K6

36. B x Pch !   Black Resigns.

White announced mate in six: 36. . . . R x B (if 36. . . . K – R1; 37. R x P mate); 37. P – Kt8 = Qch, R – K1; 38. Q x Rch, K – R2; 39. Q – K4ch, R – B4; 40. Q x Rch, P – Kt3; 41. Q x P mate.

The games in which a champion gains the title are always among the most fascinating of his career, both psychologically and technically. Here is Capa's most famous win against Lasker.

LASKER   CAPABLANCA

Havana, 1921
10th Match Game
Queen's Gambit Declined

1. P – Q4   P – Q4
2. P – QB4   P – K3
3. Kt – QB3   Kt – KB3
4. B – Kt5   B – K2
5. P – K3   O – O
6. Kt – B3   QKt – Q2
7. Q – B2   P – B4

This move is so strong that 7. Q – B2 is today infrequently seen in master play. 7. R – B1 is preferred because it prevents . . . P – B4.

8. R – Q1   . . . .

After 8. P x QP, Kt x P; 9. B x B, Q x B; 10. Kt x Kt, P x Kt; 11. P x P Black has an isolated QP; but repeated trials show that the ending is drawn.

8. . . . .   Q – R4
9. B – Q3   . . . .

Better is 9. P x QP.

9. . . . .   P – KR3
10. B – R4   BP x P
11. KP x P   P x P
12. B x P   Kt – Kt3

Securing Q4 for his Knight. The position is reminiscent of Steinitz.

13. B—QKt3	B—Q2
14. O—O	QR—B1
15. Kt—K5	. . . .

Q—K2 immediately was preferable.

15.	B—Kt4
16. KR—K1	Kt(Kt3)—Q4

17. B x Kt(Q5) ?   . . . .

Breyer's celebrated analysis showed that White can draw by 17. B x Kt(B6) e.g., 17. . . . B x B; 18. B x Kt, P x B; 19. Q—B5, B—B3; 20. Kt—Kt4, B—KKt4; 21. P—B4, P—KKt3; 22. Q—K5, KR—K1; 23. Kt—B6ch, etc.

17.	Kt x B
18. B x B	Kt x B
19. Q—Kt3	B—B3
20. Kt x B	P x Kt
21. R—K5	Q—Kt3
22. Q—B2	KR—Q1
23. Kt—K2	R—Q4
24. R x R	. . . .

To save the QP. Lasker has suggested 24. R—K3, but then . . . Kt—B4; 25. R—QKt3, Q—Q1; 26. R—Kt4, Q—Q2; 27. R—B4, P—K4 wins the QP.

24.	BP x R
25. Q—Q2	Kt—B4
26. P—QKt3	P—KR4

. . . K—R2 was more precise.

27. P—KR3 ?   . . . .

Missing his last drawing chance: 27. Kt—Kt3 !, Kt x Kt; 28. RP x Kt, R—B3; 29. Q—B4, R—B7; 30. R—Q2. From here on in Capa plays it to perfection.

27.	P—R5 !
28. Q—Q3	R—B3
29. K—B1	P—Kt3
30. Q—Kt1	Q—Kt5
31. K—Kt1	P—R4
32. Q—Kt2	P—R5
33. Q—Q2	Q x Q
34. R x Q	P x P
35. P x P	R—Kt3
36. R—Q3	R—R3

Forcing an entry behind the Pawn.

37. P—KKt4   . . . .

A desperate gamble.

37.	P x P e.p.
38. P x P	R—R7
39. Kt—B3	R—QB7

The threat is . . . Kt x QP.

40. Kt–Q1	Kt–K2
41. Kt–K3	R–B8ch
42. K–B2	Kt–B3
43. Kt–Q1	R–Kt8

Avoiding a trap. If first 43. . . . Kt–Kt5; 44. R–Q2, R–Kt8; 45. Kt–Kt2 !, R x Kt ?; 46. R x R, Kt–Q6ch; 47. K–K2, Kt x R; 48. K–Q2 only draws because Black's Kt is trapped.

44. K–K2	. . . .

Or 44. K–K1, Kt–R4.

44.	R x P !
45. K–K3	R–Kt5
46. Kt–B3	Kt–K2
47. Kt–K2	Kt–B4ch
48. K–B2	P–Kt4
49. P–Kt4	Kt–Q3
50. Kt–Kt1	Kt–K5ch
51. K–B1	R–Kt8ch
52. K–Kt2	R–Kt7ch
53. K–B1	R–B7ch
54. K–K1	R–QR7
55. K–B1	K–Kt2

White is in virtual zugzwang. Once the Black King enters the picture it will be all over.

56. R–K3	K–Kt3
57. R–Q3	P–B3
58. R–K3	K–B2
59. R–Q3	K–K2
60. R–K3	K–Q3
61. R–Q3	R–B7ch
62. K–K1	R–KKt7
63. K–B1	R–QR7
64. R–K3	P–K4
65. R–Q3	P x P
66. R x P	K–B4
67. R–Q1	P–Q5
68. R–B1ch	K–Q4

White Resigns.

He is helpless against the advance of the Black QP.

Three years after the world championship match, Capa and Lasker met again, in the New York Tournament of 1924; Lasker won first prize, but Capa had the satisfaction of again defeating him in their individual encounter.

CAPABLANCA   LASKER

New York, 1924
Queen's Gambit Declined

1. P–Q4	Kt–KB3
2. P–QB4	P–B3
3. Kt–QB3	P–Q4
4. P x P	. . . .

Capa always preferred simplicity.

4.	P x P
5. Kt–B3	Kt–B3
6. B–B4	P–K3

The safest.

7. P–K3	B–K2

. . . B—Q3 equalizes more easily.

8. B—Q3   O—O
9. O—O   Kt—KR4

Many years later Botvinnik played the obvious 9. P—KR3 to avoid this maneuver.

10. B—K5   P—B4

More consistent is . . . P—B3, to force the immediate exchange.

11. R—B1   Kt—B3
12. B x Kt   P x B !
13. Kt—KR4   K—R1
14. P—B4   R—KKt1
15. R—B3   B—Q2
16. R—R3   . . . .

An idle threat. He soon returns to the main idea.

16. . . . .   B—K1
17. P—R3   R—Kt2
18. R—Kt3   R x R
19. P x R   R—B1
20. K—B2   Kt—R4
21. Q—B3 ?   . . . .

Inexact. Q—K2 was better.

21. . . . .   Kt—B5

Attacking the KP.

22. Q—K2   Kt—Q3

Both sides have completed their development, and a battle royal is shaping up. Black will attack on the Q-side, White on the K-side.

23. R—KR1   Kt—K5ch ?

A mistake which allows a promising sacrifice. Correct was first 23. . . . B—B2 and if 24. P—KKt4, Kt—K5ch; 25. B x Kt, BP x B; and White's Queen does not reach the K-side.

24. B x Kt   BP x B
25. Q—Kt4   P—B4
26. Kt x BP !   P x Kt
27. Q x P   P—KR4
28. P—KKt4   . . . .
   28. Kt x QP, R—B7ch is inferior.
28. . . . .   R—B3
29. P—Kt5 ?   . . . .

But here, as Alekhine later showed, 29. Kt x QP would have won, e.g., 29. . . . R—B7ch; 30. K—Kt3; or 29. . . . B—R5ch; 30. P—Kt3, R—B7ch; 31. K—Kt1, B x P; 32. Q—B8ch.

29. . . . .   K—Kt1 ?

And now Lasker, in his turn, suffers from the fatal illusion that he can win. Better was 29. . . . R—Q3.

30. Kt x QP   B—B2
31. Kt x Bch   Q x Kt
32. P—KKt4   . . . .

White has acquired three Pawns for the piece and still retains a strong attack after the smoke has cleared. Both sides, however, were under the impression that they ought to win.

32. . . . .   P x P

With 32. . . . R – B7ch; 33. K – Kt3, R – K7; 34. P – Kt6, P – R5ch ! he has an easy draw, but he still hopes to do better.

33. Q – R7ch   K – B1
34. R – R6   B – Kt1

. . . R x R was simpler.

35. Q – B5ch   K – Kt2
36. R x R   P x R
37. K – Kt3   . . . .

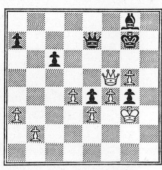

37. . . . .   Q – K3 ?

The decisive mistake. 37. . . . B – B2 ! still draws.

38. K x P !   Q x Qch
39. K x Q   B – Q4

Becker

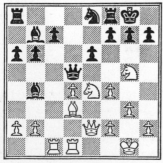

Capablanca – TO PLAY

40. P – Kt4   P – R3
41. K – Kt4 !   B – B5
42. P – B5   B – Kt6
43. K – B4   B – B7
44. K – K5   K – B2

45. P – R4 !!   K – Kt2

After 45. . . . B x P; 46. K x P, the 3 passed Pawns decide.

46. P – Q5 !   B x P
47. P – Q6   P – B4
48. P x P   B – B3
49. K – K6   P – R4
50. P – B6ch   Black Resigns.

A magnificent fighting game.

Capa's games are full of delightful surprises. Here is a choice selection.

Carlsbad, 1929

1. Kt x RP !   P – KB4
2. Kt(R7) – Kt5 !!   Black Resigns.

For there is no parrying the double threat of B – B4 and Q – R5. If 2. . . . P x Kt; 3. B – B4, or 2. . . . Q – Q2; 3. Q – R5, Kt – B3; 4. Kt x Ktch, P x Kt; 5. Q – Kt6ch, K – R1; 6. Kt x P, Q x Kt; 7. R x P, etc.

Levenfish

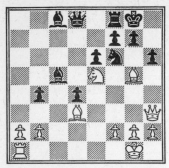

Capablanca—TO PLAY

Moscow, 1935

1. Kt—Kt4 !   B—K2
2. B x Kt !   P x B

Not 2. . . . B x B; 3. Kt x Pch,
P x Kt; 4. Q x RP, R—K1; 5. B—
R7ch, with mate to follow soon.

3. Kt x RPch   K—Kt2
4. Q—Kt4ch !   K—R1

If . . . K x Kt; 5 Q—R4ch and
mate next.

5. Q—R5   K—Kt2
6. Kt x P   R—R1

Or . . . R x Kt; 7. Q—R7ch,
K—B1; 8. Q—R8 mate.

7. Q—Kt6ch   Black Resigns.

Spielmann

Capablanca—TO PLAY

San Sebastian, 1911

1. B—B1   R x BP
2. B—B4   Q—Q1
3. R x B !   Q—KB1
4. Q x Pch   Q x Q
5. R—K8ch   Q—Kt1

6. B—K5ch and mate next
move.

Capablanca

Bernstein—TO PLAY

St. Petersburg, 1914

1. Kt x BP   Kt x Kt
2. R x Kt   R x R
3. R x R   Q—Kt7 !

Not . . . Q—Kt8ch; 4. Q—B1,
R—Q8; 5. R—B8ch !
White Resigns—for he must lose
at least a Rook.

Marshall

Capablanca—TO PLAY

8th Match Game, 1909

1.	R—K3 !!	Q x BP
2.	KR—Q3	Q—K7
3.	Kt—Q6	R x Kt
4.	B x R	B—K8
5.	Q—K8ch	K—Kt2
6.	P—R6ch	Black Resigns.

Tenerow

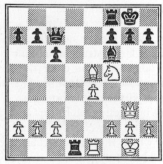

Capablanca—TO PLAY

New York, 1910?

1.	R x R	B x B

If . . . Q x B; 2. Kt—R6ch still wins.

2.	Kt—R6ch	K—R1
3.	Q x B !	Q x Q
4.	Kt x Pch	Black Resigns.

Richard Reti and the Hypermodern School

The most persuasive exponent of the hypermodern school was the Czech Richard Reti. Although he never was a serious challenger to Capablanca, he was invariably a high prize-winner throughout the 1920's. The chess world suffered a great loss when he died at a relatively early age in 1930.

The hypermodern school was essentially a revolt against the rigid formalism of Tarrasch and his followers. Tarrasch, although a great man in his day, became rather pompous and authoritarian in his later years, and expected everybody to recognize him as the man who had solved all the theoretical problems of chess. The hypermoderns rebelled, against both the man and his ideas.

Tarrasch had a simplified version of chess theory. White must open with P—K4 or P—Q4; whoever occupies the center and develops most quickly gets the better game. Not so, said the hypermoderns. It is not the *occupation* of the center per se that counts, it is *control*. In fact, it is often disadvantageous to occupy the center too soon because the occupation will soon be challenged and the result will be a collection of weaknesses, they contended. "After 1. P—K4 White's game is in its last throes," cried Breyer with typical hypermodern exuberance and exaggeration.

Since control is better than occupation, the hypermoderns reasoned, flank development is better than central. Hence all the fianchetto variations sprang up, for both White and Black, which constitute so much of the modern master's repertoire.

Development, the hypermoderns continued, need not be forced too soon, as the older masters had taught. In fact, chess was just too complicated for simple rules. The one rule that they preferred was: The opening must be treated as though it were a middle game. By this they meant that every opening move must fit into some well-conceived plan, and that the Pawn formation must be played with a view to the endgame.

This revolution enriched chess immensely. But it went too far. For the old rule *always occupy the center*, it substituted a new one, *never occupy the center*. Reti tried to see in chess a larger struggle between opposing world ideas. He wrote in 1929: "Today we see in chess the fight of aspiring Americanism against the old European intellectual life: a struggle between the technique of Capablanca, a virtuoso in whose play one can find nothing tangible to object to, and between great European masters, all of them artists, who have the qualities as well as the faults of artists in their treatment of the subject to which they devote their lives: they experimentalise and in striving after what is deep down, they overlook what is near at hand." This crude attack against American "materialism," reminiscent of the 1920's, is hardly taken seriously today. But even if it were, what Reti forgot is that chess is a game, and that the ultimate decision lies not in speculation, but in over-the-board calculation and trial. For that reason general principles can never have the same importance in chess as in other art forms. It is not, we now know, either control of the center or occupation of the center; it depends on the position. In some cases control is better, in others it is not. The ultimate test lies in variations, not in theory. This is our attitude today. But, had it not been for the hypermodern revolt, chess would not have advanced beyond the old formalism to the healthy eclecticism which characterizes it today.

Throughout the 1920's Reti was a consistent high prize winner, though he never quite reached the class of the world champions. Here is a game of immense historical importance, in which he showed how effective his new opening could be against one of the old-timers.

RETI   RUBINSTEIN

Carlsbad, 1923

Reti's Opening

1. Kt–KB3 P–Q4
2. P–KKt3 Kt–KB3
3. B–Kt2 P–KKt3
4. P–B4 P–Q5

. . . P–B3 was better.

5. P–Q3 B–Kt2
6. P–QKt4! O–O
7. QKt–Q2 . . . .

Note that Black has occupied the center with a Pawn, White proceeds to undermine and attack it.

7. . . . . P–B4
8. Kt–Kt3 P x P
9. B–Kt2 Kt–B3
10. QKt x P Kt x Kt
11. B x Kt . . . .

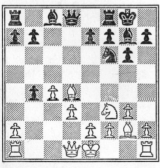

The outcome of the opening is curious.

Actually White has the better of it because he will now be able to occupy the center with his Pawns! Thus the result of the opening leads to the hypermodern paradox: if you occupy the center immediately, the Pawns

soon become weakened, and the opponent will then be able to occupy it. This means though that it is not occupation that is bad, it is in many cases *immediate occupation*.

11. . . . . P–Kt3
12. P–QR3 B–Kt2
13. B–Kt2 P x P
14. R x P Q–B2
15. Q–R1 . . . .

Kmoch writes: "One may confidently assert that Reti did not discover this move, he invented it!"

15. . . . . Kt–K1
16. B x B Kt x B
17. O–O . . . .

At last! The older masters were always horrified by the lack of precautions the hypermoderns took to defend the King.

17. . . . . Kt–K3

The RP cannot be taken because the Queen goes: 18. R x P?, R x R; 19. Q x R, R–R1.

18. R–Kt1 B–B3
19. P–Q4! B–K5
20. R–Q1 P–QR4
21. P–Q5 Kt–B4
22. Kt–Q4 B x B
23. K x B KR–Q1
24. Kt–B6 R–Q3
25. R–K3 R–K1
26. Q–K5 P–B3
27. Q–Kt2 P–K4

Reti has been hoping to provoke this move, for now the position of the Kt is secure. The next step is to concentrate on the KtP.

28. Q–Kt5 !   K–B2
29. R–QKt1   Kt–Q2

30. P–B3   R–QB1

Threatening . . . Kt–Kt1.

31. R–Q3 !   . . . .

To meet . . . Kt–Kt1 with P–B5.

31. . . . .   P–K5

A desperate liberation attempt.

32. P x P   Kt–K4
33. Q x KtP !!   . . . .

Of course. With so many Pawns for the piece the win is easy.

33. . . . .   Kt x Kt
34. P–B5 !!   . . . .

The concluding process is most elegant.

34. . . . .   R–Q2
35. P x Kt   R x R
36. Q x Qch   R x Q
37. P x R   R x P
38. R–Kt7ch   K–K1
39. P–Q4   R–R3

40. R–Kt6 !!!   . . . .

A problem-like theme.

40. . . . . .   R–R1

After 40. . . . . R x R; 41. P x R, K–Q2; 42. P–K5, P–R5; 43. P–K6ch, White queens first.

41. R x P   P–R5
42. R–B2   P–R6
43. R–R2   K–Q2
44. P–Q5   P–Kt4
45. K–B3   R–R5
46. K–K3   P–R4
47. P–R4   P x P
48. P x P   K–K2
49. K–B4   K–Q2
50. K–B5   Black Resigns.

One of the earliest triumphs of hypermodernism.

The year after the above game was played, at New York, Reti produced some classic gems with his opening, which people were now coming to take seriously. When he beat Capablanca people sat up and took notice!

RETI   **CAPABLANCA**

New York, 1924

Reti's Opening

1. Kt–KB3   Kt–KB3
2. P–B4   P–KKt3

3. P–QKt4   B–Kt2
4. B–Kt2   O–O
5. P–Kt3   P–Kt3

Alekhine writes: "Capablanca treats the opening simply as well as soundly, and, after a few moves obtains a perfectly even position."

6. B–Kt2   B–Kt2
7. O–O   P–Q3
8. P–Q3   . . . .

But Reti sticks too closely to his principles. After 8. P–Q4 I would prefer White.

8. . . . .   QKt–Q2
9. QKt–Q2   P–K4
10. Q–B2   R–K1
11. KR–Q1   P–QR4
12. P–QR3   P–R3

Stalling for time.

13. Kt–B1   P–B4

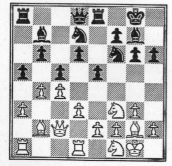

14. P–Kt5   Kt–B1
15. P–K3   Q–B2

Preparing the break with P–Q4.

16. P–Q4   B–K5
17. Q–B3   . . . .

Better was Q–B1.

17. . . . .   KP x P
18. P x P   Kt(B3)–Q2 ?

A miscalculation. After 18. . . . . Kt–K3 !; 19. P x P, QP x P; 20. Q–B1 is necessary, when Black's game is adequate.

19. Q–Q2   P x P

Simpler was . . . QR–Q1.

20. B x P   Q x P
21. B x B   K x B
22. Q–Kt2ch   K–Kt1
23. R x P   . . . .

Not 23. Kt–Q2, Q–B7.

23. . . . .   Q–B4
24. QR–Q1   R–R2
25. Kt–K3   Q–R4

A typical mid-game position of Reti's opening. The center is liquidated and White's pieces are all in commanding positions, which gives him a winning attack.

26. Kt–Q4   B x B
27. K x B   Q–K4

There are many pretty combinations afloat: if 27. . . . . R x Kt; 28. P x R, Q x R; 29. Kt–B5 ! wins.

28. Kt–B4   Q–QB4
29. Kt–B6   R–B2
30. Kt–K3   . . . .

Threatening Kt–Q5.

30. . . . .   Kt–K4
31. R(Q1)–Q5   Black Resigns.

While his victory over Capa was a great personal triumph for Reti, his win against Bogoljubow in the same tournament is one of the most beautiful games on record. It was rightly awarded the first brilliancy prize.

| RETI | BOGOLJUBOW |

New York, 1924

Reti's Opening

1. Kt–KB3	Kt–KB3
2. P–B4	P–K3
3. P–KKt3	P–Q4
4. B–Kt2	B–Q3
5. O–O	O–O
6. P–Kt3	R–K1
7. B–Kt2	QKt–Q2
8. P–Q4 !	. . . .

In a real sense the decisive move; Black is now strategically lost!

8.	P–B3
9. QKt–Q2	Kt–K5
10. Kt x Kt	P x Kt
11. Kt–K5	P–KB4

12. P–B3	P x P
13. B x P !	Q–B2
14. Kt x Kt	B x Kt
15. P–K4	P–K4

Black struggles to free himself.

16. P–B5	B–KB1
17. Q–B2	P x QP
18. P x P	QR–Q1
19. B–R5	R–K4
20. B x P	R x KBP

Leading to a brilliant finish; but . . . R–Q4; 21. QR–Q1 is equally hopeless.

21. R x R	B x R
22. Q x B	R x B
23. R–KB1	R–Q1
24. B–B7ch	K–R1

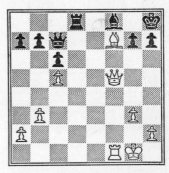

25. B–K8 !!!!   Black Resigns.

There is no defense. If 25. . . . . B x Pch; 26. Q x B, R x B; 27. R–B8 and mate next; while if 25. . . . B–K2; 26. Q–B8 and mates.

Reti was above all an artist of the chessboard. He was a problem and endgame composer of the first rank, and in his games this love for beauty crops up again and again. Here are a few of his *chef d'oeuvres.*

STUDY BY *Reti*

WHITE TO PLAY AND DRAW

1. K–Kt7   P–R5
2. K–B6   P–R6
3. K–K6   P–R7
4. P–B7   K–Kt2
5. K–Q7   P–R8 = Q
6. P–B8 = Qch

With perpetual check.

Tartakower

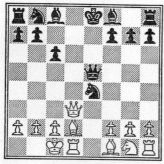

Reti–TO PLAY

Vienna, 1910

1. Q–Q8ch   K x Q
2. B–Kt5ch   K–B2
3. B–Q8 mate

Reti–TO PLAY

Euwe

Match Amsterdam, 1922

1. . . . .   B–KR6 !
2. Q x R   B–B4ch
3. K–R1   B x Pch
4. K x B   Q–Kt5ch
White Resigns.

Aron Nimzovitch

The greatest player of the hypermodern school was Aron Nimzovitch. Born in Riga, in 1886, he learned the game from his father, who was a player of considerable ability. By 1906, only twenty, he was already a master of some repute. In Russia, even then the home of many a renowned figure in the chess world, he soon became one of the leading lights. In 1914 he tied with Alekhine in the elimination rounds to decide admission to the St. Petersburg grandmasters' tournament. Thus he was a finished master long before the first World War, but it was not until the 1920's that he was recognized as a potential world champion.

During his pre-war period Nimzovitch began elaborating the ideas which were later incorporated into his monumental work, *My System.* He wrote a few articles opposing Tarrasch, which earned him much ridicule. As long as Nimzovitch was not too well known, people agreed with Tarrasch, and said of him: "a law unto himself," goes his own way, one, however, not to be recommended to the public," "mysterious." It was not until much later that the profundity of his ideas came to be appreciated.

After the war, Nimzovitch emigrated to Denmark, where he made his home until his untimely death in 1935. At first he played very little, apparently because he was suffering from ideas of persecution. Whenever he visited a restaurant, he switched the cups around for fear that he was being poisoned.

These persecutory notions eventually disappeared, or at any rate became manageable, and by 1925 he was back in the international arena. For about six or seven years his record was most impressive; his greatest success came at Carlsbad, 1929, where he finished ahead of everybody except Alekhine, who went through the tournament as chief kibitzer.

But he remained extremely nervous and was given to bizarre behavior. Smoking irritated him, and there were many stories of how annoyed he became, even though the masters knew that it bothered him and generally refrained. During one of his games with Vidmar in the New York 1927 Tournament, the latter absent-mindedly took out his cigarette case. Nimzovitch rushed up to Maroczy, the tournament director, and protested. "But," countered Maroczy, "he is not smoking." "You are a chess-master," roared Nimzovitch; "and you must know that the threat is much stronger than the execution!" Opocensky once told me of another amusing incident. In one of their games, Opocensky wanted to smoke, and walked a good distance from the board to light a cigar; he stood there for a few minutes looking at the position when suddenly Nimzovitch jumped up and shouted: "Stop shaking your belly!"

Many other eccentricities are reported of him. At one time a doctor ordered him to do calisthenics; he began to do them in the tournament room. During a particularly difficult situation once, he went to a corner and stood on his head!

Were it not for these unfortunate aberrations, Nimzovitch might well have become world champion. He had the ability, but he lacked the stamina and cold-bloodedness which is a requisite for any title holder.

For many years Nimzovitch labored over his book, which finally appeared in the late 1920's as *My System*. The title is really a misnomer, since what he had was not a system, but a collection of insights. Still it is revealing of the man—he had to have the feeling that he was revolutionizing chess from top to bottom. The need to prove his theories sometimes proved costly in tournaments, and was another factor which kept him from the chess title crown.

Nimzovitch's wizardry was most evident in so-called close positions when he made moves which were termed "mysterious." Here is a classic which has become famous as the "Immortal Zugzwang Game."

SAEMISCH	NIMZOVITCH

Copenhagen, 1923

Queen's Indian Defense

1.	P—Q4	Kt—KB3
2.	P—QB4	P—K3
3.	Kt—KB3	P—QKt3
4.	P—KKt3	B—Kt2
5.	B—Kt2	B—K2
6.	Kt—QB3	O—O
7.	O—O	P—Q4

Now a standard opening, but then radically new. . . . Kt—K5 equalizes now.

8.	Kt—K5	P—B3

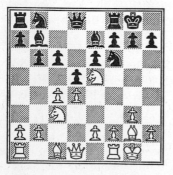

9. P x P? . . . .

Completely anti-positional. Few masters would be guilty of it today. But 9. P—K4 or P—Kt3 is much stronger.

9.	. . . .	BP x P
10.	B—B4	P—QR3
11.	R—B1	P—QKt4
12.	Q—Kt3?	. . . .

Another positional error. White is obviously lost in this hypermodern maneuvering. A plausible idea was 12. Kt—Q3, followed by P—QKt4 and Kt—B5.

12.	. . . .	Kt—B3
13.	Kt x Kt	B x Kt
14.	P—KR3	Q—Q2
15.	K—R2	Kt—R4
16.	B—Q2	P—B4

Initiating the K-side attack.

17.	Q—Q1	P—Kt5 !
18.	Kt—Kt1	. . . .

Slowly White is driven back.

18. . . . .   B – QKt4
19. R – Kt1   B – Q3 !
20. P – K4 ?   . . . .

A miscalculation in a difficult position.

20. . . . .   BP x P !!
21. Q x Kt   R x P
22. Q – Kt5   QR – KB1
23. K – R1   R(B1) – B4
24. Q – K3   B – Q6 !

Threatening . . . R – K7.

25. QR – K1   P – R3 !!!
White Resigns.

The most remarkable winning move on record. White is in literal "zugzwang" or move-compulsion – i.e., there is no direct threat, but any move that he makes loses. Here are the main possibilities:

I. 26. R – KB1, B x R.
II. 26. R – Q1, R – K7 winning the Queen.
III. 26. P – Kt4, R(B4) – B6; 27. B x R, R – R7 mate.
IV. 26. P – Kt3, P – R4 and the zugzwang continues.

The older generation had a hard time puzzling out Nimzovitch's "peculiar" moves. Here is another victory for his new ideas.

NIMZOVITCH   RUBINSTEIN
Dresden, 1926
English Opening

1. P – QB4   P – QB4
2. Kt – KB3   Kt – KB3
3. Kt – B3   P – Q4
4. P x P   Kt x P
5. P – K4 !   Kt – Kt5

Preferable was 5. . . . Kt x Kt, but Black may have been under the illusion that 6. P – Q3 was now forced, since classical dogma taught that the King must never be moved in the opening.

6. B – B4 !   P – K3

Now he rightly sees that 6. . . . Kt – Q6ch; 7. K – K2, Kt – B5ch; 8. K – B1 gets him nowhere.

7. O – O   Kt(Kt1) – B3
8. P – Q3   Kt – Q5
9. Kt x Kt   P x Kt
10. Kt – K2   . . . .

Again Rubinstein has a centrally located Pawn which proves to be his undoing. (See his game against Reti.)

10.	P–QR3
11. Kt–Kt3	B–Q3
12. P–B4	....

Q–Kt4 was a strong alternative.

12.	O–O
13. Q–B3	K–R1
14. B–Q2	P–B4
15. QR–K1	Kt–B3
16. R–K2	Q–B2
17. P x P	P x P

White's position is somewhat freer, but how should he continue? Nimzovitch has a brilliant inspiration.

18. Kt–R1 !!   ....

Beginning the long journey to KKt5.

18.	B–Q2
19. Kt–B2	QR–K1
20. KR–K1	R x R
21. R x R	Kt–Q1

If . . . R–K1; 22. Q–Q5 ! is decisive.

22. Kt–R3	B–B3
23. Q–R5	P–KKt3
24. Q–R4	K–Kt2
25. Q–B2 !	....

The genius of the hypermoderns lay in their ability to pull an attack out of what the older masters had thought of as "barren" positions.

25.	B–B4
26. P–QKt4	B–Kt3
27. Q–R4	....

Threatening to win everything.

| 27. .... | R–K1 |
| 28. R–K5 ! | Kt–B2 |

If 28. . . . P–R3; 29. P–Kt4 !

29. B x Kt	Q x B
30. Kt–Kt5	Q–Kt1
31. R x R	B x R
32. Q–K1 !	....

Nimzovitch says here: "Black is lost. In spite of the scanty material a mating attack is in the air."

32.	B–B3
33. Q–K7ch	K–R1
34. P–Kt5 !	Q–Kt2

If instead 34. . . . P x P (or 34.
. . . B x P); 35. B—Kt4, followed by B—Q6. . . . B—Q1
fails against Kt—B7ch.

35. Q x Qch	K x Q
36. P x B	Black Resigns.

Although he has become famous
for his handling of close positions, Nimzovitch was a tactical
genius of the first order. Here is
one of his most pleasing victories.

NIMZOVITCH   STOLTZ

Stockholm, 1934

Queen's Gambit Declined

1. P—QB4	P—K3
2. Kt—QB3	P—Q4
3. P—Q4	P—QB4
4. BP x P	KP x P
5. Kt—B3	Kt—QB3
6. P—KKt3	P—B5

The Folkestone Variation, which
the Swedish team popularized at
the international tournament at
Folkestone in 1933.

7. B—Kt2	. . . .

P—K4 at once is even stronger.

7.	B—QKt5
8. O—O	KKt—K2

9. P—K4 !	P x P

Forced.

10. Kt x P	B—KB4
11. Kt—K5 !	Q x P

The alternative 11. . . . Kt x
Kt; 12. P x Kt, Kt—B3; 13. Kt—
Q6ch was no better.

12. Q x Q	Kt x Q
13. P—QR3 !	B x Kt

If the Bishop moves, 13. . . . .
B—R4; 14. Kt—Q6ch is fatal.

14. B x B	B—B4
15. B x KtP	QR—Kt1
16. B—QR6	Kt—K7ch
17. K—Kt2	B—Q5

18. Kt x BP !!	. . . .

A beautiful winning move. Of
course if . . . K x Kt; 19. B x Pch
and 20. B x Kt.

18.	Kt x B
19. Kt x R	Kt—Kt6
20. QR—Q1	P—Kt3

Apparently   winning   the
Knight—

21. Kt—B7 !!	. . . .

Back again.

21.	. . . .	K x Kt
22.	B x Pch	K – B1
23.	B x Kt	B x KtP
24.	R – Q3	B x P
25.	R – B3ch	K – Kt2

The game can now be won in a variety of ways, but Nimzovitch concludes with a pretty mating attack.

26.	R – QR1	B – B4
27.	R – B7ch	K – R3
28.	R – R5 !	B – Kt3
29.	R – R4	. . . .

Nimzovitch – TO PLAY

Lund

Alapin

Nimzovitch – TO PLAY

Threatening mate in two.

29.	. . . .	Kt – B4
30.	B – K6	Kt – Q5
31.	B – Q7	Black Resigns.

Nimzovitch gives this probable variation: 31. . . . R – Kt2; 32. P – Kt4, Kt – Kt6; 33. P – Kt5ch !, K x P; 34. R – Kt4ch, K – R3; 35. R – R4ch, K – Kt4; 36. P – B4ch and mate next.

Here are some more pleasing Nimzovitch melodies.

Oslo, 1921

1.	. . . .	P – Kt5
2.	P x P	R x Kt
3.	P x R	P – Kt6
4.	P x P	P – B6ch
5.	P x P	P – R6

White Resigns – all his moves were forced.

Riga, 1913

1.	Q – Q8ch !	B x Q
2.	R – K8 mate.	

Marshall   New York, 1927

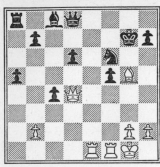

Nimzovitch—TO PLAY

1. R—K8 !   Q x R
2. Q x Ktch   K—Kt1
3. B—R6   Black Resigns.

Carlos Torre

Although the Latin countries were the leaders of the chess world in the fifteenth and sixteenth centuries, in our times they have produced few great masters. The most notable exceptions are of course Morphy and Capablanca. Another master of Latin origin who might have become world champion had his health held out was the Mexican, Carlos Torre. Born in Mexico in 1904, he moved to New Orleans, the home of Morphy, at an early age, and later to New York. In New York he quickly became one of the leading American masters. By 1925 he was sufficiently well known to be invited to a number of European tournaments, where he showed the greatest of promise. Unfortunately he suffered a nervous breakdown a year later and had to retire from chess. From time to time there have been rumors of his recovery, but he has never been well enough to return to the game he loved and enriched.

I met Torre in Monterey, Mexico, in 1934, where two exhibition games were arranged. He was still very nervous and withdrawn, and warned me not to spend too much money; aside from this, he was generally rather disinterested in what was going on. In the games he was no longer the old Torre.

In his heyday Torre was one of the bright lights of an era which produced few masters of promise. One of his most celebrated victories is the game in which he defeated Emanuel Lasker, a game played on Torre's twenty-first birthday.

TORRE   LASKER
    Moscow, 1925
    Queen's Pawn Game
1. P—Q4   Kt—KB3
2. Kt—KB3   P—K3

3. B—Kt5   P—B4
4. P—K3   P x P

A poor idea. Black should continue with . . . Q—Kt3 at an early stage.

5. P x P	B−K2
6. QKt−Q2	P−Q3
7. B−Q3	QKt−Q2
8. P−B3	P−QKt3
9. Kt−B4	B−Kt2
10. Q−K2	Q−B2
11. O−O	O−O

The great Lasker has been outplayed in the opening. White's pieces are freer and he has a strong initiative.

12. KR−K1	KR−K1
13. QR−Q1	Kt−B1
14. B−B1 !	Kt−Q4
15. Kt−Kt5	. . . .

Both sides are maneuvering to find a weakness in the enemy camp.

15.	P−Kt4
16. Kt−R3	P−Kt5
17. P x P	Kt x P
18. Q−R5 !	. . . .

A bold idea, though 18. B−Kt1 was also possible.

18.	B x Kt
19. B x B	Kt x B
20. R x Kt	Q−R4

Black is threatening P−KR3 or P−B3.

21. P−QKt4 ! . . . .

Seizing the opportunity to complicate the position.

21. . . . .   Q−KB4

Lasker is playing for a win against the relatively unknown Torre. With 21. . . . Q x P a probable draw results after 22. R−Kt1, Q−R4; 23. Kt−B4, Q−R3; 24. R x B, Q x R; 25. Kt x P, Q−Kt8ch; 26. R−Q1, Q−Kt3.

22. R−KKt3	P−KR3
23. Kt−B4	Q−Q4 ?

A mistake. Correct was . . . P x B; 24. Kt x P, Q−Kt3 !, when White regains the piece, but the endgame is drawn.

24. Kt−K3   Q−Kt4

25. B−B6 !! . . . .

Surprise decision.

25.	Q x Q
26. R x Pch	K−R1
27. R x P dis ch	K−Kt1
28. R−Kt7ch	K−R1
29. R x B dis ch	K−Kt1
30. R−Kt7ch	K−R1
31. R−Kt5 dis ch	K−R2

32. R x Q	K—Kt3
33. R—R3	K x B
34. R x Pch	K—Kt4
35. R—R3	. . . .

Torre has eaten his fill (in Spanish a colloquial expression for taking a piece is "comer"—to eat a piece). The rest is obvious.

35.	R(K1)—Kt1
36. R—Kt3ch	K—B3
37. R—B3ch	K—Kt3
38. P—QR3	P—R4
39. P x P	R x P
40. Kt—B4	R—Q4
41. R—B4	Kt—Q2
42. R x Pch	K—Kt4
43. P—Kt3	Black Resigns.

Ernst Gruenfeld

Another prominent star of the twenties was the Viennese, Ernst Gruenfeld. He stands out particularly as one of the great theoreticians of chess history. His knowledge of opening variations was simply fantastic; he knew more than any half dozen of his colleagues put together. Such encyclopedic knowledge has both good and bad features. In the early days he used it to produce vigorous games; later he became too easily contented with colorless draws. Here is a beautiful win from the earlier years.

GRUENFELD   BOGOLJUBOW
Vienna, 1922

Blumenfeld Counter Gambit

1. P—Q4	Kt—KB3
2. Kt—KB3	P—K3
3. P—B4	P—B4
4. P—Q5	P—QKt4

A gambit which was very popular in this tournament.

5. B—Kt5   . . . .

This is the refutation. If instead 5. P x KP, BP x P; 6. P x P, P—Q4 Black gets a strong attack for the Pawn.

5.	P—KR3
6. B x Kt	Q x B
7. Kt—B3	P—Kt5
8. Kt—Kt5 !	Kt—R3

Forced.

Gruenfeld now has a considerable advantage in development, which calls for a quick attack.

9. P—K4 !   Q x KtP ?

This loses. Black's best bet was . . . P—K4.

| 10. B—Q3 | Q—B3 |
| 11. P—K5 | Q—Q1 |

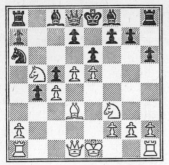

14. Q x Qch, K x Q; 15. O–O–
Och.

14. R x Q   R–QKt1
15. B–B6ch   K–K2
16. Kt x P   P–Kt4

A last gasp.

17. B–Kt5!   . . . .

Decisive. If now 17. . . . . B–
QKt2; 18. B x Kt, B x B; 19. Kt–
B6ch wins. Bogoljubow prefers
to allow mate.

17. . . . .   B–KKt2
18. Kt–B6ch   K–B1
19. R–Q8 mate.

12. P x P!   . . . .
Surprisingly effective.

12. . . . .   QP x P
13. B–K4!   Q x Qch
No better is 13. . . . . R–Kt1;

Rudolf Spielmann

Another master who began his chess career before the first World War
and rose to prominence in the Capablanca era was the Viennese, Rudolf
Spielmann. He was renowned mainly for his great tactical ability; the sacrifice he loved as nothing else. In his book, *The Art of Sacrifice in Chess,*
he brings out much of his personality. He writes:

"The beauty of a game of chess is usually assessed, and not without
good reason, according to the sacrifices it contains. Sacrifice—that is a
hallowed, a heroic thought! The individual comes forward in a spirit of
chivalry and immolates himself as did Winkelried in the battle of Sem-
pach.

"Sacrifice for an idea calls forth in us homage and admiration even
where the idea in itself may not meet with our full approval. In chess,
which we like to see as a counterpart of life, a sacrifice raises similar feelings in us. We are inclined, subconsciously, to rate a sacrificial combination more highly than positional play. We instinctively place the moral
value above the scientific. We honor Capablanca, but our hearts beat faster
at the mention of the name of Morphy. The magic of the sacrifice grips
us and we care nothing for extraneous circumstances, whether Morphy's
opponents were less strong than Capablanca's, how Morphy would fare
today, how Capablanca would have played in those far-off days. We
simply cannot resist the magic of the sacrifice, because enthusiasm for
sacrifice lies in the nature of man.

"The habit of valuing a game of chess according to the amount of material sacrificed is currently disparaged in expert-circles. In a measure this is justified, but yet is to be regretted.

"The expert has dipped so deep into the technique of the game that he cannot share in the simple-hearted joys of the people. He watches the play, not from the audience, but from the stage itself. He is also, possibly, a little case-hardened. But the ordinary chess players have preserved fresh and natural feelings, and enthuse now as ever for the combinative style."

Although he was always looking for brilliancies and sacrifices on the chessboard, in real life he was the meekest and most retiring of men. When I knew him in the 1930's his only pleasure in life apart from chess was beer. In 1935, when the Soviets invited the masters who had participated in the international tournament at Moscow to stay on, Spielmann refused because he could not stand the beer!

Over the chessboard Spielmann was frequently brilliant indeed. "I can see combinations as well as Alekhine," he used to say; "but I cannot get to the same positions." Here he put his finger on his strength and weakness.

In his book Spielmann attempted to classify the various types of sacrifices. The one in the following game he dubbed a "King hunt."

RUBINSTEIN   SPIELMANN

San Sebastian, 1912

Dutch Defense

1. P–Q4	P–K3
2. P–QB4	P–KB4
3. Kt–QB3	B–Kt5
4. B–Q2	Kt–KB3
5. P–KKt3	O–O
6. B–Kt2	P–Q3
7. P–QR3	....

Loss of time.

7.	B x Kt
8. B x B	QKt–Q2
9. Q–B2	P–B4
10. P x P ?	....

Spielmann shows mastery of hypermodern ideas which Rubinstein does not. Almost anything was better than the text.

10.	Kt x P
11. Kt–B3	Kt(B4)–K5
12. O–O	B–Q2
13. KR–Q1 ?	....

Better was 13. QR–Q1.

| 13. .... | R–B1 |

14. B x Kt   ....

This unpleasant move is forced. Spielmann points out that the alternative 14. Kt–Q2 ? is refuted by . . . Kt x BP !; 15. K x Kt, Kt–Kt5ch; 16. K–B3, B–B3ch winning. If the White Rook were still at KB1, that is, if White had played 13. QR–Q1 before, this sacrifice would not be feasible.

14.	Q x B
15. Q–Kt3	R–QB2
16. Kt–K1	Kt–B4
17. Q–Kt4	P–B5
18. Kt–Q3	P x P
19. BP x P	Kt x Kt
20. R x Kt	Q–B7ch
21. K–R1	B–B3 !
22. P–K4	. . . .

This unpleasant rejoinder is again forced. For if instead 22. B x B, Q x KP is decisive. Now Black has time to build up his attack.

22.	R(B2)–B2
23. R–K1	. . . .

If 23. Q x QP, Q x KtP.

23.	P–QR4 !
24. Q–B3	Q–QB4
25. P–QKt4	. . . .

25.	B x P !!

Spielmann says: "The hostile King is forced into the open. It is therefore a King-Hunt sacrifice. I could not calculate the combination more exactly, and I had to rely entirely on my conviction that favorable variations would occur as a matter of course. And events proved me to be right."

26. R x B . . . .

If 26. B x B, R–B8ch; 27. R x R, R x Rch; 28. K–Kt2, R–Kt8ch; 29. K–B3, Q–R4ch; 30. K–K3, Q x P and, writes Spielmann, "He who would not boldly undertake to win such a position with Black will never go far in the domain of the sacrifice." Of course the Queen could not be captured because of mate at KB8.

26.	R–B8ch !
27. B x R	R x Bch
28. K–Kt2	Q–B7ch
29. K–R3	R–KR8

"The combination had been calculated up to this point. Black is a Rook down, but drives the King to the fourth rank. Such an attack must get home!" (Spielmann)

30. R–B3	Q x RPch
31. K–Kt4	Q–R4ch
32. K–B4	Q–R3ch
33. K–Kt4	P–KKt4 !

Threatening . . . Q–R4 mate.

34. R x P . . . .

A last hope.

| 34. . . . . | Q x Rch |
| 35. R—B5 | . . . . |

K x P loses also.

35.	P—R3 !
36. Q—Q3	K—Kt2
37. K—B3	. . . .

The threat was . . . K—Kt3.

37.	R—B8ch
38. Q x R	Q x Rch
39. K—Kt2	Q x Qch
40. K x Q	P x P
41. P x P	K—B3
42. K—B2	P—R4

White Resigns.

Spielmann refers to the following game as an example of the mating sacrifice. It is chock full of surprises!

SPIELMANN   HÖNLINGER
Match: Vienna, 1929
Caro-Kann Defense

1. P—K4	P—QB3
2. P—Q4	P—Q4
3. Kt—QB3	P x P
4. Kt x P	Kt—B3
5. Kt—Kt3	P—K3
6. Kt—B3	P—B4
7. B—Q3	Kt—B3
8. P x P	B x P
9. P—QR3	O—O
10. O—O	P—QKt3
11. P—Kt4	B—K2
12. B—Kt2	. . . .

The White pieces are superbly poised for an attack against the enemy King; Black must defend precisely from here on in.

| 12. . . . . | Q—B2 ? |

A loss of time.

13. P—Kt5 !	Kt—QR4
14. Kt—K5	B—Kt2
15. Kt—Kt4	Q—Q1

Spielmann later suggested Q—KB5.

| 16. Kt—K3 | Kt—Q4 ? |

But now . . . R—B1 was essential. "There follow sacrificial revels," says Spielmann.

| 17. Q—R5 | P—Kt3 |

On the alternative 17. . . . P—KR3; 18. B x P !! wins, e.g., . . . K x B; 19. Kt(K3)—B5ch and mates soon. And if 17. . . . P—B4; again a sacrifice: 18. Kt(K3) x P, P x Kt; 19. Kt x P is decisive.

| 18. Kt—Kt4 ! | . . . . |

Threatening Kt—R6 mate.

| 18. . . . . | B—KB3 |
| 19. Kt x Bch | Kt x Kt |

Or 19. . . . Q x Kt; 20. B x Q,
P x Q; 21. Kt x P.

20. Q—R6   R—B1
21. QR—Q1   Q—K2
22. KR—K1   Kt—K1

23. Kt—B5 !!   Q—B4

The sacrifice cannot be accepted: if 23. . . . KtP x Kt; 24.
B x P, P—B3; 25. B x KPch.

24. R—K5 !   B—Q4

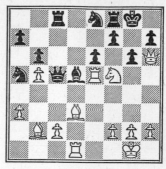

25. Kt—K7ch !!   Black Resigns.

Too bad he avoids the pretty
finish 25. . . . Q x Kt; 26. Q x
RPch !, K x Q; 27. R—R5ch and
mate next move.

Here are two more of Spielmann's brilliancies.

Gruenfeld

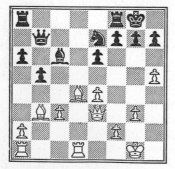

Spielmann—TO PLAY

Carlsbad, 1929

1. B x KtP !   K x B
2. Q—Kt5ch   Kt—Kt3
3. P—R6ch   Black Resigns.

Mieses   Match, 1910

1.	Q—B7 !!	Q—B8ch
2.	K—R2	Q x Ktch
3.	P—Kt3	Q—Kt4
4.	P—R4 !	Q—Kt3
5.	B—Q3ch	K—R4
6.	Q—K5ch !	P—B4
7.	R x KtP !!	R x Pch
8.	K—R3	R—Kt5
9.	R x Q	P x R
10.	Q—B7	Black Resigns.

Spielmann—TO PLAY

Savielly Tartakower

Tartakower likes to describe himself as an "old routinier." For many years now he has been part of the line-up of most big international tournaments. Although his heyday came in the 1920's, he will remain an opponent to be feared until the day he retires.

Born in Russia in 1888, Tartakower was a student of law and literature before the first World War. He is a man of broad cultural attainments, a master linguist, a poet, a wit, a philosopher, and a most delightful conversationalist.

It was not until after the war that Tartakower became a professional chess master. It is said that he was inspired by a brother who was killed in action. At any rate, he soon became a familiar figure in international tournaments. His most notable victory was first prize at London in 1927.

Tartakower has always been an inexhaustible journalist and writer. Books and articles in countless number have flowed from his prolific pen. His most lasting contribution to chess literature is the little-known *Die Hypermoderne Schachpartie.*

After the war Tartakower settled in France and became a French citizen. Were it not for his love of gambling (in which respect he was similar to another Pole who had settled in France, David Janowsky) and a dislike for the quiet life, he might well have reached the world championship class. A recent article in *Chess Review* says of him: "Since his health becomes more delicate with age, he toys with the idea of giving up practical chess and retiring to his villa in the Cote d'Azur. This plan is excellent—only for sundry reasons he has not yet acquired said villa."

Tartakower has an eclectic style and a great fondness for unusual variations, which he often regards as a challenge to his opponents. When he succeeds the results can be magnificent. Here is a case in point.

MAROCZY   TARTAKOWER

Teplitz-Schönau, 1922
Dutch Defense

1. P—Q4   P—K3
2. P—QB4   P—KB4
3. Kt—QB3   Kt—KB3
4. P—QR3   . . . .

Meaningless and not to be recommended. Better is simply P—KKt3.

4. . . . .   B—K2
5. P—K3?   . . . .

This line was abandoned a long time ago.

5. . . . .   O—O
6. B—Q3   P—Q4
7. Kt—B3   . . . .

Having made so many errors, he might at least have tried 7. KKt—K2 to follow with P—B3 and P—K4.

7. . . . .   P—B3
8. O—O   Kt—K5
9. Q—B2   B—Q3
10. P—QKt3   Kt—Q2
11. B—Kt2   R—B3!

The attack commences.

12. KR—K1   R—R3
13. P—Kt3   Q—B3
14. B—KB1   P—KKt4!
15. QR—Q1   P—Kt5
16. Kt x Kt   . . . .

Inviting the combination. But if 16. Kt—Q2, Kt x BP! is decisive.

16. . . . .   BP x Kt
17. Kt—Q2   . . . .

17. . . . .   R x P!!

According to Tartakower, this game was not awarded the brilliancy prize because the judges did not believe that he completely foresaw it to the end!

18. K x R   Q x Pch
19. K—R1   Kt—B3
20. R—K2   Q x P

Black certainly has a strong attack, but that it is worth a full Rook has yet to be demonstrated.

21. Kt—Kt1   Kt—R4
22. Q—Q2   B—Q2
23. R—B2   . . . .

To prevent . . . R—B1.

23. . . . .   Q—R5ch
24. K—Kt1   B—Kt6!
25. B—B3   . . . .

Compulsory, for if 25. R—K2, R—KB1 is conclusive.

25. . . . .   B x Rch
26. Q x B   P—Kt6
27. Q—KKt2   R—KB1
28. B—K1   . . . .

28. . . . .   R x B ch !!

This second Rook sacrifice clinches matters.

29. K x R   P—K4
30. K—Kt1   B—Kt5 !

Vidmar

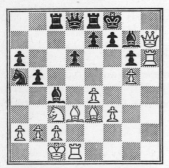

Tartakower—TO PLAY

N

Tartakower—TO PLAY

And there is no defense against . . . B—B6. A magnificent conception.

31. B x P   Kt x B
32. R—K1   Kt—B4

Not . . . B—B6; 33. Q—R2.

33. Q—KB2   Q—Kt4
34. QP x P   . . . .

Despair.

34. . . . . .   B—B6ch
35. K—B1   Kt—Kt6ch

White Resigns.

For if 36. K—R1, Kt—R8ch !!

Tartakower's games abound in tactical surprises. Here is a choice selection of some of them.

Vienna, 1906

1. P—K5 !!   B x B
2. P—K6 !!   R x Kt
3. P x R   Q—B1
4. B—Q4   P—B3
5. P x P   P x P
6. B x P   Q—Kt2
7. Q—R8ch !   B x Q
8. R x B mate.

Blindfold Exhibition, 1921

1. Q x KBPch !!   Kt x Q
2. P—K6ch   Q x P
3. Kt—B5ch   K—Q1
4. Kt x Qch   K—Q2
5. Kt—B5ch   K—Q1
6. Kt—Kt7ch   K—Q2
7. B—R3ch   P—B4
8. B x P mate.

Schlechter

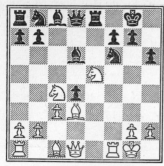

Tartakower—TO PLAY

St. Petersburg, 1909

1. Kt x P !	K x Kt
2. Q—R5ch	K—Kt1
3. R x Kt !	R—K8ch
4. R—B1	R x Rch
5. B x R	B—B1
6. B x P	Q—B3
7. B—Kt5	Q—B4
8. Kt—Q6	B x Kt
9. B—B4ch	B—K3
10. R—KB1	Q x Rch
11. B x Q and wins.	

Frederick Dewhurst Yates

After the disappearance of Blackburne and Burn from the international scene, England's outstanding representative was F. D. Yates. His first entry into international competition had a rather amusing twist to it. It took place at Hamburg in 1910. Tarrasch protested against his participation because he was too inexperienced. Yates won only one game in the tournament—against Tarrasch! In the 1920's Yates generally did reasonably well, though he was never among the top stars. His style was vigorous and forceful, and he produced many a pretty game. His most celebrated victory, against Alekhine, won him a well-deserved brilliancy prize.

ALEKHINE   **YATES**

Carlsbad, 1923

King's Indian Defense

1. P—Q4	Kt—KB3
2. P—QB4	P—KKt3
3. P—KKt3	B—Kt2
4. B—Kt2	O—O
5. Kt—QB3	P—Q3
6. Kt—B3	. . . .

Today we prefer P—K4 and KKt—K2.

6.	Kt—B3

A popular maneuver in those days.

7. P—Q5	Kt—Kt1

8. P—K4	QKt—Q2
9. O—O	P—QR4

One of the standard positions of the King's Indian. White's objective is the Q-side—Black's the K-side.

| 10. B–K3 | . . . . |

Loss of time. Better was P–KR3.

10.	Kt–Kt5
11. B–Q4	Kt(Kt5)–K4
12. Kt x Kt	. . . .

Every exchange frees Black's game.

| 12. . . . . | Kt x Kt |
| 13. P–B5 | . . . . |

If 13. P–B4, B–Kt5 !; 14. Q–Q2, Kt x P; and Black wins.

13.	P x P !
14. B x P	P–Kt3
15. B–Q4	B–QR3 !
16. R–K1	. . . .

Yates now has a strong initiative which he does not relinquish.

| 16. . . . . | Q–Q3 ! |

Preventing 17. P–B4, which would now be refuted by . . . Kt–Q6 !; 18. B x B, Q–B4ch winning.

| 17. B–B1 | B x B |
| 18. R x B | P–QB4 ! |

Seizing the proper moment to rid himself of the backward Pawn. If in reply 19. P x P e.p.?, Q x B !; 20. Q x Q, Kt–B6ch wins a piece.

19. B x Kt	Q x B
20. Q–Kt3	QR–Kt1
21. Q–Kt5 ?	. . . .

A strategical error. He should have played 21. QR–Q1, to threaten P–B4 and P–K5.

| 21. . . . . | P–B4 ! |

With secure control of the center Black begins a counterattack.

22. QR–K1	P–KB5 !
23. Q–Q7	QR–Q1
24. P x P	Q x BP
25. Q–K6ch	. . . .

He cannot take the Pawn, for after 25. Q x P, Q–Kt5ch; 26. K–R1, Q–B6ch; 27. K–Kt1, R(Q1)–K1; 28. Q–Q7, R–K4 wins.

25.	K–R1
26. P–B3	Q–Kt4ch
27. K–R1	R–Q3
28. Q–R3	B–K4
29. R–K2	R(Q3)–KB3
30. Kt–Q1	R–B5
31. Kt–K3	R–R5
32. Q–K6	Q–R4
33. Kt–Kt4	. . . .

Alekhine's position now appears to be secure, at least temporarily, but Yates produces one of the longest and most brilliant combinations on record.

33.	R x Kt !!
34. P x R	R x Rch
35. K–Kt2	Q x RPch
36. K x R	Q–R8ch

37. K—B2	B—Q5ch
38. K—Kt3	Q Kt8ch
39. K—R3	Q—B8ch
40. R—Kt2	Q—R8ch
41. K—Kt3	Q—K8ch
42. K—R3	. . . .

All White's moves have been forced.

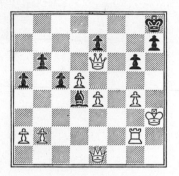

| 42. . . . . | P—KKt4 !!! |

A magnificent interpolation. The threat of . . . Q—R5 mate cannot be met without material loss.

43. R—QB2	Q—B8ch
44. K—R2	Q—Kt8ch
45. K—R3	Q—R8ch
46. K—Kt3	Q—Q8 !!!
47. R—B3	. . . .

Desperation. If instead 47. R—Kt2, Q—K8ch; 48. any, Q—K6 or Q—R5 mate, while if 47. R—R2, Q—Kt8ch; 48. K—R3, Q—K6ch; 49. K—Kt2, Q—B7ch and mate next.

47.	Q—Kt8ch
48. K—R3	Q—B8ch
49. K—Kt3	B—B7ch
50. K—B3	B—Kt8 dis ch

White Resigns—it is mate in two.

Edward Lasker

German-born Edward Lasker came to the U. S. shortly after the first World War and quickly became one of the leading American masters. In 1923 he surprised everybody by almost beating Marshall in a match for the American championship. Lasker might have gone much further in chess, but his energies were taken up by other interests; he is an engineer by profession, and a most ingenious one. In recent years Lasker has enriched chess literature considerably with a number of entertaining books.

Here is a snappy Lasker victory from his early days.

EDWARD LASKER

SIR GEORGE THOMAS

London, 1912

Dutch Defense

1. P—Q4	P—KB4
2. Kt—QB3	. . . .

This was a skittles game and the opening was played in skittles style. 2. P—K4 is a good gambit; the positionally correct move, however, is 2. Kt—KB3.

2.	Kt—KB3
3. Kt—B3	P—K3
4. B—Kt5	B—K2
5. B x Kt	B x B
6. P—K4	P x P ?

Better 6. . . . P—Q3.

7. Kt x P	P—QKt3
8. Kt—K5	O—O
9. B—Q3	B—Kt2 ?

Essential was 9. . . . Q—K1.

10. Q—R5 !	Q—K2

There is no real defense: if 10. . . . QB x Kt; 11. B x B, P—R3; 12. Q—Kt6 wins.

11. Q x P ch !!	K x Q
12. Kt x B dbl ch	K—R3

Or *12.* . . . K—R1; *13.* Kt—Kt6 mate.

13. Kt(K5)—Kt4ch	K—Kt4
14. P—R4ch	K—B5
15. P—Kt3ch	K—B6
16. B—K2ch	K—Kt7
17. R—R2ch	K—Kt8

Here White announced mate in eight moves:

18. K—Q2 mate!

7.

The Age of Alekhine

THE YEARS from 1927, when Alekhine won from Capablanca, to 1935, when he lost to Euwe were a rich period in the history of the game. It was then that chess supremacy first began to leave the Old World. By 1931 the U. S. chess team had won first prize in the International Team Tournament at Prague, and continued to be an easy winner in the three succeeding tournaments. In the wake of the world-wide depression from 1929 on a whole crop of new masters sprang up, many of them Americans. The Russians also began to develop at this time. In 1935, the year Alekhine lost his title, Botvinnik tied for first prize in the great international tournament at Moscow. Other Soviet masters were not yet up to the strength of the contemporary Bronstein and Smyslov, but they were already on a par with masters like Stahlberg and Pirc. Above all, the development of chess outside Europe, as seen in the growth of new clubs, magazines, books, tournaments, reached a height never before seen. No doubt Alekhine's travels around the world helped to inspire much activity. It was in this period that chess became the really universal game.

Alexander Alexandrovitch Alekhine

In 1925 Tartakower wrote: "Capablanca is world champion, Lasker was world champion, Alekhine plays the way a world champion ought to play." To the keen critic Alekhine's incredible talents were always evident, but the general public remained unconvinced until he won the title in spectacular style.

Alekhine was born in Moscow in 1892, scion of a wealthy Russian family. We are told that his mother taught him the game at an early age, and he soon became a rabid enthusiast. At school he would spend his time playing blindfold chess. His progress was so rapid that by sixteen he was already a master. At Hamburg, in 1910, he played in his first masters' tournament, with fair success. Chess was by now his consuming passion, and his family's fortune gave him the means to pursue it to his heart's content. (His father is reported to have lost two million rubles at Monte Carlo.)

Some successes and failures followed. His first real chance came at St. Petersburg in 1914, where the leading masters of the world were arrayed. Alekhine and Nimzovitch tied for first prize in an elimination tournament for Russian masters and were both admitted to the finals. Much to the surprise of the chess world, Alekhine finished third, outdistanced only by Lasker and Capablanca. A warm friendship grew up between Alekhine and Capablanca, which was in sharp contrast to the bitterness of the later years.

During the war and the revolution, there was no opportunity for chess activity. Many rumors about him went the rounds. One story had it that he was sentenced to be shot, but was saved at the last minute because Trotsky visited his cell to play chess with him and spared him because of his fame. Alekhine himself once told me that he spent some time in a Cheka prison, under suspicion of passing on secret information. His knowledge of languages gained him a post in the Foreign Ministry. He used this position to attach himself to a delegation sent abroad, and when he reached Germany, broke away. By 1921 he was out of the U. S. S. R., and on his own.

At this time, the only two masters who were his superiors were Capablanca and Lasker. Lasker was too old to be considered a serious rival, so he concentrated on Capablanca. Day and night he studied Capa's games. There was only one thought in his mind: to win the title.

In the period from 1921 to 1927 he played remarkable chess, technically for the most part superior to that of any of his colleagues, including Capa. One first prize after another came his way. But on the few occasions when he faced his major rivals, he faltered. Some psychological block still stood in his path.

In 1927 the Argentine financed a match between him and Capablanca. It was Alekhine's great chance, and he made the most of it. For months in advance he was in training. He did not drink or smoke; he lived the kind of ascetic existence which boxers go in for before a big event.

The chess world, impressed by the New York 1927 tournament where Capa finished ahead of Alekhine by a wide margin, expected an easy victory for the cool and confident Cuban. Much to everybody's surprise Alekhine won a gruelling contest.

For several years Alekhine was inactive in chess. He took a degree in law at the Sorbonne, which by the French rules gave him the title of doctor, and he was henceforth known as Dr. Alekhine.

In the meantime Capablanca was trying to arrange a return match. Time and again the negotiations seemed to be on the point of succeeding, when something went wrong. It soon became clear that Alekhine did not really want to play Capa again. He even went to the length of increasing his retainer demands out of all proportion if Capa were to be included in the same tournament.

But even though he did not want to play Capa, Alekhine was only too eager to play everybody else. In the years from 1929 on, he was extremely active. And apparently invincible. One first prize followed another. It was not merely that he won—but how he won that staggered the chess world! At San Remo in 1930 he allowed two draws and won every other game in grand style. At Bled, in 1931, he clinched first prize almost ten rounds before the end. After Capa's dictum that chess was played out and ought to be reformed, Alekhine's victories came like a whirlwind of rejuvenation. The young masters who were developing in the early thirties saw in him an inspiration which they had never found in any other world champion.

Then, along about 1933, something happened. He began to drink more and more. In women he had long since lost interest, prematurely of course, and he became increasingly egocentric. Stories of his drinking were freely circulated; in one simultaneous exhibition he was in such poor condition that it had to be cancelled. For a while he worked on a theory of winning by hypnotism.

By 1935 he was faced by a whole army of young aspirants. Euwe was the first to arrange the necessary backing, and defeated him by the odd point.

Alekhine now had a goal, to regain the title. But it was no longer the old Alekhine who strode and conquered. After 1934 he never again won first prize in a big international tournament, and even in the smaller ones he did none too well. Although he regained the title from Euwe in 1937, his victory was anticlimactic. There were by now many other challengers, any one of whom might have beaten him.

The war years are not easy to record. Alekhine remained in Nazi-occupied Europe although he had no personal ties to hold him there, and became a collaborationist. He wrote a series of ridiculous articles "proving" that only Aryans can play chess well.

The upshot of his wartime activities was that in the first post-war tournament the other masters unanimously refused to play with him. He was rescued from isolation by Botvinnik's challenge to a match in the summer of 1946. A few months later he suddenly died in Portugal.

At his best Alekhine may have had equals, but he did not have any superiors. For sheer originality, profundity and technical perfection he was never surpassed. He ranks among the really great artists of the chessboard.

Besides his over-the-board activities, Alekhine was also pre-eminent as an author. His notes appeal more to the expert than to the layman; they are so profound and full of so many insights that generations of aspiring masters will continue to profit from them.

In style Alekhine was the great exponent of the attack. He would almost literally shake combinations out of his sleeve. But it was not merely the combinations; others made combinations too. It was the painstaking preparation, the build-up that characterized him. His feel for positions was uncanny; he could sense an attack where others never dreamed that anything was brewing. Reti has pointed out that the surprise move in an Alekhine attack comes at the end rather than at the beginning.

Alekhine was a man who loved chess and loved to win. When he reached a winning position he never relaxed his grip; his sheer joy in beating his opponent was too great. It was for this reason that he could devote his entire life to chess and derive so much enjoyment from it; being world champion was a boost to his ego which none of his predecessors had felt, with the possible exception of Steinitz. Alekhine lived only to prove that he could beat anyone; and when he lost his only thought was to continue until he won. I recall when he visited New York in the early part of 1933, he came to the Marshall Chess Club, where I was then champion, and played a number of offhand games with me. This was in itself most unusual, as I was impressed by the throng of famous masters who kept themselves aloof from chess outside of tournament play. But not Alekhine. In these games I just about held my own with him, and at this he became so furious that he demanded that a skittles match be arranged for a small stake; he could not bear the thought that anyone might beat him, even in offhand games. In other games his need to win was just as great and soul-consuming. When he lost at ping-pong he would crush the ball in anger!

Out of this need to win came the peculiar characteristic of his style: in a won position he played to perfection. Other masters win games, but not in the way that Alekhine did. He literally revelled in every move as the end approached. There were no mistakes, no slips; once the game was won he was in his element. He simply enjoyed it too much to falter. For this reason so many of his games are models of technical precision, and the collection of his best games is among the three most beautiful that we have (I would rank Botvinnik and Rubinstein as the other two).

Alekhine was also a superb blindfold player, and his record was 32 games at the Chicago World's Fair in 1933, a feat surpassed quantitatively only by Koltanowsky and Najdorf.

Alekhine considered the following two games his most brilliant tournament victories.

BOGOLJUBOW   ALEKHINE
Hastings, 1922
Dutch Defense

1. P–Q4   P–KB4

A defense which Alekhine rarely adopted in those days. But he was a half a point behind Rubinstein and had to play for a win at all costs.

2. P—QB4   Kt—KB3
3. P KKt3   P—K3
4. B—Kt2   B—Kt5ch

Nowadays . . . . B—K2 is preferred.

5. B—Q2   B x Bch

Many years later Alekhine ex-
perimented with the dubious
. . . B—K2.

6. Kt x B   . . . .

Stronger is Q x B.

6. . . . .   Kt—B3
7. KKt—B3   O—O
8. O—O   P—Q3

White has mishandled the
opening, and Black has a comfortable position. The immediate intention is . . . P—K4.

9. Q—Kt3   . . . .

A useless misconception. He
hopes for 9. . . . P—K4?; 10.
P—B5 dis ch, with attacking
chances.

9. . . . .   K—R1
10. Q—B3   P—K4!

Now Bogoljubow realizes that
his play was completely at fault.
Naturally the Pawn cannot be
taken because the QKt is loose at
the end: 11. P x P?, P x P; 12.
Kt x P?, Kt x Kt; 13. Q x Kt,
Q x Kt.

11. P—K3   P—QR4
12. P—Kt3   . . . .

To hold Black's Kt out. If 12.
P—QR3? immediately, then 12.
. . . P—R5! is too strong.

12. . . . .   Q—K1
13. P—QR3   Q—R4!

To build up threats on the other
wing. Again the Pawn is taboo:
after 14. P x P, P x P; 15. Kt x P?,
Kt x Kt; 16. Q x Kt, Kt—Kt5!
wins the Queen.

14. P—KR4   . . . .

Threatening P x P.

14. . . . .   Kt—KKt5!
15. Kt—Kt5   . . . .

This is a game where it is all too
easy to criticize White's play, but
difficult to suggest satisfactory al-
ternatives. With the text he prepares . . . P—B5.

15. . . . .   B—Q2

. . . P—B5 was also to be considered.

16. P—B3   Kt—B3
17. P—B4   . . . .

To prevent . . . P—B5.

17. . . . .   P—K5
18. KR—Q1   P—R3
19. Kt—R3   . . . .

Alekhine recommended 19. P—Q5 ! instead. After the text Black ingeniously demolishes the opponent's center and shifts his initiative to the Q's wing.

| 19. . . . . | P—Q4 ! |
| 20. Kt—B1 | Kt—K2 |

Threatening . . . P—R5.

21. P—R4	Kt—B3 !
22. R—Q2	Kt—QKt5
23. B—R1	. . . .

Bogoljubow is going through the exertions of a contortionist to get some counterplay; but it is in vain.

| 23. . . . . | Q—K1 ! |
| 24. R—K2 | . . . . |

He decides to give up a Pawn. On the alternative 24. P—B5, P—QKt4 !; 25. P x P e.p., P x P Black soon penetrates on the QB file.

24.	P x P
25. P x P	B x P
26. Kt—B2	B—Q2

Alekhine is a Pawn ahead. For other masters there would still be a note on "technical difficulties," but he is in his element.

| 27. Kt—Q2 | P—QKt4 ! |
| 38. Kt—Q1 | Kt—Q6 ! |

Flexing for an explosive finish.

| 29. R x P | P—Kt5 ! |
| 30. R x R | P x Q !! |

The Alekhine touch. This and the following he of course foresaw some moves back.

| 31. R x Q | . . . . |

| 31. . . . . | P—B7 !!! |

The point. Black must queen.

32. R x Rch	K—R2
33. Kt—B2	P—B8 = Qch
34. Kt—B1	. . . .

Theoretically the material is still even: White has two Rooks and a Pawn for the Queen, but Black's attack is decisive.

34.	Kt—K8 !
35. R—R2	Q x BP
36. R—QKt8	B—Kt4
37. R x B	. . . .

Alekhine has played with foresight. If instead 37. Kt—Q2, Q—

B8 is murderous, e.g., 38. R x B, Kt—B6 dbl ch and mate in two.

37.	Q x R
38. P—Kt4	. . . .

Desperation

38.	Kt—B6ch
39. B x Kt	P x B
40. P x P	Q—K7 !

Another beautiful point: White is in zugzwang. If 41. Kt—Kt4, Kt x Kt !; and if 41. R—R3, Kt—Kt5 !

41. P—Q5	K—Kt1
42. P—R5	K—R2

Now White's Pawn moves are almost exhausted and he must lose material.

43. P—K4	. . . .

Now all the Pawns go.

43.	Kt x P
44. Kt x Kt	Q x Kt
45. P—Q6	P x P
46. P—B6	P x P
47. R—Q2	Q—K7 !

Exact to the end!

48. R x Q	P x R
49. K—B2	P x Kt = Qch
50. K x Q	K—Kt2
51. K—B2	K—B2
52. K—K3	K—K3
53. K—K4	P—Q4ch

White Resigns.

RETI   **ALEKHINE**

Baden-Baden, 1925
King's Fianchetto Opening

1. P—KKt3	P—K4
2. Kt—KB3	. . . .

Now we have an Alekhine's opening in reverse! (1. P—K4, Kt—KB3).

2.	P—K5
3. Kt—Q4	P—Q4
4. P—Q3	P x P

In Alekhine's defense proper 4. . . . P—QB4 is good; here it was also a strong alternative.

5. Q x P	Kt—KB3
6. B—Kt2	B—Kt5ch
7. B—Q2	B x Bch
8. Kt x B	O—O

The opening has resulted in an even game, but both sides thirst for complications.

9. P—QB4 !	Kt—R3
10. P x P	Kt—QKt5
11. Q—B4	QKt x QP
12. Kt(Q2)—Kt3	P—B3
13. O—O	R—K1
14. KR—Q1	B—Kt5 !

To prevent P—K4.

15. R—Q2	Q—B1 !
16. Kt—QB5	B—R6 !

The fun begins. Reti must have thought that he had prevented this move.

17. B—B3   . . . .

There is a subtle combination involved: 17. B x B ?, Q x B; 18. Kt x KtP, Kt—KKt5; 19. Kt—B3, Kt(Q4)—K6; 20. P x Kt, Kt x KP; 21. Q x Pch !, K—R1 !; 22. Kt—R4, R—KB1 and wins.

17. . . . .   B—Kt5
18. B—Kt2   B—R6
19. B—B3   B—Kt5

Alekhine is content with a draw.

20. B—R1   . . . .

Reti decides to play for a win.

20. . . . .   P—KR4 !
21. P—Kt4   P—QR3
22. R—QB1   P—R5
23. P—R4   P x P
24. RP x P   Q—B2
25. P—Kt5 !?   . . . .

Alekhine recommends instead 25. P—K4, Kt—Kt3; 26. Q—Kt3.

25. . . . .   RP x P
26. P x P   . . . .

26. . . . .   R—K6 !!

Now we are in for Alekhine's most celebrated combination.

27. Kt—B3   . . . .

Alekhine suggests 27. B—B3 as the only chance, but Black still retains an advantage after 27. . . . B x B; 28. P x B, P x P; 29. Kt x P(Kt5), Q—R4 !. Of course, if 27. P x R, Q x Pch is devastating.

27. . . . .   P x P
28. Q x P   Kt—B6 !
29. Q x P   Q x Q
30. Kt x Q   Kt x Pch
31. K—R2   . . . .

If 31. K—B1, Kt x Pch wins.

A fantastic position; so much is en prise. Yet the material is even, and one would ordinarily expect a quick draw. But Alekhine has a trick up his sleeve: he will win White's QKt at Kt7 after twelve forced moves!

31. . . . .   Kt—K5
32. R—B4   . . . .

Relatively best. If 32. P x R, Kt x R(Q7); 33. Kt x Kt, Kt x R.

32.	Kt x BP
33. B–Kt2	B–K3 !
34. R(B4)–B2	Kt–Kt5ch
35. K–R3	. . . .

Forced, for if 35. K–R1, R–R8ch.

35.	Kt–K4 dis ch
36. K–R2	R x Kt !
37. R x Kt	. . . .

On 37. B x R, Kt x Bch Black comes out a piece ahead.

37.	Kt–Kt5ch
38. K–R3	Kt–K6 dis ch
39. K–R2	Kt x R
40. B x R	Kt–Q5 !

The final point. If now 41. R–KB2, Kt x Bch; 42. R x Kt, B–Q4 and White's Kt is lost!
White Resigns.

From a technical point of view the game which won Alekhine the title from Capablanca is unquestionably the finest of his career.

ALEKHINE   CAPABLANCA

Match, 1927, 34th Game
Queen's Gambit Declined

1. P–Q4	P–Q4
2. P–QB4	P–K3
3. Kt–QB3	Kt–KB3
4. B–Kt5	QKt–Q2
5. P–K3	P–B3

The Queen's Gambit Declined was almost played to death in this match. Alekhine essays an unusual wrinkle to avoid the Cambridge Springs Defense.

6. P–QR3	B–K2
7. Kt–B3	O–O
8. B–Q3	P x P
9. B x BP	Kt–Q4
10. B x B	Q x B

| 11. Kt–K4 ! | . . . . |

A new idea at the time. The fifth game, with Capablanca as White, had continued 11. R–QB1, Kt x Kt; 12. R x Kt, P–K4 and while White kept the initiative he could do little with it.

11.	Kt(Q4)–B3
12. Kt–Kt3	P–B4
13. O–O	Kt–Kt3

Not too bad, but . . . P x P first was better; for if then 14. Kt x P, Kt–K4.

| 14. B–R2 | P x P |
| 15. Kt x P | P–Kt3 |

Preparing . . . P–K4.

| 16. R–B1 | B–Q2 |

If at once 16. . . . P–K4; 17. Kt–Kt5 is strong.

| 17. Q–K2 | QR–B1 |
| 18. P–K4 | P–K4 |

19. Kt—B3   K—Kt2
20. P—R3   P—KR3?

Needless loss of time. 20. . . . R x R followed by R—QB1 was preferable.

21. Q—Q2!   . . . .

Threatening Q—R5, and posing for Capa many problems.

The counter-threat 21. . . . B—B3 is refuted by 22. Kt—R4!, for if then . . . Kt x P; 23. Kt(R4)—B5ch, P x Kt; 24. Kt x Pch, K—Kt3; 25. Q x Pch, K x Kt; 26. P—Kt4 mate.

21. . . . .   B—K3?

A mistake which costs a Pawn and the game, match and title. Emanuel Lasker later pointed out that the only saving move is 21. . . . Kt—R5!, for if then 22. Q—R5, Kt x KtP; 23. Q x RP, R—QR1 with the better game for Black.

In an analogous situation Lasker made a crucial blunder against Capa. It is easy to criticize from the sidelines!

22. B x B   Q x B
23. Q—R5   Kt—B5
24. Q x RP   Kt x KtP

The only chance. If first . . . P—QKt4; 25. P—Kt3 is adequate.

25. R x R   R x R
26. Q x P   Kt—B5

Alekhine has won a Pawn, but the technical difficulties are still enormous. A lesser master might well have faltered against Capablanca.

The first step is to consolidate the position.

27. Q—Kt4   R—QR1
28. R—R1   Q—B3
29. P—QR4!   Kt x P!
30. Kt x P!   . . . .

. . . . Black's move had been foreseen.

30. . . . .   Q—Q3
31. Q x Kt   Q x Kt
32. R—K1   Kt—Q3!
33. Q—B1!   Q—B3
34. Kt—K4!   Kt x Kt
35. R x Kt   . . . .

Now an endgame is reached which is almost a facsimile of the first and twenty-first match games.

35. . . . .   R—QKt1
36. R—K2   R—QR1
37. R—R2   . . . .

His immediate objective is to tie up Black's pieces.

37. . . . .   R—R4
38. Q—B7   Q—R3

It certainly is not easy to see how White can proceed in this position.

39. Q—B3ch   K—R2

40. R—Q2 !!   . . . .

Now the point becomes clear: mating threats are developed on the K-side while Black's pieces are tied up on the other wing. Black must then either defend against mate or allow the Pawn to advance.

40. . . . .   Q—Kt3

After . . . R x P?; 41. R—Q8 wins.

41. R—Q7   Q—Kt8ch
42. K—R2   Q—Kt1ch
43. P—Kt3   R—KB4

He prefers an active defense.

44. Q—Q4   Q—K1
45. R—Q5 !!   . . . .

Of course not 45. R—Q8 ?, R x Pch !

45. . . . .   R—B6

After 45. . . . R x R; 46. Q x R, Q x P; 47. Q x Pch, K—R1; 48. Q x P White wins easily.

46. P—R4   . . . .

An inaccuracy; 46. K—Kt2 wins more quickly, for if then . . . R—Kt6; 47. R—Q8.

46. . . . .   Q—KR1
47. Q—Kt6 !   . . . .

White must be very careful. After 47. Q x Qch ?, K x Q; 48. P—R5, R—R6 Black draws.

47. . . . .   Q—R8
48. K—Kt2   R—B3
49. Q—Q4 !   . . . .

Forcing the exchange of Queens at a favorable moment. As long as Black's Rook cannot get behind the passed Pawn the game is won.

49. . . . .   Q x Q
50. R x Q   K—Kt2
51. P—QR5   R—R3
52. R—Q5   R—QB3
53. R—Q4   R—R3
54. R—R4   K—B3
55. K—B3   K—K4
56. K—K3   P—R4

If Black's King goes to the Queen side, then White allows the exchange of Rooks and enters the opposite wing.

57. K—Q3   K—Q4
58. K—B3   K—B4
59. R—R2   K—Kt4
60. R—Kt2ch   K—B4
61. R—R2   K—Kt4
62. K—Q4   R—Q3ch

On 62. . . . R—R1; 63. P—R6.

63. K—K5   R—K3ch
64. K—B4   K—R3

Black's Rook and King have exchanged positions. The decisive action now takes place on the King's side.

65. K–Kt5	R–K4ch
66. K–R6	R–KB4
67. P–B4	R–B4
68. R–R3	R–B2
69. K–Kt7	R–Q2
70. P–B5 !	....

The most precise.

| 70. .... | P x P |
| 71. K–R6 | P–B5 |

72. P x P	R–Q4
73. K–Kt7	R–KB4
74. R–R4	....

Black must weaken himself further.

74.	K–Kt4
75. R–K4 !	K–R3
76. K–R6 !	....

A pretty idea.

76.	R x RP
77. R–K5	R–R8
78. K x P	R–KKt8
79. R–KKt5	R–KR8
80. R–KB5	K–Kt3
81. R x P	K–B3
82. R–K7	Black Resigns.

The remainder is "book."

There are so many Alekhine brilliancies to choose from that it is difficult to make a selection. Here are some of my favorites.

Feldt

Alekhine—TO PLAY

Blindfold Display, Tarnapol, 1916

| 1. Kt–B7 ! | K x Kt |
| 2. Q x Pch !! | K–Kt3 |

If . . . K x Kt; 3. Kt–Kt5 mate.

| 3. P–KKt4 | B–K5 |
| 4. Kt–R4 mate. | |

Bogoljubow

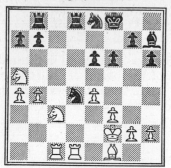

Alekhine—TO PLAY

Alekhine—TO PLAY

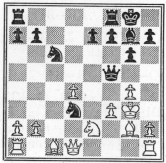

Potemkin

Alekhine—TO PLAY

Yates

Match, 1929

White won a Pawn by means of the following tactic:

1. Kt–Kt5 !	Kt x Kt
2. R x R	R x R
3. Kt x P !!	R–Kt1

If . . . R–Q7ch; 4. K–K3, R–Kt7; 5. B x Kt, R x QKtP; 6. R–B8 and wins.

4. Kt–B5 !	K–K2
5. P x Kt and wins.	

St. Petersburg, 1912

1.	Kt x QP !!
2. P x Q	Kt x Pch
3. K–R3	Kt–B7 mate.

Kecspkemet, 1927

1.	K–R4 !!
2. Q x Kt	P–R8Kt mate!

Yates   London, 1922

Alekhine—TO PLAY

1. R x P   R x Kt
2. K—K5 !!   Black Resigns.

The Rook is trapped in the middle of the board! If either Rook to KB1, then follows mate in two.

Sterk   Budapest, 1921

Alekhine—TO PLAY

1. B—B6 !!   KR—B1

If . . . P x B ? 2. R—Kt4ch wins the Queen.

2. Q—K5   R—B4

If 2. . . . Q x R; 3. Q—KKt5, K—B1; 4. Q x Pch, K—K1; 5. Q—Kt8ch, K—Q2; 6. Kt—K5ch, K—B2; 7. Q x Pch, winning the Queen.

3. Q—Kt3   P—Kt3
4. R x Kt and wins.

Ewfim D. Bogoljubow

Of all the masters who were Alekhine's contemporaries, the only one before Euwe who could obtain backing for a title match was his compatriot, Ewfim Bogoljubow. The results of the matches showed conclusively that the challenger, though a great player in his own right, could not stand up to Alekhine.

Bogoljubow was born in Russia, and remained there until 1925, when he scored the biggest success of his life by winning first prize at Moscow ahead of Lasker and Capablanca. Then he emigrated to Germany where he remained and eventually became a naturalized citizen. His greatest victories came during the period 1925–1931 when he was outdistanced only by Alekhine and Capablanca. After that he could not hold his own against the new masters. "The young people have read my book," he would wail in his jovial manner. "Now I have no chance."

In style Bogoljubow was pre-eminently an attacking player; the subtleties of position play held little interest for him. Like other attacking geniuses, such as Marshall and Anderssen, he could produce atrociously poor games as well as sparkling gems; his play was generally uneven. At his best, though, he was a dangerous opponent. We begin with a Bogoljubow classic.

BOGOLJUBOW   AMATEUR
Stockholm, 1919
French Defense

1. P—K4   P—K3
2. P—Q4   P—Q4
3. Kt—QB3   Kt—KB3
4. B—Kt5   B—K2
5. P—K5   KKt—Q2
6. P—KR4   . . . .

Alekhine's attack, still new then.

6. . . . .   B x B
7. P x B   Q x P?

A mistake which meets with a brilliant refutation.

8. Kt—R3   Q—K2
9. Q—Kt4   P—KKt3

For his Pawn, White has a much freer development.

10. Kt—B4   P—QR3
11. O—O—O   P—QB4
12. Q—Kt3!   Kt—Kt3?
13. P x P   Q x P
14. B—Q3   . . . .

Threatening Kt x KtP and B x Pch.

14. . . . .   Q—B1

15. B—K4!!   . . . .

An astonishing conception; the White attack now crashes through.

15. . . . .   P x B

If he declines with 15. . . . . Kt —B3; 16. B x P! leads to a quick win.

16. Kt x P(K4)   QKt—Q2
17. Q—QB3   Q—K2
18. Kt—B6ch!   Kt x Kt
19. P x Kt   Q—B1
20. Q—B7   Kt—Q2

Black is almost stalemated although he is a full piece ahead. The finish is pretty.

21. Kt—Q5!!   P x Kt

If 21. . . . Q–B4; 22. Q x Q, Kt x Q; 23. Kt–B7ch.

22. KR–K1ch   Kt–K4
23. R x Ktch   B–K3

24. K–Kt1 !!   . . . .

A beautiful preparatory move. If 24. R(Q1) x P? immediately, 24. . . . Q–R3ch ! gets Black out of his trouble.

24. . . . .   R–Q1
25. R(Q1) x P !!   R x R
26. R x R   B x R
27. Q–B8 mate.

The following game is the finest positional victory of Bogoljubow's career.

KASHDAN   BOGOLJUBOW

Bled, 1931

Gruenfeld Defense

1. P–Q4   Kt–KB3
2. P–QB4   P–KKt3
3. Kt–QB3   B–Kt2
4. Kt–B3   . . . .

Better was P–K4.

4. . . . .   O–O
5. P–KKt3   P–Q4

6. P x P   Kt x P
7. B–Kt2   Kt x Kt

. . . P–QB4 was a strong alternative.

8. P x Kt   P–QB4
9. O–O   Kt–B3
10. P–K3   . . . .

When such a weakening move is necessary, White has definitely been outplayed. Black will now concentrate on the exposed white squares.

10. . . . .   Q–R4
11. Q–Kt3   R–Kt1
12. Kt–Q2   . . . .

White is floundering. More aggressive was 12. B–QR3 at once.

12. . . . .   Q–B2 !
13. B–QR3   P–Kt3 !
14. P x P ?   B–QR3
15. KR–Q1   P x P
16. Q–Q5 ?   . . . .

Meets with a brilliant refutation. Q–B2 was essential.

16. . . . .   Kt–Kt5 !!
17. Q–Kt3   . . . .

The Knight cannot be taken: if
17. P x Kt, B x R; 18. R x B, KR—
Q1 wins.

17.	Kt—Q6
18. Q—B2	Q—R4
19. Kt—Kt1	P—B5 !

Ingenious. On 20. B x P, R—
Kt7 ! wins White's Queen.

| 20. B—QB1 | R—Kt3 |

White is practically stalemated.
In desperation he sacrifices a
Pawn to get some counterplay.

21. Kt—R3	B x P
22. R—Kt1	R x R
23. Kt x R	B—K8 !

Another pretty idea.

| 24. P—B4 | B—B7ch |
| 25. K—R1 | Q—R4 ! |

The attack begins!

| 26. Kt—Q2 | B x KtP |
| 27. Kt—B3 | . . . . |

| 27. . . . . | B x RP ! |

A final elegant coup.

28. Kt x B	Q x Rch !
29. Q x Q	Kt—B7ch
White Resigns.	

Here is an extraordinary game
with a tragi-comical end-game position.

BOGOLJUBOW   DANIELSSON
Match: Germany-Sweden,
1935
French Defense

1. P—K4	P—K3
2. P—Q4	P—Q4
3. Kt—QB3	B—Kt5
4. P—K5	P—QB4

Bogoljubow usually played 5.
B—Q2 here, but he plays the
modern move.

| 5. P—QR3 | P x P |

Better was . . . B x Ktch followed by . . . Kt—K2.

| 6. P x B | P x Kt |
| 7. Q—Kt4 | . . . . |

7.	P—KKt3
8. Kt—B3	Q—B2
9. B—Q3	Kt—QB3
10. O—O	KKt—K2

Black cannot castle after 10.
. . . Kt x KP; 11. Kt x Kt, Q x Kt;

12. B—Kt5ch. Now he concentrates on defense, and the result is amusing.

11. R—K1	B—Q2
12. P x P	O—O—O
13. P—Kt5	Kt—QKt1
14. Q—Kt4	B—K1
15. B—KKt5	R—Q2
16. R x RP	Q—Kt3
17. R—R8	Q—Q1
18. Kt—Q4	P—KR3
19. B—B6	R—Kt1
20. P—Kt6	Black Resigns.

Przepiorka

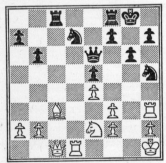

Bogoljubow—TO PLAY

Mieses

Bogoljubow—TO PLAY

FINAL POSITION

Here are a few choice morsels from Bogoljubow's masterpieces.

Pistyan, 1922

1. R x Kt(5) !	P x R
2. R x Kt !	R x B !
3. Kt x R	Q x R
4. Q—Kt5ch	K—R1
5. Q—B6ch	K—Kt1
6. Kt—Q5	R—K1
7. Q—Kt5ch	K—R1
8. Kt—B6	Q—Q1
9. Q—R6	Q—Q8ch
10. K—Kt2	R—Kt1ch
11. Kt x R	K x Kt
12. Q—Kt5ch	K—B1
13. Q x KP and wins!	

Baden-Baden, 1925

An interesting psychological interplay as Mieses purposely allowed the sacrifice because he did not consider it dangerous.

1. B x P !	P x B
2. R x Pch	K x R
3. Q—B6ch	K—Kt1
4. R—Kt1ch	Q—Kt5
5. R x Qch	P x R
6. P—B5	KR—QB1
7. P—K6	B—B3

8. Q–B7ch   K–R1
9. P–B6   R–KKt1
10. Q–B7   QR–QB1
11. Q–K5   P–Q5ch
12. K–Kt1   B–Q4
13. P–B7ch   R–Kt2
14. Q x B   Black Resigns.

Rubinstein

1. R x Bch   R x R
2. Kt(R7) x Pch Black Resigns.

Bogoljubow—TO PLAY

Salo Flohr

In the years from 1929 to 1933, when Alekhine was at his peak, Flohr was universally recognized as his most serious challenger. Although he did poorly in individual games with Alekhine, his results were outstanding against the others. On the basis of his past record he was selected as the official challenger at the FIDE (International Chess Federation) meeting at Stockholm in 1937.

Flohr was born in Horodenka, Russian Poland, in 1908. His parents were killed in a pogrom when he was still young, and during the war he fled to Czechoslovakia where he made his home until the second World War again uprooted him. He showed an unusual aptitude for chess at an early age, and he soon discovered that a good living could be made by playing skittles in the cafés. Here he developed his fantastic abilities for quick chess, which later stood him in such good stead in tournaments and simultaneous exhibitions.

In 1929, when he was only 20, he won second prize at Rogaska Slatina, behind Rubinstein. Then he began a long string of tournament successes which placed him second only to Alekhine.

This period lasted until about 1935, when his style underwent a considerable change and his play fell off somewhat. His play became increasingly cautious; he avoided complications and steered for the endgame as soon as possible. Although he still won some important tournaments, such as the one at Leningrad-Moscow in 1939, he became more and more of a drawing master and was content to win a high prize, say fourth or fifth, rather than go after top honors. After the second World War he settled in the U. S. S. R. and became naturalized there.

What happened to Flohr? We see in him a development similar to that of so many other great masters—a spectacular beginning, loss of the creative urge, tapering off to become a "routine" tournament player who always has a sufficient command of technique to win a high prize, yet no longer capable of the brilliant flights of imagination of his youth. How are we to explain this process? It is not unlike that seen in artists in other fields. Many a writer has written one book—or a few books—and then repeated himself over and over; Sinclair Lewis is an example. Many an artist has done some magnificent painting and then lost his zest for the art; Theodore Dreiser has a splendid description of such a man in his novel *The Genius.*

In Flohr's case the roots of his frantic emphasis on "safety first" are not hard to discover. In 1936, when his play was beginning to fall off, Czechoslovakia, his second homeland, was faced with the growing threat from Nazi Germany. Flohr was a hero in Czechoslovakia, where chess was extremely popular. There were Flohr cigars, Flohr collars, Flohr pastries. With this support endangered, Flohr found it impossible to concentrate on his own growth as a chess master. His childhood had left psychological scars which he was unable to eradicate. And so he chose, unconsciously perhaps, the method most suited to keep him near enough to the top to make him feel safe; nothing else mattered. He was content to demonstrate himself equal to any master.

In his early days Flohr established a reputation as a master of the attack. Here are two beautiful victories from that golden epoch.

FLOHR   LANDAU
Antwerp, 1930
Queen's Gambit Declined

1. P—Q4   Kt—KB3
2. P—QB4   P—B3
3. Kt—KB3   P—Q4
4. P—K3   P—K3
5. QKt—Q2   B—K2

Too passive. . . . B—Q3 is better, to prepare . . . P—K4.

6. B—Q3   QKt—Q2
7. O—O   O—O
8. P—QKt3   P—B4
9. B—Kt2   BP x P

Weak . . . P—QKt3 is preferable.

10. KP x P   P x P
11. P x P   P—QKt3

White is now ideally prepared for a K-side attack.

12. Q–B2   B–Kt2
13. Kt–K5   Q–B2
14. P–B4   KR–Q1
15. Kt(Q2)–B3   P–KR3

After . . . Kt–B1; 16. Kt–Kt5 ! wins a Pawn.

16. Q–K2   Kt x Kt

If now 16. . . . Kt–B1; 17. P–Kt4 gets the attack going.

17. BP x Kt   Kt–Q2

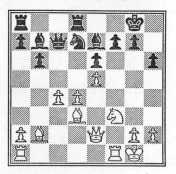

18. P–Q5 !   . . . .

Such a move can be played intuitively.

18. . . . . .   B–B4ch

Or 18. . . . P x P; 19. P–K6.

19. K–R1   P x P

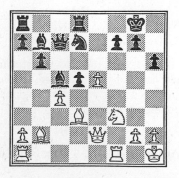

20. Kt–Kt5 !!   Kt–B1

What else was there? If 20. . . . P x Kt; 21. B–R7ch !!, K x B; 22. Q–R5ch, K–Kt1; 23. Q x Pch, K–R2; 24. R–B3.

21. Kt x P   R–K1
22. Q–Kt4   R–K3

The threat was Kt x Pch.

23. B–B5 !   QR–K1

Forced. On 23. . . . Q x Kt; 24. B x R, Q x B; 25. R x Ktch! is decisive.

24. B x R   R x B
25. Kt–Q6 !   B x Kt
26. P x B   Q–Q2

There is no defense. If 26. . . . R x P; 27. B–K5 wins.

27. B–R3 !   . . . .

With a most ingenious threat: R x Ktch, followed by Q x R and P–Q7 dis ch.

27. . . . . .   Kt–R2

To play . . . Kt–B3.

28. P–R3 !   . . . .

So that if . . . Kt–B3; 29. R x Kt !

28. . . . . .   P x P
29. Q x P   Kt–B3
30. R x Kt !   . . . .

Of course.

30. . . . . .   P x R
31. R–K1   B–B1

On 31. . . . K—B2; 32. R x R,
Q x R; 33. Q—B7ch wins a piece
(and Black has no perpetual).

32. R—QB1 !	B—Kt2
33. Q—Kt4ch	K—R1
34. R—B7	R—K8ch
35. K—R2	Q x Q
36. P x Q	Black Resigns.

Flohr was not admitted to the
Masters' Tournament at Hastings in 1930–31; he had to
content himself with the Premier
Reserves. But he still won the
prettiest game of the Congress!

FLOHR   RELLSTAB

Hastings, 1930–31
English Opening

1. P—QB4	P—QB4
2. Kt—QB3	Kt—KB3
3. P—KKt3	P—Q4
4. P x P	Kt x P
5. B—Kt2	Kt—B2
6. P—Kt3	P—K4
7. B—Kt2	B—K2
8. R—B1 !	. . . .

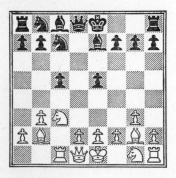

We really have a Sicilian Defense with colors reversed. Black

has the better of it if he can consolidate his position, but the tactical question remains, can he?

| 8. . . . . | O—O |

Better . . . P—B3, to counter
9. Kt—R4 with . . . Kt—K3.

9. Kt—R4	Kt—Q2
10. Kt—KB3	P—B3
11. Q—B2	Kt—K3

With the other Knight at Q2,
this move is no longer so effective.

| 12. Kt—R4 ! | Kt—Kt3 |
| 13. Kt—B5 ! | . . . . |

Excellent. He prepares an attack
on both flanks.

| 13. . . . . | Kt x Kt |
| 14. P x Kt | R—Kt1 |

To play . . . P—QKt3.

| 15. P—B4 !! | . . . . |

A most original conception. If
now 15. . . . P x P; 16. P x P,
Kt x P; 17. Q—B4ch, Kt—K3; 18.
B—Q5, K—B2 White can regain
his Pawn by 19. Kt x P, or play
for the attack with 19. R—KKt1.

15.	P x P
16. P x P	R—K1
17. R—KKt1 !	. . . .

As a result of his masterful
handling of both wings, Flohr
now has a powerful attack against
the enemy King.

| 17. . . . . | B—B1 |

Again if 17. . . . Kt x P ?; 18.

Q—B4ch, Kt—K3; 19. B—Q5
wins (19. ... B—B1; 20. Kt—
R6ch, K—R1; 21. Kt—B7ch). 17.
... K—R1, however, was the
best try.

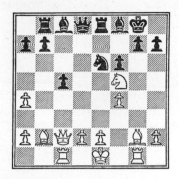

18. B—B6 !!   . . . .

Decisive. The immediate threat
is not only B x R, but the more
important Kt—R6ch and Kt—
B7ch.

18. . . . .   Kt—Q5
19. Kt—R6ch   K—R1
20. Kt—B7ch   K—Kt1
21. Kt—R6ch   . . . .

To gain time on the clock.

21. . . . .   K—R1
22. Kt—B7ch   K—Kt1
23. Q—B4 !!   . . . .

Flohr is absolute master of the
complications. The immediate
threat is mate in two.

23. . . . .   R x Pch
24. Q x R !!   Kt x Q
25. Kt x Q   . . . .

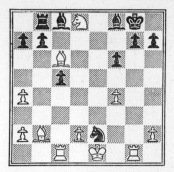

25. . . . .   Kt x R (Kt8)

There was nothing better. If 25.
... P x B; 26. K x Kt, R x B; 27.
R—Kt1 !, R x P; 28. R—Kt8 with
an easy win.

26. B—Q5ch   K—R1
27. Kt—B7ch   K—Kt1
28. K—B2 !   Kt—R6ch
29. K—Kt3 !   . . . .

And now Black's Kt is stuck.
The rest is simple.

29. . . . .   P—QKt4
30. P x P   B—Kt2
31. B—B4   P—QR3
32. P—R4   P x P
33. P x P   Kt x P

Desperation.

34. K x Kt   P—R4
35. R—KKt1   K—R2
36. B x P !!   Black Resigns.

A final pretty point. After 36.
... P x B; 37. B—Q3ch leads to
mate.

Flohr's mastery of the endgame
has rarely been equalled. Here is
one of his most famous, against
present world champion, Botvinnik.

FLOHR   BOTVINNIK
Match, 1933
Nimzoindian Defense

1. P–Q4	Kt–KB3
2. P–QB4	P–K3
3. Kt–QB3	B–Kt5
4. Q–B2	P–B4
5. P x P	Kt–R3
6. P–QR3	B x Ktch
7. Q x B	Kt x P
8. P–B3 !	P–Q3
9. P–K4	P–K4

To prevent P–K5.

White has emerged from the opening with a clear-cut advantage.

10. B–K3	Q–B2
11. Kt–K2	B–K3
12. Q–B2	O–O
13. Kt–B3	KR–B1

Botvinnik's only hope for counterplay lies in the QBP.

14. B–K2	P–QR3

To stop Kt–Kt5; if at once 14. . . . Kt(B4)–Q2; 15. Kt–Kt5, Q–Kt1; 16. R–Q1.

15. R–QB1	Kt(B4)–Q2
16. Q–Q2	Q–Kt1

Of course not . . . B x P ?; 17. Kt–Q5.

17. Kt–Q5	. . . .

Playing for the endgame. On the alternative 17. P–QKt3, Kt–B4 gives Black some counterplay.

17.	B x Kt
18. BP x B	R x Rch
19. Q x R	Q–Q1
20. O–O	R–B1
21. Q–Q2	Q–B2
22. R–B1	Q x Rch
23. Q x Q	R x Qch
24. B x R	. . . .

White's only advantage lies in his two Bishops. Yet even against a lesser master Flohr would not be expected to win this position; that he does so against Botvinnik is a real tribute to his endgame skill.

24.	K–B1
25. K–B2	K–K2
26. B–K3	K–Q1
27. K–K1	K–B2
28. K–Q2	Kt–B4
29. P–QKt4	. . . .

As a rule with the two Bishops any move to close the position must be made with caution. Nevertheless, the text is well timed; for if 29. . . . Kt–R5; 30. B–Q1, P–QKt4; 31. B x Kt, P x B; 32. K–B3, K–Kt2; 33. K–B4, Kt–Q2; 34. P–Kt5, P–QR4; 35. P–Kt6 ! leads to a won ending for White.

29.	Kt(B4)–Q2
30. P–Kt3	Kt–Kt3
31. K–B2	Kt(Kt3)–Q2

But here . . . Kt–R5 was preferable.

| 32. P–QR4 | Kt–Kt3 |
| 33. P–R5 | Kt(Kt3)–Q2 |

White has conquered more space and strengthened his position. The next step is to seek points at which a breakthrough can be achieved.

34. B–QB1	K–Q1
35. B–Kt2	Kt–K1
36. K–Q2	Kt–B2
37. K–K3	K–K2
38. B–KB1	Kt–Kt4
39. P–R4	Kt–B2
40. B–KR3	Kt–K1
41. P–B4 !	. . . .

Threatening to win a Pawn.

| 41. . . . . | P–B3 |
| 42. B–B5 ! | . . . . |

To further weaken the Pawns.

| 42. . . . . | P–KKt3 |
| 43. B–KR3 | . . . . |

Now P–B5 will be threatened under the proper circumstances.

| 43. . . . . | P–R3 |

To answer P–B5 with P–Kt4 without allowing White a passed Pawn.

| 44. B–QB1 | Kt–Kt2 |

| 45. P x P ! | . . . . |

Surprising and pretty. If now 45. . . . Kt x P ?; 46. B–B8, and if 45. . . . BP x P; 46. K–B3 !, P–R4; 47. B–Kt5ch, K–K1; 48. B–R6 ! and White wins a piece –a most remarkable variation!

| 45. . . . . | QP x P |

Thus this ugly reply is forced.

46. K–B3	P–R4
47. B–K3	K–Q3
48. B–R6	Kt–K1
49. P–Kt4	P x Pch
50. B x P	Kt–B2
51. B–K3	Kt–Kt4
52. K–K2	Kt–B2

Black has little choice; if 52. . . . Kt–Q5ch; 53. B x Kt, P x B; 54. B x Kt, K x B; 55. K–Q3.

53. K—Q3   . . . .

Threatening K—B4 followed by B—B5ch.

53. . . . .   P—B4

The only chance.

54. P x P   P x P
55. B x P   Kt x P
56. B—Q2   Kt(Q2)—B3
57. K—B4   K—B3
58. B—Kt6   . . . .

To advance the RP. As a result of his maneuvering, White has the decisive outside passed Pawn.

58. . . . .   P—Kt4ch
59. K—Q3   Kt—K2
60. B—K4ch !   . . . .

The two Bishops are no longer important—the RP is now sufficient.

60. . . . .   Kt(K2)—Q4
61. B—Kt5 !   Kt—R4

If instead . . . Kt x B; 62. K x Kt, Kt x P; 63. P—R5 wins.

62. B—B3 !   Kt—Kt6

Saemisch

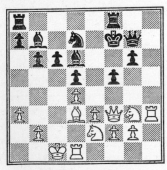

Flohr—TO PLAY

63. B—Q2 !   . . . .

Not P—R5 at once because of . . . P—K5ch. First the Kt must be driven.

63. . . . .   K—Q3
64. B—Kt4   Kt—B3

Offering the RP. If instead 64. . . . Kt—K2; 65. P—R5.

65. B—B8   K—B3
66. B—K1   . . . .

More precise than the immediate 66. B x P, Kt—B4.

66. . . . .   P—K5ch
67. K—Q4   Kt(Kt6)—R4
68. B—B5   . . . .

B x P can also be played.

68. . . . .   K—Q3
69. B—Q2   Black Resigns.

After the KP goes there is no real play left. One of the classic two Bishop endings in chess history.

Here are a few more examples of Flohr's genius.

Rogaska-Slatina, 1929

The game that made Flohr famous.

1. B x P !   Kt—B3
2. Kt—B4   B x Kt
3. Q x B   QR—K1
4. QR—R1   K—Kt1
5. R—R8ch   Q x R
6. R x Qch   K x R
7. Q—R6ch   K—Kt1
8. Q x Pch   K—R1
9. Q—R6ch   K—Kt1
10. Kt—R5 ! and wins.

Flohr—TO PLAY

Blechschmidt

Zwickau, 1930

1.	P—Kt4 !!
2. Q x KtP	R—QKt1 !
3. Q—B6 !	Q x Pch
4. K—B3	P—B4 !!
5. R x Rch	K—B2
6. B—Q4	Kt—K4ch !
7. B x Kt	Q—K5ch !
8. K—Kt3	Q—Kt5ch
9. K—R2	R x P mate.

Flohr—TO PLAY AND DRAW

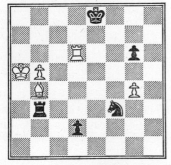

Sultan Khan

London, 1932

| 1. . . . . | Kt—K4 ! |

The only saving move in an apparently lost position.

| 2. B x P | . . . . |

The point is that if 2. K—R4, Kt—Q6; 3. B x P, Kt—B4ch; 4. K—R5, Kt—Kt2ch and Black wins a Rook or draws by perpetual check.

2.	Kt—B5ch
3. K—R4	Kt x R
4. K x R	Kt x P

Drawn.

Isaac Kashdan

Next to Flohr the most likely challenger for Alekhine's crown in the early 1930's was the American, Isaac Kashdan. This was a novelty, since he was the first American since Marshall to achieve any prominence in the international arena. There was no question in anybody's mind that had he played a match with Marshall in 1931 or 1932 Kash would have won the title; but those were depression years and it could not be arranged. Kashdan's superiority, however, was recognized in that he was placed on first board in the team tournaments.

Kashdan was the strongest American player for three or four years;

then he was outdistanced by Reshevsky and Fine. His play was solid, unspectacular, yet thorough. What he lacked was knowledge of the openings, and the willingness to risk tactical adventures; eventually, in spite of his comprehensive grasp of the game, his overcautiousness began to take its toll.

At his best Kashdan was nicknamed "The Little Capablanca" because of his great emphasis on position play and endgame technique. Here is one of the games which earned him this nickname.

RELLSTAB   KASHDAN

Stockholm, 1930

Queen's Gambit Declined

1. P—Q4   Kt—KB3
2. P—QB4   P—K3
3. Kt—QB3   P—Q4
4. B—Kt5   QKt—Q2
5. P—K3   B—K2
6. Kt—B3   O—O
7. R—B1   R—K1

More precise is 7. . . . . P—B3.

8. B—Q3   . . . .

Better is 8. P—B5 !, for if then
. . . P—B3; 9. B—KB4 with a
strong bind.

8. . . . .   P x P
9. B x P   P—QR3
10. B—Q3   P—B4

11. O—O   P x P
12. Kt x P   . . . .

White plays with too passive a spirit. P x P ! was more aggressive.

12. . . . .   Kt—K4
13. B—Kt1   . . . .

Now the attack is misplaced. Better 13. B—K2.

13. . . . .   Q—R4
14. Q—R4   . . . .

Playing for a draw, but he underrates Kashdan's endgame skill.

14. . . . .   Q x Q
15. Kt x Q   . . . .

In the pre-Capablanca days, such positions were almost automatically considered draws; Capa showed how many hidden potentialities lay in them. Kashdan, as the sequel shows, was also a past master at such positions.

15. . . . .   Kt(K4)—Q2 !!

Threatening . . . P—QKt4 and . . . B—Kt2, with a free game.

16. Kt—QB3   . . . .

So that if 16. . . . . P—QKt4;
17. Kt—B6.

16.	Kt–Kt3
17. KR–Q1	B–Q2
18. Kt–B3	R(K1)–Q1
19. Kt–K4	QR–B1
20. Kt x Ktch?	....

Overlooking the strength of Black's reply.

20.	P x Kt !
21. B–R6	....

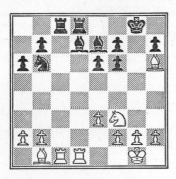

21.	Kt–R5 !

Forcing an entry.

22. R x R	B x R !
23. R x Rch	B x R
24. P–QKt3	Kt–B6
25. Kt–Q2	....

The only way to hold the Pawn.

25.	B–Q2
26. P–QR3	....

To free the Bishop.

26.	P–QKt4 !
27. B–Q3	....

If instead 27. P–QKt4, P–QR4; 28. P x P, B x P; 29. B–Q3, B–B2 ! and ... B–Q3, winning a Pawn.

27.	P–R4
28. P–K4	B–K2

Cashing in on his profound strategy; Black now wins a Pawn.

29. Kt–B3	....

Or 29. B–K3, B x P; 30. B–Q4, B–Kt7; 31. B x BP, Kt–K7ch; 32. B x Kt, B x B followed by advance of the QRP wins.

29.	B x P
30. B–Q2	B–Kt7
31. Kt–Q4	P–R5

Decisive.

32. P x P	....

A pretty alternative is 32. B x Kt, B x B; 33. Kt x KtP, B x Kt; 34. B x B, P–R6 ! and queens.

32.	P x P
33. Kt–B2	Kt–Kt8 !
34. B–Kt4	P–R6
35. B–B4	B–R5
36. Kt–K1	B–B6 !
37. Kt–Q3	B–B7

White is completely bottled up. There is no defense against the threat of ... B x Kt and ... P–R7.

38. P—B3   P—R7
White Resigns.

Kashdan first attracted international attention by his play at the team tournament in Hamburg, 1930. Here is his best game from that event.

STAHLBERG   KASHDAN

Hamburg, 1930

Nimzoindian Defense

1. P—Q4   Kt—KB3
2. P—QB4   P—K3
3. Kt—QB3   B—Kt5
4. Q—Kt3   P—B4
5. P x P   Kt—B3
6. Kt—B3   Kt—K5
7. B—Q2   Kt x QBP
8. Q—B2   O—O
9. P—K4?   . . . .

An error which is most instructively punished. P—QR3 is correct.

9. . . . .   Q—B3 !
10. O—O—O !   . . . .

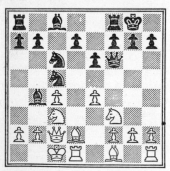

10. . . . .   P—QKt3 !

Black cannot afford to win the Pawn with 10. . . . B x Kt; 11.

B x B, Q—B5ch; 12. Kt—Q2 !, Q x BP ?; for after 13. P—QKt4 ! he loses a piece. Now he does threaten it because the Knight can return to Kt2.

11. B—Q3   . . . .

Unappetizing, but forced.

11. . . . .   P—QR4 !
12. K—Kt1   Q—Kt3
13. KR—Kt1   . . . .

White's pieces are bottled up. 13. P—QR3 ? would threaten nothing.

13. . . . .   B—R3
14. B—K3   . . . .

A desperate attempt to free himself.

14. . . . .   Kt x B
15. Q x Kt   B x Kt
16. P x B   . . . .

16. . . . .   P—Q4 !

A pretty deciding move.

17. KP x P   Q x Qch
18. R x Q   B x P
19. R—Q2   B x QP

20. B x P   KR—Kt1
21. R—Kt2   P—R5 !

The real point of the combination. If now 22. B—B5, P—R6 !;
23. R x Rch, R x Rch; 24. K—R1,
R—Kt7 ! and wins.

22. B—B7   R—QB1

23. B—B4   Kt—R4
24. R—QB1   . . . .

Losing neatly. 24. Kt—Q2, R x
P loses more slowly.

24. . . . .   B—K5ch
25. K—R1   Kt—Kt6ch !
White Resigns.

Edgar Colle

While he was never a serious contender for the world championship,
the Belgian master, Edgar Colle, was one of the tournament stalwarts of
the Alekhine era. He is best known for the opening named after him, the
Colle System, which, as he showed, packs a terrific wallop in spite of its
placidity. Colle was primarily an attacking player; here is one of his most
brilliant efforts.

COLLE   GRUENFELD
Berlin, 1926
Queen's Indian Defense

1. P—Q4   Kt—KB3
2. Kt—KB3   P—K3
3. P—K3   P—QKt3

Avoiding the Colle System
proper, which arises after 3. . . . .
P—Q4.

4. B—Q3   B—Kt2
5. QKt—Q2   P—B4
6. O—O   B—K2
7. P—QKt3   P x P

Weakening.

8. P x P   P—Q3
9. B—Kt2   QKt—Q2
10. P—B4   O—O

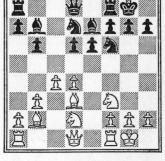

Colle could pull the most brilliant combinations out of placid
positions of this sort.

11. R—B1   R—K1
12. R—K1   Q—B2

Loss of time.

13. Q—K2   QR—B1
14. Kt—B1   Q—Kt1
15. Kt—Kt3   Q—R1
16. Kt—Kt5 !   . . . .

On 16. . . . B x P he intends 17. P—B3, P—KR3; 18. Kt x BP !

16. . . . .   P—Kt3 ?

Evidently believing the sacrifice unsound. Better was 16. . . . Kt—B1.

17. Kt x BP !   . . . .

This offer, which occurred so often in Colle's games, was the hidden point of his system.

17. . . . .   K x Kt
18. Q x Pch   K—Kt2

On 18. . . . K—B1; 19. P—Q5, Kt—B4; 20. Q—K3, Kt x B; 21. Q x Kt, Kt—Q2; 22. R—K6, Kt—B4; 23. Q—Q4, Kt x R; 24. P x Kt wins.

19. P—Q5 !   Kt—B4

20. Kt—B5ch !!   K—B1

After 20. . . . P x Kt; 21. Q x BP Black's position rapidly disintegrates.

21. Q—K3 !   P x Kt
22. Q—R6ch   K—B2
23. B x P !   B x P

Desperation.

24. R x Bch !   R x R
25. Q x Ktch   K—K1
26. Q—R8ch   K—B2
27. B x R   Black Resigns.

Lajos Steiner

The Hungarian, Lajos Steiner, comes of a family of chess masters. His father was a well-known Budapest master in the years before the first World War; his brother, Endre, was a master who was strong enough to take part in international tournaments. Lajos rarely managed to win top honors, but he was renowned for his ability to topple the great, and for the creative intuition which he so often displays in his play. Before the war he moved to Australia where, although he still plays serious chess, he settled down to his profession of engineering.

L. STEINER   KERES
Warsaw Team Tourney, 1935
Ruy Lopez

1. P–K4   P–K4
2. Kt–KB3   Kt–QB3
3. B–Kt5   P–QR3
4. B–R4   Kt–B3
5. O–O   P–Q3
6. P–B3   B–Q2

Black can also play . . . Kt x P.

7. R–K1   B–K2
8. P–Q4   O–O
9. QKt–Q2   . . . .

9. . . . .   P x P ?

A risky maneuver which is ef-
ficiently punished.

10. P x P   Kt–QKt5
11. P–Q5 !   Kt–Q6
12. R–K3   B x B
13. Q x B   Kt–B4
14. Q–B2   Kt–Kt5
15. R–K2   R–K1
16. P–KR3   Kt–K4
17. Kt x Kt   P x Kt
18. Kt–B4   . . . .

White has a solid position with
considerable potential pressure

on the Q-side. Keres therefore
decides to try something.

18. . . . .   P–B4 !?
19. P x P   P–K5
20. Kt–K3   B–Q3

Evidently hoping for an even-
tual K-side attack.

21. B–Q2   Kt–Q6
22. Kt–B1   Q–B3
23. P–B3 !   Q–Q5ch
24. B–K3   Q x QP
25. R–Q1 !   . . . .

Black's pieces are badly tied up.
If here 25. . . . P x P ?; 26. P x
P ! wins the Kt.

25. . . . .   Q x RP
26. P x P   Kt–Kt5
27. Q–B3   R x P ?

Loses nicely, but on the alternative 27. . . . Kt–B3; 28. B–B2
followed by Kt–K3–B4 pre-
serves the pressure.

28. R x B !!   R–QB5

The point is that if instead 28.
. . . P x R; 29. B–R6 ! decides.

29. Q–K5   P x R

30. Q—K6ch   K—R1
31. P—B6   . . . .

Now the attack is decisive.

31. . . . .   R—B2
32. Q x P   Q—B5
33. R—KB2   R—B2
34. R—B4   Q—B3

35. P x Pch !   R x P

Equally useless is 35. . . . K x P; 36. B—Q4ch.

36. R—B8ch   Black Resigns.

It is mate after 36. . . . R x R; 37. Q x Rch, R—Kt1; 38. B—Q4ch.

Sultan Khan

The appearance of an Indian on the tournament scene was one of the sensations of the early 1930's. Sultan (a first name, not a title) was a serf on the estate of an Indian Maharajah, who was impressed by his extraordinary ability at chess. His master took him to England, where Sultan Khan had to learn the European rules, which were not adhered to in India. In spite of this handicap, his native genius was such that he soon became British champion. When the Maharajah returned to India Sultan Khan went with him, and has not been heard from since.

Because he had to relearn the rules, his games often had a peculiar appearance. Here is one of his best efforts.

SOULTAINBEIEFF

SULTAN KHAN

Liege, 1930
Queen's Indian Defense

1. P—Q4   Kt—KB3
2. Kt—KB3   P—QKt3
3. P—B4   P—K3
4. P—KKt3   B—Kt2
5. B—Kt2   B—Kt5ch
6. B—Q2   B x Bch
7. QKt x B   . . . .

Better is 7. Q x B.

7. . . . .   O—O
8. O—O   P—B4

Sultan Khan handles the positional maneuvering with admirable skill.

9. Q—B2   Kt—B3
10. P x P   P x P
11. P—K4 ??   . . . .

A positional blunder which opens the Q5 square to Black.

11. . . . .   Q—B2
12. KR—K1   P—Q3
13. QR—B1   P—KR3
14. P—QR3   Kt—Q2
15. Q—B3   . . . .

Hoping to be able to play P—QKt4.

15. . . . .   P—QR4
16. Kt—R4   P—Kt4
17. Q—K3   . . . .

Planning on 17. . . . P x Kt; 18. Q x P, with a complicated attack.

17. . . . .   Q–Q1 !

Rightly refusing the sacrifice since his game is positionally won.

18. Kt(R4)–B3   Q–K2
19. P–R3   QR–Kt1
20. P–Kt3   B–R1
21. Kt–Kt1   Kt(Q2)–K4
22. P–QR4   . . . .

Afraid of . . . P–R5. White flounders aimlessly, while Sultan Khan continually strengthens his position.

22. . . . .   Kt x Ktch
23. B x Kt   Kt–Q5
24. B–Q1   . . . .

He must prevent . . . Kt–B7.

24. . . . .   P–B4 !

Decisive. The lines are now opened for the concluding attack.

25. P x P   R x BP
26. R–B3   R(Kt1)–KB1
27. R–KB1   R–B6 !!

The finish is pretty. If in reply 28. Q–Q2, Q–Kt2 ! leads to mate.

28. B x R   R x B
White Resigns.

For on 29. Q–Q2, Black can win with either 29. . . . R x R ! or . . . Q–Kt2.

Erich Eliskases

The Austrian master, Erich Eliskases, started in the early 1930's, though his great success came at Noordwijk in 1938, where he took first prize. Since the war he has settled in Brazil, and has done much to enrich chess life in that country.

Eliskases first rose to prominence with a victory over Spielmann in a match in 1932. The most brilliant game of that match is an enduring masterwork.

SPIELMANN   ELISKASES

7th Match Game, 1932
Queen's Gambit Declined

1. P—Q4	P—Q4
2. Kt—KB3	P—K3
3. P—B4	P—QB3
4. Kt—B3	P x P
5. P—K4	. . . .

A gambit-like variation which Spielmann was fond of.

5.	P—QKt4
6. P—K5	B—Kt2
7. B—K2	Kt—K2
8. Kt—K4	Kt—Q4
9. O—O	Kt—Q2
10. KKt—Kt5	B—K2
11. P—B4	. . . .

Intending P—B5.

11.	P—Kt3

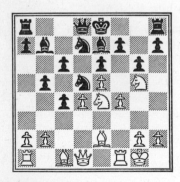

12. P—B5 !?   . . . .

Typical Spielmann—it might have worked against a lesser master.

12.	KP x P

Traps are numerous! If 12. . . . . KtP x P; 13. Kt x KP ! wins beautifully, e.g., 13. . . . . P x Kt(K3); 14. B—R5ch, K—B1; 15. B—R6ch, K—Kt1; 16. Q—Kt4ch !!, P x Q; 17. B—B7 mate.

13. P—K6	P x P
14. Kt x KP	Q—Kt3
15. P—QR4	. . . .

Fumbling for a continuation. If 15. R x P !?, P—B4 ! wins.

15.	P x Kt !
16. P—R5	Q—R3
17. Q—B2	Kt(Q2)—B3
18. R x Kt !	B x R !!
19. Q x KP	. . . .

Winning the Queen . . . and losing the game. Black's defense is superb.

19.	K—B2 !
20. Kt—B5	QR—K1
21. Q—B3	R x B !!

The point. If 22. Q x R ?, B x Pch saves everything. Black now gets Rook and two pieces for the Queen, or a potent counterattack.

22. Kt x Q	R—K8ch
23. K—B2	R(R1)—K1
24. Kt—B5	B—B1
25. P—QKt4	K—Kt1

Black has Rook, Bishop and Pawn for the Queen—quite sufficient in this position. White has no more good moves.

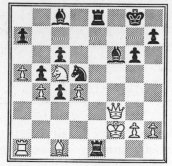

26. B—Kt2   R(K8)—K6
27. Q—Q1   P—B6

Bogoljubow

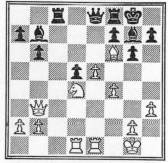

Eliskases—TO PLAY

28. B—B1   P—B7!
29. Q x P   R—K7ch!
30. Q x R   B x Pch
31. B—K3   R x B

Finis. If in reply 32. Q x R, B x Qch; 33. K—B3, Kt x P! and it is all over.

32. Q—B1   R—QR6ch
White Resigns.

Here is a pretty finish from another of Eliskases' games.

Match Game, 1939

1. Kt—B5!   Black Resigns.

For if 1. . . . P x Kt; 2. Q—Kt3 mates. On other moves Black loses the exchange.

The Swedish School

While Sweden and the Scandinavian countries in general have long been important chess centers, it was not until the 1930's that they produced a number of masters of international stature. Most prominent among them were Stoltz and Stahlberg, who led the Swedish team in its outstanding showing at international team tournaments.

Stoltz has always been brilliant and erratic. Here is his most famous game, in which he unseats a great tactician.

SPIELMANN   STOLTZ

Stockholm, 1931
French Defense

1. P—K4   P—K3
2. P—Q4   P—Q4

3. Kt—Q2   Kt—KB3
4. P—K5   KKt—Q2
5. B—Q3   P—QB4
6. P—QB3   Kt—QB3
7. Kt—K2   Q—Kt3

In this variation Black must

smash White's Pawn center quickly.

8. Kt–B3	P x P
9. P x P	B–Kt5ch
10. K–B1	P–B3
11. Kt–B4	....

Spielmann, as usual, attacks.

| 11. .... | P x P ! |

A most ingenious defense.

| 12. Kt x P(K6) | P–K5 |
| 13. B–KB4 | .... |

The attack seems overwhelming; but Black has surprises in store.

| 13. .... | P x Kt !! |

A queen sacrifice . . . is it sound?

| 14. B–B7 | .... |

Accept it and see.

| 14. .... | Kt–B3 |
| 15. Kt x Pch | K–B2 |

| 16. B x Q | B–Kt5 |

An extraordinarily complicated position in which both sides must rely on intuition. But post-mortem analysis has never demonstrated a really satisfactory defense for White.

17. P–KKt3	B–R6ch
18. K–Kt1	K x Kt
19. B–B7	KR–K1
20. B–K5	....

Better 20. Q x P, but White is naturally anxious to exchange pieces.

20.	Kt x B
21. P x Kt	R x P
22. Q–Kt3	B–QB4 !!

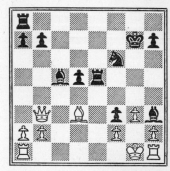

An astounding position. Black, already a Queen behind, blithely offers another Rook. Shudders must have gone through Spielmann at the sight of this usurpation of his style.

| 23. B–B5 | .... |

To deflect the Bishop. If 23. Q x Pch, R–K2; 24. Q x R, Kt–Kt5 !; 25. R–KB1, Kt x BP and wins. And on 23. B–B1, B x Pch ! 24. K x B, Kt–K5ch is decisive.

| 23. .... | B x B |
| 24. Q x Pch | K–Kt3 |

25. Q x R   R—K7!

Black has a mating attack in spite of his material handicap.

26. P—KR4   . . . .

Despair. On 26. R—KB1, B—KR6! and there is no defense, e.g., 27. Q—B6, B x Pch; 28. R x B, R—K8ch and mate next.

26. . . . .   B x Pch
27. K—B1   B—Q6

Threatening mate.

28. P—R5ch   K—Kt4
White Resigns.

A most remarkable position. There is no defense against the discovered check. If 29. R—Q1, R—Q7 mate. It is easier to compose such positions than to produce them over-the-board!

Gideon Stahlberg

After the team tournament of 1939 in Buenos Aires, Stahlberg settled in Argentina. Here is his finest game from down south.

PILNIK   STAHLBERG

Mar del Plata, 1943
French Defense

1. P—K4   P—K3

Stahlberg's favorite defense.

2. P—Q4   P—Q4
3. Kt—QB3   B—Kt5
4. Kt—K2   P x P
5. P—QR3   B x Ktch
6. Kt x B   P—KB4

A defense considered bad since Alekhine's sensational victory against Nimzovitch at San Remo in 1930. But Stahlberg has some improvements up his sleeve.

7. B—KB4   . . . .

Alekhine had played 7. P—B3, but after 7. . . . P x P; 8. Q x P, Q—R5ch! gives Black an adequate defense.

7. . . . .   Kt—KB3
8. Q—Q2   O—O

9. O—O—O   Kt—R4
10. B—B4   Kt—QB3
11. Kt—K2?   . . . .

Here he should have proceeded to open the KKt file with *11. P—B3!* After *11. . . . P x P; 12. P x P, Kt x B; 13. Q x Kt, Q—Q3; 14. Q—K3, K—R1; 15. P—B4* White has attacking possibilities.

11. . . . .   Kt—K2!
12. P—KB3   Kt x B
13. Kt x Kt   Kt—Q4
14. P—KKt3   Q—Q3!

An active defense, even if it involves return of the extra material.

15. P x P   P x P
16. Kt—Kt2   . . . .

White seems to be pulling out, but he is in for a surprise!

16. . . . .   P—QKt4!
17. B—Kt3?   . . . .

Too timid. With *17. B x P!* he can hold the position satisfactorily.

17. . . . .   B—Kt2
18. KR—K1   P—QR4
19. R x P   P—R5
20. B x Kt   . . . .

Dire necessity. On *20. B—R2, Kt—B6!* wins the exchange.

20. . . . .   Q x B
21. R—K2   Q—R7

With this penetration the game is virtually decided.

22. P—B3   B—B6

Black wins the exchange, but even more important is the strengthening of the attack.

23. Kt—B4   . . . .

23. . . . .   P—Kt5!!

A pretty surprise.

24. RP x P   . . . .

If *24. BP x P, R x Kt!; 25. P x R, Q—B5ch* and Black emerges a piece ahead.

24. . . . .   P—R6
25. P x P   Q x Pch
26. Q—Kt2   . . . .

Loses a piece, but there was nothing to be done. On *26. K—B2, Q—R3!* wins.

26. . . . .   R x Kt
27. P x R   B x R
28. Q x Q   R x Q
29. K—Kt2   R x P
30. R—K1   R—K6
31. R—QB1   B—B6
32. R x P   B—Q4
White Resigns.

Sir George Thomas

After Yates, Sir George was England's major representative in international competition. Although not on a par with Blackburne and Burn, he was always a dangerous opponent. His great success came at Hastings, 1934, where he tied for first with Flohr and Capablanca, ahead of Botvinnik and others. Here is one of his most elegant efforts.

THOMAS   FLOHR

Margate, 1939
Ruy Lopez

1. P–K4	P–K4
2. Kt–KB3	Kt–QB3
3. B–Kt5	P–QR3
4. B–R4	Kt–B3
5. O–O	B–K2
6. Kt–B3	. . . .

An older line, rarely seen nowadays. Flohr is evidently not too familiar with it and does not defend well.

6.	P–QKt4
7. B–Kt3	P–Q3
8. Kt–Q5 !	B–Kt5

Not the best; 8. . . . Kt–QR4 equalizes more easily. On 8. . . . Kt x P; 9. Kt x B, Kt x Kt; 10. P–Q4 gives White a strong attack for the Pawn.

9. Kt x B	Q x Kt
10. P–B3	O–O
11. P–Q3	. . . .

As a result of his opening maneuvering White has gained the advantage of the two Bishops.

11.	Kt–QR4
12. B–B2	P–B4
13. P–KR3	B–R4
14. Q–K2	Kt–Q2
15. Q–K3 !	. . . .

Releases the pin.

15.	Kt–QB3
16. Kt–R2	Kt–Kt3 ?

A very careless move which is promptly punished.

17. P–QKt4 !	QR–Kt1
18. P–R3	KR–B1
19. P x P	P x P
20. P–KB4 !	. . . .

Black has been thoroughly outplayed and White now has the

initiative on both sides of the board.

20.	P x P
21. Q x KBP	Kt—K4
22. Q—Kt3 !	B—Kt3

He had to guard against R—B5.

23. B—B4	Kt(Kt3)—Q2
24. Kt—Kt4	R—K1
25. Kt—K3 !	. . . .

Well played. On the tempting 25. Kt x Kt, Kt x Kt; 26. P—Q4 ?, Black can reply 26. . . . P x P !; 27. P x P, QR—B1 !

25.	R(Kt1)—B1
26. Kt—Q5	Q—Q1
27. P—QR4 !	. . . .

With everything else temporarily stabilized he creates new threats.

27.	P—Kt5
28. P—R5 !	. . . .

Fixing Black's QRP as a target.

28.	P x P
29. Kt x P	Kt—QB3
30. Kt—Q5	. . . .

Preventing . . . Kt x P.

30.	Kt—Q5
31. R—B2	Kt—K3

He had to stop B—B7.

| 32. B—Kt3 | . . . . |

Threatening B—B4, which would prove decisive.

32.	P—B5

The best chance.

33. B x P	B x P
34. Kt—K3 !	B—Kt3

Forced, for if 34. . . . B—Kt2; 35. Kt—B5, threatening B x Kt, is decisive.

35. B x P	R—R1
36. B—QKt5	Kt—Q5
37. B—B7	Q—K2
38. B x Kt	Q x B
39. B—Kt6	Kt—Kt6
40. R—R3	Kt—B8
41. P—Q4	. . . .

The complications are temporarily calm. White's Pawn plus is secure, but the situation is still fluid and there are many technical difficulties.

41.	Kt—Q6
42. R—Q2	Q—Kt4
43. K—R2	P—R4
44. Kt—Q1	. . . .

To chase the Knight away.

44.	. . . .	Kt—B8
45.	R—K3	R x R
46.	Q x R	R—K1
47.	R—Kt2 !	Q—B3
48.	Q—QB3	Q—Q3ch
49.	Q—Kt3	Q—Q4
50.	Kt—B3	Q—KB4
51.	Kt—Kt5	Q—B8
52.	Q—B2	Q—Q8
53.	R—Q2	Q—Kt6
54.	Kt—B7	R—K2
55.	P—Q5	Kt—Q6

56. P—Q6 !   . . . .

Very pretty. If 56. . . . R—Q2;

51. Q—Q4 followed by P—R6 with an easy win.

56.	. . . .	Kt x Q
57.	P x R	P—B3
58.	R x Kt	. . . .

White has Rook and Knight for the Queen and will soon win the Bishop.

58. . . . .   Q—Kt5

There is no defense: on 58. . . . Q—R5; 59. P—R6 decides.

59.	P—K8 = Qch	B x Q
60.	Kt x B	P—R5
61.	Kt—B7	K—B2
62.	K—Kt1	K—Kt3
63.	Kt—Q5	Q—R6
64.	Kt—K3	K—B2
65.	R—B1	P—Kt3

Black is lost anyhow, but this hastens the end.

66.	Kt—Kt4	P—B4
67.	Kt—K5ch	K—B3
68.	B—Q4 !	Black Resigns.

8.

The Age of Euwe

ALEKHINE had waned slightly by 1934. He was still the perennial first prize winner, but his rivals were much less impressed by his play. The first to overthrow him was the Dutchman, Max Euwe.

In the two years that Euwe held the title, from 1935 to 1937, a whole generation of new masters suddenly sprang up. Chess supremacy continued moving away from Central Europe; during this period the Americans held the world chess leadership, later the Russians. At the historic Nottingham tournament of 1936 four world champions, Alekhine, Capablanca, Lasker, and Euwe fought it out with four challengers, Botvinnik, Fine, Flohr and Reshevsky; the next year a fifth, Keres, was added. Although Capa could still win first prize at Nottingham, it was not long before the newcomers definitely held the center of the stage.

Dr. Max Euwe

Euwe is the embodiment of logic in chess. Since chess is "theoretically" a mathematical exercise, one would expect every chess master to play according to the rules of logic. Nothing could be further from the truth. One man relies on imagination, a second on intuition, a third on authority. Only a rare genius like Euwe can consistently attempt to play logical chess.

Euwe was born near Amsterdam, Holland, in 1901. His chess career began early; at the age of ten he won a one-day tournament in Amsterdam, but his family preferred not to push him as a wonder child, and he finished his schooling quietly. In 1921, when he was 20, he won the Dutch championship and drew a match against Maroczy. Although he had already come pretty far, he preferred to devote himself to his academic work, and played little chess until after he had received his doctorate in mathematics in 1926. He has always been a mathematics teacher by profession.

Paradoxically, Euwe's main international successes came in the form of defeats by narrow margins. In 1926 he lost a match to Alekhine by the score of 4½–5½ (two wins, three losses, five draws), a much better score than Capablanca made the next year in the world championship match.

Euwe's progress was gradual. In 1932 he drew a match with Flohr, and tied for second at Berne behind Alekhine. From that time on he was generally recognized with Flohr as Alekhine's most dangerous rival.

His chance came in 1935. Alekhine, playing somewhat too over-confidently, was defeated by a one-point margin, and Euwe was proclaimed world champion. In the two years that followed before the return match, Euwe's strength increased. Although he never enjoyed the supremacy over his rivals that his predecessors had, he had no superiors in this period.

The Euwe-Alekhine matches were always full of surprises for the chess world. The games, moreover, were of a high fighting quality. In the 1935 encounter Euwe won when everybody expected him to lose. In 1937, when everybody thought he would win, he lost. The reason for this is that Euwe becomes too nervous under pressure. In the 1937 match at times he had a barber come in and give him a massage during the games, but even that did not suffice to reduce the tension.

After the war, Euwe took a five-year leave of absence from his school activities to devote himself entirely to chess. He travelled all over the world and played a great deal, but his tournament results were no longer on a par with his pre-war standards.

Euwe's strength always lay in his theoretical grasp of the game. He is one of the greatest theoreticians of the age; his contributions to opening theory are voluminous. Once he builds up a superior position out of the opening, his handling of it can be perfection itself. But he too often lacks the stamina to pull himself out of bad positions.

The game which virtually clinched the title for Euwe in 1935 has come to be known as the "Pearl of Zandvoort."

EUWE   ALEKHINE

26th Match Game, 1935
Dutch Defense

1. P–Q4   P–K3
2. P–QB4   P–KB4

The two-edged Dutch was Alekhine's favorite during this period.

3. P–KKt3   B–Kt5ch
4. B–Q2   B–K2

The maneuver which Alekhine popularized. The idea is that White's Bishop is poorly placed at Q2.

5. B–Kt2   Kt–KB3
6. Kt–QB3   O–O
7. Kt–B3   Kt–K5
8. O–O   P–QKt3
9. Q–B2   B–Kt2
10. Kt–K5   Kt x Kt !

Similar to a sacrifice seen in the Euwe-Capablanca match. After 11. B x B? Kt x Pch; 12. K—R1, Kt x QP; 13. Q—Q3, QKt—B3, Black has more than enough for the exchange.

11. B x Kt   B x B
12. K x B   Q—B1

It does not seem as if White has been able to get any advantage from the opening, but Euwe comes through with a dynamic surprise.

13. P—Q5!   P—Q3
14. Kt—Q3   P—K4
15. K—R1   . . . .

A far-sighted maneuver, the point of which soon becomes clear.

15. . . . .   P—B3
16. Q—Kt3   K—R1
17. P—B4   P—K5
18. Kt—Kt4   P—B4
19. Kt—B2   Kt—Q2
20. Kt—K3   . . . .

Now it is clear what White had in mind: he plans to play P—KKt4 and play for the attack.

20. . . . .   B—B3?

A mistake which gives White a great chance. Better was . . . Kt—B3.

21. Kt x P !!   . . . .

This must have taken Alekhine by surprise.

21. . . . .   B x B
22. Kt x QP   Q—Kt1
23. Kt x P   B—B3
24. Kt—Q2   . . . .

White has three Pawns for his piece and good attacking chances.

24. . . . .   P—KKt4!

Alekhine never defends passively. The threat of P—K4—K5 is met by a counterattack.

25. P—K4   P x P
26. P x P   B—Q5
27. P—K5   Q—K1
28. P—K6   R—KKt1

So that if 29. P x Kt?, Q—K7.

29. Kt—B3?   . . . .

Inaccurate. 29. Q—KR3 ! would have led to a forced win.

29. . . . .   Q—Kt3
30. R—KKt1 !   B x R
31. R x B   Q—B3 ??

The losing move. Subsequent analysis showed that 31. . . . Q —B4 ! was sufficient to draw, for if then 32. Kt—Kt5, P—KR3 !

32. Kt—Kt5 !!   . . . .

A Rook behind—and he makes combinations! The immediate threat is unpleasant.

32. . . . .   R—Kt2
33. P x Kt   R x P
34. Q—K3   R—K2
35. Kt—K6   . . . .

White has two Pawns for the exchange and a strongly posted Knight; the rest is not difficult.

35. . . . .   R—KB1

Or . . . Q x KtP; 36. P—Q6, R —Q2; 37. Kt—Kt5 !

36. Q—K5   Q x Q
37. P x Q   R—B4

The two Pawns decide in any event, but 37. . . . R x Kt; 38. P x R, R—B4 offered better chances.

38. R—K1   . . . .

Even stronger was 38. R—Kt5 !

38. . . . .   P—KR3

Time pressure. 38. . . . R x Kt; 39. P x R, K—Kt2 makes life harder for White.

39. Kt—Q8 !   R—B7
40. P—K6   R—Q7

41. Kt—B6   R—K1
42. P—K7   P—Kt4

Desperation—nobody likes to resign.

43. Kt—Q8   K—Kt2
44. Kt—Kt7   K—B3
45. R—K6ch   K—Kt4
46. Kt—Q6   R x KP
47. Kt—K4ch   Black Resigns.

For sheer logic the following game can scarcely be matched in the annals of chess.

KERES   EUWE

Zandvoort, 1936
French Defense

1. P—K4   P—K3
2. P—Q4   P—Q4
3. P—K5   . . . .

Keres was then fond of this variation.

3. . . . .   P—QB4
4. Kt—KB3   P x P
5. Q x P   . . . .

Nimzovitch preferred 5. B—Q3.

5. . . . .   Kt—QB3
6. Q—KB4   P—B4

At first sight this looks illogical because Black usually must keep . . . P—B3 in reserve, to break up the White center. But Euwe has a different idea—he will leave White's Pawn at K5 and prove that it is a source of weakness. The idea reminds one of something that Rubinstein once tried against Euwe.

7. B–Q3	KKt–K2
8. O–O	Kt–Kt3
9. Q–Kt3	B–K2
10. R–K1	O–O
11. P–QR3	....

The opening phase is over; now we are in for some mid-game jockeying.

11.	Kt–Kt1 !!

A profound regrouping idea; the Knight is headed for K5.

12. QKt–Q2	P–QR4
13. Kt–Kt3	Kt–R3
14. P–QR4	....

To stop . . . P–R5. 14. B x Kt is preferable, but the attacker is always loath to part with his King's Bishop.

14.	Kt–Kt5
15. Kt(B3)–Q4	B–Q2
16. B–QKt5	Kt–B3

White's Q-side has been weakened, therefore the Knight can return.

17. P–QB4 ?	....

Gives Black a chance. 17. P–QB3 was better.

17.	Kt x Kt
18. Kt x Kt	B–B4 !

Almost out of nowhere Black has built up a menacing K-side attack.

19. Q–Q3	B x B
20. Kt x B	Q–R5 !

Thoroughly consistent.

21. Q–B1	....

To avoid a weakening. If 21. P–KKt3, Q–R6 threatens . . . P–B5–B6.

21.	QR–Q1 !
22. B–K3	P–Q5 !
23. B–Q2	P–Q6

First fruits of the attacking threats: a strong passed Pawn.

24. P–QKt3	....

The Bishop is artificially pinned. If 24. B x P, P–Q7; 25 KR–Q1, Kt x P; 26. R x P, Kt–Kt5 ! wins.

24.	P–B5
25. R–K4	R–B4
26. QR–K1	R–R4

The attack continues raging.

27. P–R3   R–Kt4
28. Kt–Q6   . . . .

On 28. K–R1, B x P is decisive,
e.g., 29. R–Q1, Q–Kt6; 30. B x
RP, P–B6!

28. . . . .   Q x P
29. B x BP   Kt x B
30. R x Kt   Q–Kt6!

Finis.

31. R(B4)–K4   R–R4

White Resigns.

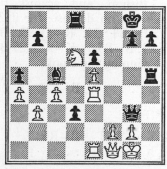

It's mate!

Euwe's phenomenal knowledge
of the openings led to mathemat-
ically precise victories. Here is a
beautiful one against Alekhine.

EUWE   **ALEKHINE**
5th Match Game, 1937
Queen's Gambit Declined

1. P–Q4   P–Q4
2. P–QB4   P x P
3. Kt–KB3   P–QR3
4. P–K3   Kt–KB3
5. B x P   P–K3
6. O–O   P–B4
7. Q–K2   Kt–B3

In this much analyzed position,
Euwe springs a surprise move.

8. Kt–B3!   . . . .

A considerable improvement
over the older 8. R–Q1, P–
QKt4; 9. B–Kt3, P–B5; 10. B–
B2, Kt–QKt5.

8. . . . .   P–QKt4

On 8. . . . P x P here or later
on the reply is R–Q1.

9. B–Kt3   . . . .

White's eighth move has allowed
him to preserve this Bishop.

9. . . . .   B–K2
10. P x P   B x P
11. P–K4!   . . . .

Black is virtually lost after only
11 moves. If 11. . . . O–O; 12.
P–K5, Kt–Q2; 13. Kt–K4, B–
K2; 14. R–Q1 and Black's position is untenable.

11. . . . .   P–Kt5

Allowing dazzling fireworks.

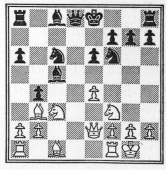

12. P–K5!   P x Kt
13. P x Kt   KtP x P

Not 13. . . . . Q x P; 14. Q–B4,
Q–K2; 15. B–K3 !, winning a
piece.

14. Q–B4   Q–Kt3
15. Q̄ x BP   K̄t–Q5

Other moves are no better.

16. Kt x Kt   B x Kt
17. B–R4ch   K–K2

Or 17. . . . B–Q2; 18. B x
Bch, K x B; 19. R–Q1.

18. B–K3 !   B x Q ?

The best chance was 18. . . . .
R–Q1, though White still main-
tains the pressure after 19. B x
B !, R x B; 20. QR–Q1.

19. B x Q   B–K4
20. QR–Q1 !   K–B1

The threat was B–B5ch.

21. P–B4 !   B x KtP
22. R–B3 !   . . . .

A curious position. The immedi-
ate threat is R–QKt3 winning
the Bishop, and against this
Black has no defense; for if 22.
. . . P–B4; 23. R–QKt3, B–
B3; 24. B–B5ch, K–Kt2; 25 B–
B6 ! winning the Rook.

22. . . . . .   B–Kt2

Despair.

23. R–QKt3   B–R6
24. R x B   . . . .

The rest is simple.

24. . . . .   R–KKt1
25. R–KKt3   R x R
26. P x R   B–Q4
27. B–Kt3   B x B
28. P x B   K–K1
29. P–QKt4   R–QKt1
30. B–B5   R–B1
31. R–R1   R–B3
32. K–B2   P–B4
33. K–K3   P–B3
34. K–Q4   K–B2
35. K–B4   K–Kt3
36. R–Q1   K–R4
37. R–Q6   R x R
38. B x R   K–Kt5
39. B–K7   K x P

40. B x P	K x BP	Here are some more products of
41. K−B5	Black Resigns.	Euwe's artistry.

Max Euwe

Loman

Euwe−TO PLAY

Rotterdam, 1923

1. Kt x QP   B x Kt
2. Q−R8ch   B x Q
3. R̄ x B mate.

Alekhine

Euwe−TO PLAY

2nd Match Game, 1935

1. Q̄−R1 !   R−Kt7
2. R̄−B7   Q−K1

This loses at once. The main variation was 43. . . . Q−B4; 44. Q−Q5 ! (threatening R x Pch), Q x Q; 45. B x Q, B−K6 !; 46. P−B7, B−Kt8; 47. B−Kt2 !, R−QB7; 48. K−R4 !, P−Kt4ch; 49. K̄−R3 followed by R−B6ch and wins. (Euwe)

3. P−B7   R−QB7

Either 4. Q−Q5 or Q−K6 could not have been parried.

4. Q−Kt7 !   Black Resigns.

Weenink   Amsterdam, 1923

Euwe—TO PLAY

1. R x P !	P x R
2. P—Kt7	R—QKt1
3. Q x QRP	Q—K2
4. B—Kt5 !	Q x B
5. Q—Q6ch	K—K1
6. Q x QRch	K—B2
7. Q x Rch	K x Q
8. P—Kt8 = Qch	Black Resigns.

Samuel Reshevsky

Reshevsky has had two chess careers: one as a child prodigy, the other as a grandmaster.

Born in a small Polish town in 1911, Sammy learned the moves when he was three or four, and at five he was already so strong that he was giving simultaneous exhibitions. During the war his town was occupied by the Germans, and the German general in charge of the province called Sammy to his headquarters and commanded him to play some chess. Sammy of course won and told the general, "You play war, I play chess." Oh for the privileges of childhood!

After the war the child prodigy was taken on a grand tour. There have been a few other child prodigies in the history of the game—Capablanca, Morphy, Pomar—but none could compare with Reshevsky. Added to his phenomenal ability at chess was the uninhibited personality of a child who has the feeling that he can get away with anything. This combination made Sammy tremendously popular; wherever he went the houses were sold out. Many people who came to see him thought it was some kind of hoax, but all came away convinced. His strength at the age of eight or nine was that of a master, though not what it is today. In 1919 he played a serious game with Grandmaster Vidmar in Vienna, and lost (he took his revenge seventeen years later at Nottingham), but it was clear that he was good enough to play in master tournaments.

Just what made him so strong puzzled everybody. Psychologists in Switzerland put him through a number of tests, but could find little; evidently his chess gift was specific and unique.

Sammy soon received an invitation to visit the United States, and he toured this country for several years. Charlie Chaplin offered him a movie job, but his advisers turned it down for religious reasons. In 1923 he played in a small masters' tournament in New York; while he did not do too well he showed that he had to be taken seriously.

At that time the philanthropist Julius Rosenwald took an interest in him, and financed his education until he became of age, on condition that Sammy stay away from chess. He became an accountant by profession, but recently abandoned it to devote all his time to his first love.

In 1931 Reshevsky returned to the chess world; he played in a Western Championship Tournament at Tulsa and captured first prize. For a few years after that his results were good but not outstanding. Then, in 1934 he won first prize at Syracuse ahead of all the leading American players, and immediately assumed top ranking among American masters. He has held this ranking to the present time, though it is regrettable that the rivalry with the writer was never definitively settled by a match.

In 1935 Reshevsky returned to the international arena in a tournament at Margate, England. Here he astonished everybody by beating Capablanca and finishing first. The next year he won the first U. S. Championship title and tied for third at Nottingham, thus placing himself definitely among the elite who were considered serious challengers for the world championship.

In the ensuing years Reshevsky almost invariably won a high prize in every contest in which he took part. However, his results in the United States have been better than his results abroad. He won the U. S. Championship four times (tied once). But in the world championship tournament in 1948 he was somewhat of a disappointment.

Reshevsky's style is a curious one. Time and again he gets into lost or impossible positions—yet he wins. How does he do it?

* Twenty-five years ago, when Sammy was touring the world as a boy wonder, another prodigy, who was then getting his Ph.D from the University of Chicago at fifteen, was asked to explain Reshevsky's success. "Sammy has a secret move," he replied, "and whenever he gets into a tight spot he plays it."

Many people who watch Reshevsky today are often inclined to think that explanations involving secret moves have a great deal of truth to them. Time and again he gets into a poor or mediocre or even lost position, with fifteen or twenty moves to make in two minutes. Bang-bang-bang is all the spectators hear; and when the smoke has cleared—Sammy has won. How does he do it?

Several years ago Reinfeld was preparing a book of Reshevsky's games, and he asked me to contribute an introductory article. Why he asked me of all people I can't imagine, but anyhow I wrote the article. My main

* This passage is reproduced from my book, *The World is a Chessboard*, by courtesy of the David McKay Co.

point was that Sammy's success is primarily due to a will-to-win which was far stubborner than that of any other grandmaster. Others get tired, or excited, or rattled, or lose interest, or lose hope; Reshevsky never.

But, the reader may well object, surely that is not enough. Lots of lesser mortals want to win just as fiercely, and it does them no good. True enough, the will-to-win is only one aspect in which he differs from other masters.

There is more. Technically, Reshevsky is characterized above all by superb tactical skill. Unlike Euwe and Fine he does not bother much about the openings. Unlike Botvinnik he is little concerned with the strategical backbone of the game. What he cares about are tactical combinations, and these he handles to perfection. That is why he does well in time-pressure: with both players moving fast there is no opportunity for deep strategy—all that counts is tactics. And Reshevsky generally manages to see a little farther than the other fellow.

At his best, Reshevsky is notable for his mastery of the subtleties of position play. His style has often been likened to Capablanca's. Here is his celebrated win against the Cuban, which showed the chess world that the former child prodigy was now an adult prodigy.

RESHEVSKY	CAPABLANCA

Margate, 1935
Queen's Gambit Declined

1. P–Q4	Kt–KB3
2. P–QB4	P–K3
3. Kt–QB3	P–Q4
4. B–Kt5	QKt–Q2
5. P x P	. . . .

One of Reshevsky's favorite variations. Against Capa it has a psychological value since he lost an important game with it to Alekhine in their match.

5.	P x P
6. P–K3	B–K2
7. B–Q3	O–O
8. Q–B2	. . . .

Keeping the development of his KKt in reserve. Alekhine's idea, 8. KKt–K2 and castling Q-side, is excellent.

8.	P–B4

A weakening move, perhaps played to avoid the Alekhine variation. 8. . . . P–B3 is preferable.

9. Kt–B3   P–B5
10. B–B5   R–K1
11. O–O   P–KKt3
12. B–R3   Kt–B1

Better was 12. . . . P–QR3. Reshevsky now evolves an interesting combination.

13. B x B   R x B
14. B x Kt   B x B

It looks as though Black has overcome the opening difficulties; he is in for a surprise.

15. P–QKt3 ! . . . .

A subtle and profound idea. If in reply 15. . . . P x P ?; 16. Q x P wins the QP.

15. . . . .   Q–R4?

The fatal mistake, though Black could hardly have known it. 15. . . . Q–Q2 was essential.

16. P–QKt4 ! . . . .

A beautiful move which artificially isolates the QP and builds up a variety of threats.

16. . . . .   Q–Q1

Forced; if 16. . . . Q x KtP; 17. QR–Kt1, Q–Q3; 18. R x P is crushing.

17. Q–R4 !   P–QR3
18. P–Kt5 ! . . . .

Now Black's Pawns are attacked in many ways.

18. . . . .   R–K3
19. QR–Kt1 . . . .

Threatening to win a Pawn by P x P and Q–Kt5. The move also prevents the blockade of the Q-side with . . . P–QR4, for then 20. P–Kt6 ! wins a Pawn, e.g., 20. . . . R x P; 21. R x R, Q x R; 22. Kt x P, Q–Q3; 23. Q x RP.

19. . . . .   R–Kt1
20. R–Kt2   B–K2

Hoping to prepare . . . P–QR4.

21. P x P   . . . .

Keeps the Q-side open.

21. . . . .   R x P
22. Q–B2   Kt–K3
23. KR–Kt1   R–R2
24. P–QR4   Kt–B2
25. Kt–K5   . . . .

Threatening Kt–B6. Black has managed to defend against all the threats thus far, but his pieces are awkwardly placed and his position uncomfortable.

25. . . . .   Q–K1
26. P–B4   . . . .

Planning P–B5 by opportunity.

26. . . . .   P–B3
27. Kt–Kt4   Q–Q2
28. P–R3   K–Kt2

29. Kt−B2   B−R6
30. R−R2   B−Q3
31. Kt(B2)−Q1 . . . .

Maneuvering to find an opening. One possibility is Kt−Kt5, Kt x Kt; R x Kt and Kt−B3; another is P−B5.

31. . . . .   P−B4

Better was 31. . . . R−R3 to reply to Kt−Kt5 with . . . Kt−K1.

32. Kt−Kt5   R−R4
33. Kt x Kt   B x Kt
34. Kt−B3 !   . . . .

The grand tour of the Kt from KB3 to K5 to KKt4 to KB2 to Q1 to QB3 is striking. Now the threat is R(R2)−Kt2 and R−Kt5.

34. . . . .   Q−K3
35. Q−B2   P−Kt3
36. Q−B3   R−Q1
37. R(R2)−Kt2 . . . .

Now it looks as though the QP cannot be defended, but Capa finds something.

37. . . . .   Q−K2 !

So that if 38. R−Kt5, R x R; 39. R x R, Q−R6 !; e.g., 40. Kt x P, P−B6 ! and Black wins!

38. R−Kt4   R−Q2
39. K−R1   B−Q1

R−Kt5 is still not feasible; what is White to do?

40. P−Kt4 !   . . . .

With so many of Black's pieces tied to the defense of the QP, he prepares a K-side attack.

40. . . . .   P x P
41. P x P   Q−Q3
42. K−Kt1   B−B2
43. K−B2 !   . . . .

Another remarkable theme: the White King is headed for QB2.

43. . . . .   R−B2 !

And again Capa finds an ingenious defense. If now 44. K−K2, P−Kt4 gives Black a dangerous counterattack.

44. P−Kt5 !   B−Q1
45. K−K2   B x P ?

The only inaccuracy in an otherwise perfect defense. After 45. . . . Q−K3, threatening Q−B4 White's task would have been much harder.

46. R x P   Q−R6
47. K−Q2 !   . . . .

A comparison of this with the previous diagram shows the profundity of White's winning scheme. By defending the Kt with his King, White is free to attack.

| 47. | . . . . | B–K2 |
| 48. | R–Kt7 | R x RP |

Desperation. If 48. . . . . Q–Q3; 49. R(Kt7)–Kt5, R x R; 50. P x R !, R–B4; 51. P–Kt6 and wins.

| 49. | Q x P | . . . . |

Of course not 49. Kt x R ??, Q–Q6ch and Black wins!

| 49. | . . . . | R–R4 |
| 50. | Q x P | . . . . |

Finis. Reshevsky's strategy has torn apart Black's position. The remainder is easy.

50.	. . . .	R–R4
51.	K–Q3	Q–R1
52.	Q–K6	Q–R6
53.	R–Q7	. . . .

| 53. | . . . . | R(R4)–KB4 |
| 54. | R–Kt3 ! | . . . . |

Wins a piece.

| 54. | . . . . | Q–R8 |
| 55. | R x B | Q–B8ch |

One last spite check.

| 56. | K–Q2 | Black Resigns. |

Reshevsky is one of the greatest masters of the defense in the history of the game. Here is an outstanding effort.

LANDAU   RESHEVSKY

Kemeri, 1937
Queen's Gambit Accepted

1.	P–Q4	P–Q4
2.	P–QB4	P x P
3.	Kt–KB3	Kt–KB3
4.	P–K3	P–QR3
5.	B x P	P–K3
6.	O–O	P–B4
7.	Q–K2	P–QKt4
8.	B–Q3	. . . .

Better 8. B–Kt3.

| 8. | . . . . | P x P |
| 9. | P x P | B–Kt2 |

Landau was an attacker par excellence, and Reshevsky of course

knew what he was letting himself in for.

10. P—QR4!	P—Kt5
11. QKt—Q2	B—K2
12. Kt—B4	P—QR4

To stop P—R5.

13. B—B4	O—O
14. KR—Q1	Kt—B3
15. B—K5!	. . . .

An ingenious idea. Landau now
manages to conjure up many
threats.

15.	Kt—Q4
16. Q—K4	P—Kt3
17. Q—Kt4	. . . .

The battle is taking on a more
difficult shape. White is preparing to make inroads on the K-
side, and Black must tread care-
fully.

| 17. . . . . | Kt—B3 |
| 18. Q—B4 | Kt—R4 !? |

To shift this Kt from Q4 to
KR4, let the White Queen pene-
trate to KR6 . . . what's up?
We shall soon see.

19. Q—K3 !   . . . .

Avoiding the trap. If 19. Q—R6,
Kt x B !; 20. P x Kt, B x Kt; 21.
B x P, BP x B !; 22. R x Q, QR x
R; 23. P x B, Kt—B5 ! wins.

19.	R—B1
20. QR—B1	Kt x B
21. P x Kt	B—B4 !
22. Q—R6	Q—K2 !
23. Kt—Kt5 ?	. . . .

White finally falls for a trap. 23.

Kt x P ? is refuted by . . . B x
Kt, but 23. B—K2 ! was excellent.

| 23. . . . . | P—B3 |
| 24. P x P | . . . . |

Expecting the routine . . .
Kt x P.

24. . . . .   B x Pch !!

A bolt from the Black.

25. K x B   . . . .

White suddenly discovers that
he is lost. If 25. K—R1, R x P; 26.
Kt x QRP, R x R; 27. R x R, B—
K6 and wins.

| 25. . . . . | Q x Pch |
| 26. Kt—B3 | . . . . |

Or 26. K—Kt1, Q—B7ch and
mates.

26.	B x Kt
27. P x B	Q x Pch
28. K—Kt1	R—B5 !

Nothing can be done against
. . . R—Kt5ch.

29. Q x R   . . . .

Resigning is no better.

| 29. . . . . | Kt x Q |
| 30. B—B1 | R—B4 |

More "brilliant" but a little less effective was 30. . . . R x Kt.

31. R—Q8ch . . . .

Spite check.

31. . . . . K—Kt2
32. R—Q7ch K—R3

White Resigns.

A typical Reshevsky game.

Reshevsky can also produce brilliancies a la Morphy with the best of them. Here is one of his snappiest.

RESHEVSKY VASCONCELLOS

Boston, 1944
French Defense

1. P—K4 . . . .

Sammy rarely opens with the KP, but here he already had first prize clinched and had nothing to lose.

1. . . . . P—K3
2. P—Q4 P—Q4
3. P—K5 . . . .

Reshevsky obviously has a prepared variation.

3. . . . . P—QB4
4. P x P Kt—Q2
5. Kt—KB3 B x P?

Inconsistent. . . . Kt—K2 is best.

6. B—Q3 . . . .

Now simple development gives White an overwhelming game.

6. . . . . Kt—K2

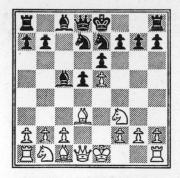

7. O—O Kt—QB3
8. B—KB4 Q—B2

More loss of time. 8. . . . B—Kt3—B2 was a preferable idea.

9. Kt—B3! . . . .

Ingeniously defending the KP: if 9. . . . Kt x KP?; 10. Kt x Kt, Kt x Kt; 11. Q—R5!, B—Q3; 12. Kt—Kt5, winning a piece.

9. . . . . P—QR3
10. R—K1 Q—Kt3

In despair he goes Pawn-hunting.

11. B—Kt3 Q x P

12. Kt x P !   P x Kt
13. R — Kt1   Q — R6
14. P — K6   Kt — B3 ?

Vasconcellos is in one of those positions where almost anything looks better than what he does, but is not really. However, here 14. . . . P x P; 15. R x Pch, Kt — K2 was a stronger defense.

15. P x Pch   K x P
16. B — R4   Kt — QKt5 ?

Another mistake which seals his doom with trumpets. 16. . . . B — K2 was absolutely necessary.

17. Kt — K5ch   K — B1
18. B x Kt   Kt x B

Or 18. . . . P x B; 19. Q — R5 !!!, P x Kt; 20. R x P with numerous mating threats.

19. B x Pch !!   K x B
20. R x Pch !!!   . . . .

This is the hidden point. On 19. . . . B x R; 20. Q — Kt4ch leads to a quick mate: 21. . . . K — B3; 22. Q — B3ch, K — Kt2; 23. Q — B7ch, K — R3; 24. Q — B6ch, K — R4; 25. P — Kt4 mate.

20. . . . .   B — K2
21. Q — R5 !   . . . .

Every White piece except the Queen is en prise — and still he wins. Mind over matter!

21. . . . .   R — B1

There are many ways to lose. The prettiest is 21. . . . B x R; 22. Q — B7ch, K — R3; 23. Kt — Kt 4ch, K — Kt4; 24. Q — Kt7ch, K — R4; 25. Q — R6ch !, K x Kt; 26. P — R3ch, K — B4; 27. P — Kt4 mate.

22. Q — Kt5ch   K — R1

Now every White piece is en prise.

23. Kt — Kt6ch !   P x Kt
24. Q — R6ch   K — Kt1
25. Q x Pch   K — R1
26. R(Kt7) x B   Black Resigns.

It is mate. Even the loser must have enjoyed this game.

Here are some more samples of Sammy's skill.

Santasiere

Reshevsky—TO PLAY

U. S. Championship, 1938

1. R(B5) x QPch !	P x R
2. Q x Pch	K—B2
3. Q—B5ch	K—Q2
4. Q—K7ch	K—B3
5. Q—K6ch	Black Resigns.

Treysman

Reshevsky—TO PLAY

U. S. Championship, 1938

1. P—B6ch ! K—R3

Or . . . K x P; 2. Kt—K8 dbl ch wins the exchange.

2. K—Kt3 !	K—R2
3. R x R	R x R
4. P—Kt5	R—Kt3
5. R—R6	R—Kt1
6. B—B6	B—B4
7. R—R8	R x R
8. B x R	B—Q6
9. P—Kt6	B—R3
10. B—Kt7 !	Black Resigns.

Fine

Reshevsky—TO PLAY

Western Championship, Detroit, 1933

1. R x P !	Kt x R
2. R x Kt	Q—R3 ?

Best was . . . Q—Kt2; 3. Kt—Q5, K—B1; 4. Q—K4, P—B3 !

3. Q—K4	R—K2
4. Q—Kt4ch	K—B1
5. R—R5	Q—Kt2
6. Q—R4	K—K1
7. Kt—Q5	P—B4
8. Kt x R	Black Resigns.

Reuben Fine

My first impulse was to ask Euwe to write an article about me. My second impulse, since I am now a psychoanalyst, was to free associate about my chess past. The second impulse sounds more attractive.

First, in brief, the outlines of my chess career. I was born in New York in 1914, learned the moves when about eight. Chess did not become important until my last term in high school, in 1929. After that I became active at it. Throughout college I spent much of my spare time playing; and though I hate to admit it because it will probably cut down the sale of my books, I never read a book until I was already a master. In college I continued to improve and, by the time I was a senior, qualified for the United States team which went to Folkestone. For a few years after that chess occupied all my time. In 1936 I went to Europe and toured it for about two years. My major success came at the AVRO tournament in Holland in 1938, where I tied for first prize with Keres and had the pleasure of beating Alekhine twice. After 1941 there was less and less time for chess. During the war I was busy in Washington. Afterwards I took my Ph.D. in psychology, and became a psychoanalyst.

And now for some free associations . . . Alekhine was my first chess hero. In my formative years—1930, 1931—he scored his most tremendous successes, at San Remo, 1930 and Bled, 1931. The next year I met him at Pasadena; he was still very impressive, though his chess had become a little shaky. I managed to draw with him in a hard-fought game . . . Several years later stories of his goings-on began to circulate . . . Drinking . . . Wife-beating . . . He was supposed to have written two letters, one to the Russians extolling the Communist system, the other to the Germans praising the Nazi system, and put them in the wrong envelopes. Apocryphal or symbolic? . . . A great chess genius, but a sick man . . . Emanuel Lasker, the calmest chess master I ever met. I never heard him utter an angry word, or make a really unkind remark. Devoid of alibis; when I beat him at Nottingham in 1936 all he said to me was, "Young man, you play well." I wrote a book about him in collaboration with Reinfeld; the old man was so free of egotism he would not even talk about it . . . Masters I have read about and later met . . . Tartakower, at Folkestone in 1933. He no sooner met me than he said, "Young man, give me a penny for a stamp. You Americans are all rich. We Europeans are all poor." Tartakower and Yates—Yates and Tartakower—they were the backbone of every tournament. Tartakower was brilliant, but too cynical. Had he written less and studied more he might have hit the top . . . Spielmann turned out to be a frightened old man whose brilliance came out only in chess . . . Political squabbles among the chess masters, which in those times were no laughing matter . . . In Nazi Germany a famous grand-master tried to force his journalistic rivals into concentration camps to get their columns away . . . The Indian Sultan Khan. In 1933 his Maharajah invited the American team, then in London, for an evening; when we came in the Maharajah said: "It is an honor for you to be here; ordinarily I converse only with my greyhounds." Sultan Khan, the great chess master, waited on table. The "Sultan" was just a first name, and he was really a serf to the Maharajah . . . Monterey in 1934; two games with Torre. He warned me to stay away from women because they cost too much money. Poor Carlos—he could still play good chess in spite of his sickness . . . Eminent psychoanalysts with whom I've played chess; even their personalities came out over the chessboard. One kept on saying to me after every move, "What is your diagnosis?" . . . Countries where chess is popular, and countries where it is not. In Holland, where everybody plays chess, only one really great chess master has been produced. And in America, where so few play, so many have been produced. In Russia chess is the national sport. I once gave an exhibition at a Moscow University, where literally half the student body attended . . . A chess tournament in Hollywood in 1945, just before the war ended. Lots of movie stars came to kibitz. Marlene Dietrich came with her entourage and asked us how we could play chess when men were dying. Linda Darnell, the most beautiful woman I've ever seen, stayed through the last two days, and helped Gregory Ratoff distribute the prizes. Her husband played me some games, and had his own version of the rules. When I beat him with the usual rules, he complained, "If you play my way, I can beat you." The movie stars were so famous and so insecure. . . . Capa fighting his battle with Alekhine to the bitter end. In 1937 he showed me some of the correspondence with Alekhine about the world championship match and asked me to support some of his claims . . . A chess tournament at Semmering, the famous mountain resort near Vienna; it was out of season and there were more players than spectators . . . Keres, the innocent; once we went to a night club, he left, said he was going to visit the zoo the next day . . . stories about the old days; how Tchigorin accepted the invitation to Cambridge Springs in 1904 only on condition that women be available in the town . . . memories of my first days at the Marshall Chess Club. Frank Marshall with his Windsor tie, always willing to analyze any position. Most chess masters do not like to play chess in their spare time, but Frank was an exception . . . Gruenfeld with his fantastic knowledge of the openings; he must have known everything by heart . . . curious coincidences—the other day at a high school reunion dinner I met a fellow alumnus, now a physician, who had done an autopsy on Capablanca. The impression of his brain was that it was larger than average and had more convolutions . . . Flohr once told me in 1932 that a brain research institute in Hamburg had offered him 300 marks for the right to examine his brain after he died . . . Jews in chess; why are so many chess masters Jewish? Concert violinists too . . . People I have met through chess; chess players are a kind of international brotherhood, an independent society . . . Once I saw a chess master become so absorbed in his game that one of the spectators burned a hole in his pants and he did not even notice it . . . Few games absorb people as completely as chess; that is the reason for its universal appeal . . . Euwe-Alekhine match in 1937, where I was Euwe's second. I analyzed adjourned games; everybody knew it, but nobody was supposed to say so. I always had the impression that Euwe remained unnaturally calm during games; better, like Alekhine, to be continually jumping up and down . . . my second try on an American team, at Warsaw, in 1935. They put me on first board and everybody commented on the foolishness of the Americans putting a twenty-year-old at top board. Keres and I battled out a battle royal there, that year two unknowns, two years later two very-well-knowns . . . Andre Steiner who came to Kemeri in 1937 chaperoned by his father, who was still bossing him around like a schoolboy; a comical sight . . . and many other memories better left unsaid, even in free association . . . maybe at some future time it can all come out. . . .

In master tournaments, prepared opening variations are a most feared weapon; sometimes days of analysis are required to find the right reply, and in the crowded two and one-half hours allotted the tournament player he can only too easily go wrong. Here is a game where I had the satisfaction of beating world champion Botvinnik with a prepared variation.

FINE   BOTVINNIK

AVRO tournament, Holland, 1938

French Defense

1. P—K4   . . . .

Before this tournament I was known as a 1. P—Q4 player, hence my first move must have come as somewhat of a surprise to Botvinnik.

1. . . . .   P—K3

Botvinnik does not vary. Against 1. P—K4 he almost invariably

plays the French; sometimes he tries the Sicilian.

2. P—Q4	P—Q4
3. Kt—QB3	B—Kt5
4. P—K5	P—QB4

5. P x P !?   . . . .

This is the prepared move. Unlike Euwe, I make it a rule not to analyze such lines too profoundly before the game because it is most essential to be able to meet whatever surprises come up over-the-board, and not everything can be foreseen.

5. . . . .   **Kt—K2**

The advance 5. . . . P—Q5; 6. P—QR3 is favorable for White.

6. Kt—B3   **QKt—B3**
7. B—Q3   **P—Q5**

Accepting the complications. On 7. . . . B x P; 8. O—O, White's game is freer.

8. P—QR3   **B—R4**
9. P—QKt4   **Kt x KtP**
10. P x Kt   **B x P**
11. B—Kt5ch . . . .

Another possibility was O—O, but the text was part of the prepared variation.

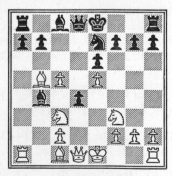

11. . . . .   **Kt—B3?**

The fatal error. Necessary was 11. . . . B—Q2; 12. Q x P, B x

Ktch; *13.* Q x B, B x B; *14.* Kt—Q4 with about equal chances.

12. B x Ktch **P x B**
13. R—R4 !   **B x Ktch**
14. B—Q2   . . . .

Suddenly Black discovers that he is lost. The Bishop is hopelessly shut in, and it is only a question of time before White's superior development makes itself felt.

14. . . . .   **P—B3**

Desperately striving to free his Bishop.

15. O—O   **O—O**
16. B x B   **P x B**
17. Q—K1   **P—QR4**
18. Q x P   **B—R3**
19. KR—R1   **B—Kt4**

Hoping for 20. R x P, which would bring some freedom to the Black pieces.

20. R—Q4 !   **Q—K2**
21. R—Q6   **P—R5**

To tie White's Rook down.

22. Q—K3 !   . . . .

Threatening to win a Pawn, but not in an obvious way.

22. ....   R—R2
23. Kt—Q2!   ....

The point: the poor Bishop will be driven away.

23. ....   P—R6

The Pawn goes anyhow.

24. P—QB4   B—R5
25. P x P   Q x P
26. R x RP   R—K1
27. P—R3   ....

After this quiet move Black might as well resign.

27. ....   R(R2)—R1
28. Kt—B3   Q—Kt7
29. Kt—K5   Q—Kt8ch
30. K—R2   Q—B4
31. Q—Kt3!   Black Resigns.

There are too many threats on all sides. The most immediate one is R—Q7. If in reply 31. .... R—K2; 32. R x B!, R x R; 33. R —Q8ch. And if 31. .... R—R2; 32. R—B3, Q—K5; 33. Kt—Q7!, K—R1; 34. R—B7, R—KKt1; 35. Kt—K5 and so on.

In terms of over-all strategic planning and tactical execution, I consider the following to be the best game I have ever played.

FINE   FLOHR

AVRO tournament,
Holland, 1938

1. P—K4   P—K3
2. P—Q4   P—Q4

3. Kt—QB3   B—Kt5
4. P—K5   P—QB4
5. B—Q2   ....

5. P x P, which I tried against Botvinnik (see the previous game), no longer had any surprise punch to it.

5. ....   Kt—K2
6. Kt—B3   Kt—B4?

Meaningless. 6. .... QKt—B3 equalizes.

7. P x P!   B x P
8. B—Q3   Kt—R5

After his weak sixth move he must lose more time. On 8. .... Kt—K2; 9. O—O, he still cannot castle because of the routine sacrifice at KR7.

9. O—O   Kt—B3
10. R—K1   P—KR3

To castle. On 10. .... O—O? at once, 11. B x Pch wins.

11. Kt—R4!   B—B1

Black is faced by a choice of evils. On 11. .... B—K2; 12.

Kt x Kt, B x Kt; 13. Q–Kt4 is
powerful.

12. R–QB1   . . . .

Preparing P–QB4, which would
get this Rook into the game.

12. . . . .   B–Q2

Threatening to win a Pawn by
. . . Kt x Ktch followed by . . .
Kt x KP.

13. Kt x Kt !   Q x Kt
14. P–QB4 !   P x P
15. R x P   Q–Q1

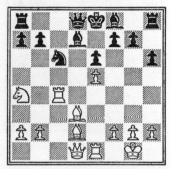

White's development is plainly
superior, but the problem of how
to continue is still not easy to answer. In such positions it is necessary to find moves that keep the
attack going.

16. Q–R5 !!   . . . .

Prevents 16. . . . P–QKt4 because of 17. R–KB4, and prepares other threats.

16. . . . .   Kt–K2

On the immediate . . . P–
KKt3; 17. B x KtP crashes
through.

17. R–Q4   P–KKt3
18. Q–B3   Q–D2
19. Kt–B3   . . . .

This Kt must be remobilized.

19. . . . .   Kt–B4
20 Kt–Kt5 !   Q–Kt3

21. R x B !!   . . . .

Decisive. Now Black's game
falls apart.

21. . . . .   K x R
22. P–KKt4   Kt–R5

If instead 22. . . . Kt–K2; 23.
Q x BP and the position is hopeless. The best chance was 22.
. . . Q–B3, although 23. R–K4
still wins.

23. Q x BPch   B–K2
24. B–Kt4   QR–K1

Threatening . . . R–KB1.

25. B x B   R x B
26. Q–B6   P–R3

White can regain his material,
but he has an even stronger variation in mind.

27. R–Q1!   P x Kt
28. B–K4 dis ch Black Resigns.

After 28. . . . K–B2; 29. Q x
R(R8), R–Q2; 30. R–B1ch, the
Queen must be given up to stop
mate.

We are often asked how many
moves we see ahead. Sometimes,
as in the following game, we do
not see ahead at all except for
the crucial combinations. Our
feel for the position tells us that
something will happen and, as
here, it does.

FINE   STEINER

Hollywood, 1945
Queen's Gambit Accepted

1. P–Q4	P–Q4
2. P–QB4	P x P
3. Kt–KB3	Kt–KB3
4. P–K3	P–K3
5. B x P	P–B4
6. O–O	P–QR3
7. Q–K2	P–QKt4
8. B–Kt3	B–Kt2

Black has advanced his Q-side
Pawns too quickly, and they must
be broken up.

9. P–QR4	P–B5?

Surprisingly, the fatal mistake.
9. . . . P–Kt5 was essential.

10. B–B2	Kt–B3
11. P x P	P x P
12. R x R	Q x R
13. Kt–B3	Q–R4

Forced, for if 13. . . . P–Kt5;
14. Kt–QKt5 wins a Pawn.

14. P–K4   . . . .

The position where I did not
bother to look ahead; I felt confident that something would turn
up.

14. . . . .   Kt–Q2

If 14. . . . P–Kt5; 15. P–Q5,
Kt–Q1; 16. B–R4ch wins.

15. P–Q5   Kt–Q1

Black is beginning to consolidate his position, and here I had
to look ahead.

16. Kt–Q4!   P–Kt5

17. Kt(B3)–Kt5!   . . . .

Offering a piece for the attack.

17. . . . . P–K4

On the alternative 17. . . . P–
Kt6; 18. P x P ! wins, e.g., 18.
. . . P x P; 19. Q–R5ch ! K–K2
(forced); 20. B–Kt1.

18. Q x P P x Kt
19. Kt–B7ch K–K2
20. P–K5 ! . . . .

The immediate threat is mate.

20. . . . . . Kt x P

Forced.

21. R–K1 P–B3
22. P–Q6ch !! . . . .

The decisive move.

22. . . . . . K x P

22. . . . K–Q2; 23. B–B5ch is
hopeless.

23. Kt–Kt5ch . . . .

When I originally annotated
this game I wrote: "It is a pity
that Steiner did not allow the
continuation which is really the
crux of the entire combinative
series beginning with White's
sixteenth move. It runs 23. . . .
K–K2; 24. R x Ktch !, P x R; 25.
B–Kt5ch, K–K1; 26. Kt–B7ch,
K–Q2; 27. B–B5ch, K–Q3; 28.
Kt–K8 mate."
Returning now to the game.

23. . . . . Q x Kt
24. Q x Q K–B2
25. Q–R5ch Black Resigns.

One of my most satisfying
games.
Here are some more combinations from my collection.

Dake   Chicago, 1933

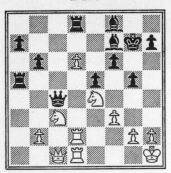

Fine—TO PLAY

1. Kt x BP !!   K x Kt
2. Kt—K4ch   K—Kt2
3. R—QB2 !   Q—R5
4. Q x Pch   B—Kt3
5. R—B7ch   K—Kt1
6. Q x Bch   Black Resigns.

Grossman   New York, 1933

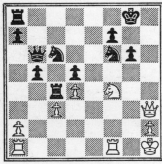

Fine—TO PLAY

1. Kt x KtP !   K—Kt2
2. R—KKt1 !!   P x Kt
3. R x Pch   K x R
4. Q—K6 !   Kt x P ?

4. . . . Kt—K4 !! draws.

5. R—Kt1ch   K—R3
6. Q—K3ch   K—R2
7. Q—K7ch   K—R3
8. Q—Kt7ch   Black Resigns.

Georges Koltanowsky

The Belgian, Georges Koltanowsky, occupies a unique position in the history of chess—he is a specialist in blindfold play. His over-the-board strength is not outstanding, that of a good master, but in blindfold exhibitions he has few peers. One of his favorite tricks is to have the name of a city entered on each of the sixty-four squares of a board before he begins an exhibition. When he finishes he does a Knight's tour blindfold from city to city! He knows the chessboard better than many men know their own homes.

Shortly before the war Kolty moved to this country, where he has since settled down and become an American citizen.

KOLTANOWSKY   WALPOLE

One of eight blindfold games
England, 1937
Queen's Pawn Opening

1. P–Q4   Kt–KB3
2. Kt–KB3   P–K3
3. P–K3   . . . .

Koltanowsky has always been fond of his countryman Colle's system.

3. . . . .   P–Q4
4. B–Q3   QKt–Q2
5. QKt–Q2   B–Q3
6. P–K4   P x P
7. Kt x P   Kt x Kt
8. B x Kt   Kt–B3
9. B–Q3   O–O
10. O–O   P–KR3

To stop the pin.

11. Q–K2   B–Q2

White has come out of the opening with greater mobility, but to convert it into a win with seven other games going blindfold is quite a feat.

12. Kt–K5   P–B4
13. P x P !   B x P

14. R–Q1   Q–K2
15. B–KB4   QR–Q1
16. Q–B3   B–B1
17. P–B3   P–KKt4

A frantic effort to get some air.

18. B–Kt3   K–Kt2
19. P–KR4   R–KR1
20. B–B2   P–Kt3
21. Kt–B6   B–Kt2
22. P–Kt4 !   . . . .

So that if 22. . . . . B–Q3; 23. Kt x Q, B x Q; 24. R x B, winning a piece.

22. . . . .   Q–K1

Allows a neat finish, but there was no real defense.

23. Q x Ktch !! K x Q
24. B–K5 mate.

William Winter

For a number of years Winter was one of England's outstanding representatives in international chess. His play, as in the following game, is notable for its combination of strategic accuracy and brilliance.

WINTER   MIKENAS

Lodz, 1935
Dutch Defense

1.	P–Q4	P–K3
2.	Kt–KB3	P–KB4
3.	P–KKt3	Kt–KB3
4.	B–Kt2	B–K2
5.	O–O	O–O
6.	P–B4	P–Q3

Better is . . . P–Q4 immediately.

7.	Kt–B3	Q–K1
8.	R–K1	. . . .

Q–B2 is also strong. The present game helped to refute Black's set-up.

8.	. . . .	Q–R4
9.	P–K4	P x P
10.	Kt x P	Kt x Kt
11.	R x Kt	Kt–B3
12.	B–B4 !	. . . .

Finely conceived. The point will soon be clear.

12.	. . . .	B–B3
13.	P–KR4	P–KR3

14. R–B1 !   . . . .

Now we see what White is driving at: P–B5 is a serious threat.

14.	. . . .	P–R3
15.	P–B5 !	Kt x P !

A combinative reply. On the stodgy 15. . . . . P–Q4; 16. R–K2, R–B2; 17. Q–Q2 White's game is as good as won.

16. R x Kt !   . . . .

An elegant rejoinder. The alternative 16. Kt x Kt ?, Q x Qch; 17. R x Q, P–K4 is much weaker.

16.	. . . .	P–K4
17.	R–Q5 !	P–B3

Apparently regaining the piece with a good game: after 18. R x QP ?, P x B Black should win.

18. P x P !!   . . . .

A brilliant reply.

18.	. . . .	P x R
19.	Q x Pch	K–R1
20.	Kt x P	. . . .

White has a powerful attack and two Pawns for the exchange; the rest is easy.

20.	B x Kt	25.	B−K3
21. B x B	Q−B2	26. B x P	B x P
22. R−B7	B−Q2	27. P−QKt4	B−K3

22. . . . Q x P ch is good only
for a spite check.

28. P−Kt5	R−Q2
29. P−Kt6	R−QKt1
30. P−Kt7	K−Kt1

23. Q x Q	R x Q	31. R−B8ch	R−Q1
24. B x P	R−K1	32. P−Q7 !	Black Resigns.
25. P−B4	. . . .		

White has too many Pawns.

A neat conclusion: if 32. . . . .
B x P; 33. B x R.

Paul Keres

Keres stands out as one of the great combinative geniuses in chess history. Unlike Alekhine, who was his hero in the beginning, his combinations do not so much arise out of solid positional play, but seem to come almost from nowhere. In fact, his style is in some respects closer to that of Anderssen than to that of anyone else. Almost alone among the contemporary grandmasters, Keres essays gambits in serious play, and is responsible for many crucial innovations in them.

Paul Keres was born in 1916 in Narva, a small town in Estonia. He tells us in his autobiography that he learned chess at the age of four, by looking on when his father played; the same was true of Capablanca. His chief rival then was his brother, three years older than himself, with whom he agreed on a set of rules which only approximated the actual ones. Chess literature was virtually nonexistent in the small town in which he lived. But such was his zeal for the game that he copied down every single game that came his way, eventually reaching a total of 800 games, each of which he had played over at least twice.

His first competition came in a ten-second chess tournament at Parnu in 1929. At first he was denied admittance because of his youth, but after breaking even with the champion of Parnu in two games he was allowed to play and amazed everybody by scoring 100%. In 1930 he won first prize in a national students' tournament at Tallinn, and was already recognized as one of the leading Estonian masters.

But opportunities for play in Estonia were of course extremely limited, so Keres turned to correspondence chess. The competition was quite keen, equivalent in fact to grandmaster strength, yet the young Keres' results were outstanding. His play, however, was extraordinarily risky; he tried every conceivable gambit, one game was even opened with 1. P−KKt4. Yet he won. By 1934 he was strong enough to win the Estonian championship, and has been head and shoulders above his compatriots ever since.

The next year, in 1935, he had his chance in international competition. A small tournament was arranged at Tallinn, where he finished second, and the Estonians decided to send a team to the Warsaw tournament; Keres played first board. At Warsaw he did rather well, ending up with a 67% score, and several fantastically brilliant games focused the attention of the chess world on him.

In 1936 he took part in a number of individual international tournaments. Here he gave evidence not only of great ability, but also of great unsteadiness, which has remained characteristic of him ever since. At Bad Nauheim in 1936 he tied for first with Alekhine; shortly thereafter, at Dresden, in a weaker field, he tied for eighth place in a ten-man tournament.

The earlier unsteadiness was ironed out somewhat in 1937, where he scored a brilliant series of victories, culminating in first prize at Semmering-Baden, ahead of Fine, Reshevsky, Flohr and Capablanca. By this time he was definitely in the ranks of the contenders for the world championship.

He then returned to his studies, and was inactive in chess until late the next year, when he tied for first prize with Fine at the AVRO tournament in Holland. By the application of the Sonnenborn-Berger system he was declared the official winner and challenger for the world title. Needless to say, negotiations for a match with Alekhine fell through.

Shortly after his great success at the AVRO tournament, Keres went to Russia to play in the Leningrad-Moscow tournament, where he finished twelfth in a field of eighteen players. As he puts it, "what a fall after so brilliant an achievement!"

During and after the war years Keres' play has fallen off slightly. He has a way of overestimating certain opponents. Before that was true of Alekhine; now it is true of Botvinnik. In Russian tournaments he has never been able even to come close to Botvinnik, and this has had a depressing effect on his play against the other masters. Several times he has won the Soviet championship; at other times he has done quite badly. While still in the foremost ranks of the contenders for the world's championship he must still get over the troublesome unsteadiness in his play if he is ever to win top honors.

Keres himself gives this description of his style:

"My style is generally considered one that tends towards combinative complications. This was unquestionably true of the period 1935–37, in which the influence of my correspondence play dominated. When playing by correspondence, I sought to complicate positions as much as possible, even in the opening stage, as I feared that a positional struggle might become boring. I retained the same policy in my early tournaments, but after several disastrous experiences, I had to change my views. I first adopted a more sensible style in the Semmering tournament, and with excellent results. In 1938 my chief problem was, therefore, to become more familiar with this new style, which gives preference to the more solid and positional aspects of the game. My experiences have taught me that this is the style which is the proper one against opponents of equal strength. Hence I have become a devotee of the solid openings, and in the middle game I undertake risky attacks only when the chances favor me. My inclination is now toward the accumulation of slight advantages, although to translate these into victory is more arduous than to win—or lose!—by means of direct attack."

No one is a good objective judge of himself, and what Keres wrote was more wish than reality. His great forte remains in the area of the sudden unforeseen attack; when the accumulation of small advantages is involved, he often does quite poorly. But clearly a struggle is going on in his mind—to attack or not to attack, and this struggle must account for the unsteadiness he sometimes displays.

In personality Keres is again the opposite of what one would expect an attacking genius to be. He is modest and quiet to the point of being withdrawn. For a while he was a student of mathematics, but the war interrupted his plans, and he has become a professional chess master, with all his energies devoted to the game.

At the Warsaw Team Tournament in 1935 Keres was still a young unknown. Here is the game which catapulted him to world fame.

KERES   WINTER

Warsaw Team Tournament,

1935
Sicilian Defense

1. P—K4   P—QB4
2. Kt—KB3   Kt—KB3

The Nimzovitch Variation—a risky line against Keres. But how could Winter know who Keres was?

3. P—K5   Kt—Q4
4. Kt—B3   P—K3

Better 4. . . . Kt x Kt and . . . P—Q4.

5. Kt x Kt   P x Kt
6. P—Q4   P—Q3

At first sight it looks as though White has nothing; one would expect the Pawns to be exchanged and a drawish position to be reached. Keres, however, comes up with something.

7. B—KKt5!   Q—R4ch

The point is that after 7. . . . B—K2; 8. B x B Black must play 8. . . . K x B, since 8. . . . Q x B loses a Pawn after 9. P x BP.

8. P—B3   P x QP

Apparently strong, for if 9. Q x P, Kt—B3; 10. Q—KB4, P x P;

11. Kt x P, Q—B2 ! with a good game.

9. B—Q3 !   P x BP
10. O—O !   P x KtP ?

But this is too much. With 10.
. . . Kt—B3; 11. R—K1, B—K3
Black still has an adequate defense.

11. R—Kt1   P x P
12. Kt x P   B—Q3

After twelve moves the opening looks more like a King's Gambit than a Sicilian Defense! Black expects 13. R—K1, O—O; 14. Q—R5, P—B4 ! with good defensive possibilities.

13. Kt x P !!   . . . .

Tears Black's position apart.

13. . . . .   K x Kt
14. Q—R5ch   P—Kt3

There is nothing better. If 14.
. . . K—B1; 15. KR—K1, B—Q2;
16. R—K3 and R—B3ch.

15. B x Pch   P x B
16. Q x R   . . . .

Black's King is now too exposed. The rest is easy, though still pretty.

16. . . . .   B—KB4
17. KR—K1 !   . . . .

Threatening mate. R x P is also good.

17. . . . .   B—K5
18. R x B !   P x R
19. Q—B6ch   Black Resigns.

Mate follows in a few moves, e.g., 19. . . . K—Kt1; 20. Q x Pch, K—B1; 21. Q x Bch, K—B2; 22. Q—B6ch and so on.

Even against first-class competition Keres essays gambits at times. Here is one of his most successful efforts.

KERES   ELISKASES
Semmering-Baden, 1937
Sicilian Defense

1. P—K4   P—QB4
2. Kt—KB3   P—Q3
3. P—QKt4 !?   . . . .

The Wing Gambit deferred, introduced in this game.

3.	P x P
4. P–Q4	Kt–KB3
5. B–Q3	P–Q4
6. QKt–Q2	P x P
7. Kt x P	QKt–Q2

8. Kt(K4)–Kt5 !   . . . .

A brilliant idea: if in reply 8. . . . P–KR3; 9. Kt–K6 ! and Black's position is disrupted. And if 8. . . . P–K3; 9. Q–K2, threatening Kt x BP.

8. . . . .   Q–B2

Prevents 9. Kt–K6 and prepares . . . P–KR3.

9. P–B4 !!!   . . . .

The power of this move is fantastic. On 9. . . . P x P e.p.; 10. Q–Kt3 wins, for if 10. . . . P–K3; 11. Kt x BP !, K x Kt; 12. Kt–Kt5ch with a mating attack.

9.	P–KR3
10. Kt–R3	P–KKt4

Wins a tempo, but leads to a further weakening of Black's Pawns. 10. . . . P–K3 was more prudent.

11. Kt(R3)–Kt1	B–Kt2
12. Kt–K2	. . . .

This Kt has made six of White's twelve moves, yet White's position is incredibly strong.

12. . . . .   P–K4

Eliskases prefers an active defense.

13. Kt–Kt3 !	O–O
14. O–O	P–K5
15. Kt x KP	Kt x Kt
16. B x Kt	Q x P

Black's defense is as subtle as White's attack is bold. As a result of the maneuver initiated with his fourteenth move Black has forced some exchanges, always favorable for the defender, and liberated himself somewhat —but not enough!

17. B–Q3	Q–Q4
18. R–K1	P–Kt5

Playable, though 18. . . . Kt–Kt3 was simpler.

19. Kt–R4   Kt–Kt3 ?

Eliskases decides belatedly to forego the Pawn, but without good reason. If 19. . . . B x P ??; 20. Kt–B5 ! wins a piece. But 19. . . . Q x P was feasible, for if then 20. Kt–B5 ?, Q x R; 21. Q x P, K–R1 ! and should win, while if in reply to 19. . . . Q x P; 20. R–Kt1, Kt–B4 forces another favorable exchange.

20. R–Kt1	B–Q2
21. R–K4	KR–K1
22. R–B4	. . . .

A typical Keres position—the pieces are scattered all over, but the attack continues!

22. ....   Q–Q3

To play ... Kt–Q4.

23. B–Q2   Kt–Q4

Black must have been expecting 24. R–K4, R x R; 25. B x R, R–K1 with a good game.

24. R x KtP !   ....

With this sacrifice White gets an overwhelming attack against the King.

24. ....   B x R
25. Q x B   ....

The immediate threat is now Q x Bch and Kt–B5ch, winning a piece.

25. ....   Q–KB3
26. Kt–B5   K–B1
27. Kt x B !   Q x Kt
28. Q–R5   Kt–B3

Forced, to stop B x RP.

29. Q–R4   P–KR4
30. R x P   QR–B1

31. P–KR3   R–B2
32. R–Kt5 !   ....

This powerful move decides.

32. ....   R–K3
33. R x RP !   Black Resigns.

For if 33. ... Kt x R; 34. Q–Q8ch wins.

Keres can also produce masterpieces of position play. Here is one of the most impressive of his career.

RESHEVSKY   KERES

Semmering-Baden, 1937
Queen's Indian Defense

1. Kt–KB3	Kt–KB3
2. P–B4	P–K3
3. P–Q4	P–QKt3
4. P–KKt3	B–Kt2
5. B–Kt2	B–Kt5ch
6. B–Q2	B x Bch
7. Q x B	O–O
8. O–O	P–Q3
9. Q–B2	QKt–Q2
10. Kt–B3	Q–K2
11. P–K4	....

White has emerged from the opening in command of slightly

more terrain, but in this position it means little.

11.	QR—B1
12. KR—K1	P—K4
13. QR—Q1	P—B3
14. Q—R4	. . . .

A faulty plan which gets White in trouble. Better was 14. Q—Q2.

14.	R—B2 !

For if 15. Q x RP ?, R—R1 wins the Q.

15. Q—R3	R—K1
16. P—Kt3	P—Kt3
17. P x P	. . . .

Premature. It leads to an endgame in which White thought he had the better of it because of his command of the Queen file, but this advantage is deceptive. He should have waited with the exchanges.

17.	P x P
18. Q x Q	R x Q
19. B—R3	B—B1
20. P—QKt4	Kt—B1
21. B x B	R x B
22. R—Q6	. . . .

It looks as though White has a little the better of it, but Black has many resources.

22.	Kt—K1
23. R—Q3	P—B3
24. R(K1)—Q1	K—B2
25. P—QR4 ?	. . . .

The point is obscure.

25.	K—K3
26. R—Q8	R(K2)—QB2

27. K—B1	K—K2
28. R(Q8)—Q3	R—Q2

Relieves the pressure of the doubled Rooks.

29. R x Rch	Kt x R
30. K—K2	Kt—Q3

After all the maneuvering Keres finally begins to come into his own. The first step is to prod the weakened Pawns.

31. Kt—Q2	Kt—B1
32. R—QR1	Kt—K3
33. P—R5	P—QKt4
34. P x P ?	Kt—Q5ch !
35. K—Q3	P x P
36. R—QB1	K—K3
37. Kt—K2	. . . .

Hoping for a liberating exchange.

37.	Kt—B3 !

Ties down White's pieces further.

38. R—QKt1	R—Q1
39. K—B3	P—B4 !

With so many of the White

pieces immobilized, this break is decisive.

40. P x Pch   . . . .

Forced, for if 40. P—B3, P x P; 41. P x P, R—KB1 and the Rook makes a decisive entry.

40. . . . .   P x P
41. P—B3   R—QB1
42. K—Q3   Kt—K1 !

The next step is to centralize this Knight at Q4.

43. Kt—B3   Kt—B3 !

To reply to 44. Kt x P with . . . Kt—Q4.

44. R—Kt2   P—QR3
45. P—Kt4   . . . .

A desperate attempt at counter-play.

45. . . . .   P—K5ch !
46. BP x P   . . . .

On 46. K—K3, Kt—K4 is decisive.

46. . . . .   Kt—K4ch
47. K—B2   P x KtP

Black now has the majority of Pawns of the K-side, and White's pieces are still awkwardly placed.

48. K—Kt3   Kt—B5
49. Kt x Kt   R x Kt
50. R—K2   K—K4
51. R—K1   P—KR4

Stronger than capturing the Pawn.

52. R—Q1   P—R5
53. R—Q8   P—Kt6
54. P x P   P x P
55. R—Q3   . . . .

The Rook cannot get behind the passed Pawn effectively.

55. . . . .   P—Kt7 !!

A problem-like finish. If in reply 56. R—Kt3, R x Ktch ! wins, for if 57. K x R, Kt x Pch.

56. Kt—K2   R x KP
57. Kt—Kt1   R—K8 !
White Resigns.

After 58. Kt—B3ch, K—K5 it is all over.

Here are some more samples of Keres' skill.

Keres—TO PLAY

Euwe

Ninth Match Game, 1940

1.	Q x R !!
2. Q x Q	B — Q5ch
3. R — B2	R x B
4. K — B1	QR — K1 !
5. P — B5	R — K4
6. P — B6	P x P
7. R — Q2	B — B1 !
8. Kt — B4	R — K6 !
9. Q — Kt1	R — B6ch
10. K — Kt2	R x Kt !
11. P x R	R — Kt1ch
12. K — B3	B — Kt5ch

White Resigns.

Flohr

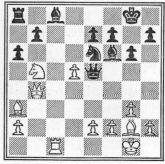

Keres—TO PLAY

Semmering-Baden, 1937

| 1. Kt — R7 !! | Kt — Q5 |

If . . . R x Kt; 2. R x Bch, Kt — B1; 3. Q — Kt6, Q — Q5; 4. B — B5, etc.

2. R x Bch	R x R
3. Kt x R	Q x KP
4. P — R4	Kt — B4
5. Q — K4	Black Resigns.

André Lilienthal

The Hungarian master André Lilienthal has been one of the tournament regulars since the early 1930's. His style at its best is on the highly imaginative side, though he is somewhat lacking in originality. Since 1935 he has settled in Russia and become a Soviet citizen. Here is his most celebrated victory.

LILIENTHAL   CAPABLANCA

Hastings, 1934–35

Nimzoindian Defense

1. P–Q4	Kt–KB3
2. P–QB4	P–K3
3. Kt–QB3	B–Kt5
4. P–QR3	. . . .

The Saemisch variation, in vogue at that time and Lilienthal's favorite.

4.	B x Ktch
5. P x B	P–QKt3

Generally 5. . . . P–B4 or 5. . . . P–Q4 is preferred.

6. P–B3	P–Q4

Thus his fifth move was a loss of time.

7. B–Kt5	P–KR3
8. B–R4	B–R3

9. P–K4 !   . . . .

An invitation to complications. If in reply 9. . . . P–KKt4; 10. B–Kt3, P x P; 11. B–K5, QKt–Q2; 12. Q–R4 !, B–Kt2; 13. P–B5 ! with a strong attack.

9.	B x P

Capa, perhaps fearing a prepared variation, decides to play it safe.

10. B x B	P x B
11. Q–R4ch	Q–Q2
12. Q x BP	Q–B3
13. Q–Q3	QKt–Q2
14. Kt–K2	R–Q1
15. O–O	P–QR4

To stop Q–R6.

16. Q–B2	. . . .

To play P–QB4, which cannot be done at once because of . . . Kt–K4.

16.	Q–B5
17. P–B4	. . . .

If 17. P–K5, Kt–Q4. The text keeps the initiative.

17.	R–QB1
18. P–B5 !	. . . .

The introduction to a beautiful combination.

18.	P–K4
19. P x P !	Q x KP

Thinking "now I'm out of it.". . .

20. P x Kt !!   . . . .

Only to find himself really in it!

20. . . . .   Q x Q
21. P x P   R – KKt1
22. Kt – Q4   Q – K5

Or 22. . . . Q – R5; 23. QR –

K1ch, Kt – K4; 24. R x Ktch, K –
Q?; 25. R – Q5ch, K – K1; 26.
R – K1 mate.

23. QR – K1   Kt – B4
24. R x Qch   Kt x R
25. R – K1   R x P
26. R x Ktch   Black Resigns.

C. H. O' D. Alexander

Although England was the leading chess country in the first half of the nineteenth century, in our times it has produced few top-notch masters. The man with the most talent, who could have gone much farther had he devoted more time to it, is C. H. O'D. Alexander. By profession Alexander is a mathematician. At one time he had the desire to become a professional chess master, but financial support was lacking.

Alexander's style is very enterprising. He avoids stereotyped variations, and prefers to go his own way, which often produces chess of much freshness and originality. Here is one of his finest efforts, a truly great game.

ALEXANDER   BOTVINNIK

Radio Match: England– U. S. S. R., 1946

French Defense

1. P – K4   P – K3
2. P – Q4   P – Q4
3. Kt – QB3   B – Kt5
4. P – K5   P – QB4
5. P – QR3   . . . .

The most aggressive line, well suited to Alexander's temperament.

5. . . . .   B x Ktch
6. P x B   Kt – K2
7. Q – Kt4   . . . .

All this is book – and Botvinnik's favorite variation.

7. . . . .   P x P

A move, says Botvinnik, which leads to a very intense struggle. This is quite in keeping with his style.

8. Q x KtP   R – Kt1
9. Q x P   Q – R4

A new idea. The older 9. . . . Q – B2 is refuted by 10. Kt – K2 !

10. R – Kt1 !   Q x Pch
11. B – Q2   Q – B2

Inconsistent. Since he is playing to win Pawns he might as well have tried 11. . . . Q x RP.

12. P – KB4   QKt – B3
13. Kt – B3   B – Q2

14. Kt–Kt5 ! ....

Botvinnik's innovation has failed; after only fourteen moves he has a lost position.

Black cannot castle because of the disintegrating effect of Kt x BP, and if *14. . . . R–KB1; 15. P–KR4* and the RP will march on to happy hunting grounds.

14. . . . .   R x Kt

The only chance; but it still requires play of a high order to refute it.

15. P x R	O–O–O
16. Q x P	Q x Pch
17. K–Q1	Kt–B4
18. P–Kt6	....

Lo and behold—he has a choice of winning lines against a Botvinnik. *18. B–Q3* was also quite sufficient.

18. . . . .   Kt–K6ch

On *18. . . . QKt–K2; 19. P–Kt7 !* wins.

19. K–B1	Q–K5
20. B–Q3	Q x P(Kt7)
21. R–K1	....

21. . . . .   Kt–K4

Botvinnik cabled after the game: "Congratulations on victory. You made the best of my mistake on the 21st move."

What he thought he could do remained a mystery until it was cleared up in his notes. He maintained that *21. . . . Kt–B5* would have held the position. But subsequent analysis showed that White can still win, the main variation running *21. . . . Kt–B5; 22. B x Kt, P x B; 23. Q–B6 !, Q x RP; 24. B–Kt5, Q–Kt6; 25. K–Kt2 !, Q–B6ch; 26. K–R2, Q x BPch; 27. R–Kt2, Q–B6; 28. P–Kt7 !, Q x R; 29. Q x Rch !, Kt x Q; 30. P–Kt8 = Q and wins.*

| 22. Q–B4 | Kt–B6 |
| 23. R–K2 | .... |

Good enough, though *23. B–R5 !* was more forceful.

23.	Q–R6
24. B x Kt	P–K4
25. Q–B7	P x B
26. P–Kt7	Q–Kt5
27. P–R3 !	Q–Kt8ch

28. K—Kt2   Q—Kt6
29. B—Kt6 !   Kt—Q5

The rest is easy.

30. P—Kt8 = Q   R x Q
31. Q x Rch   K—B2
32. Q—R7 !   . . . .

Never a dull moment. On 32.
. . . Kt x R; 33. B—B5 is decisive.

32. . . . .   K—Q3
33. B—Q3   P—K5
34. Q—R6ch   K—B2
35. R x P   Q—K4
36. K—R2 !   Kt—B4
37. Q—Kt5   B—K3
38. B—K2   P—Q5 dis ch
39. R(3)—Kt3   P—Kt4
40. Q—Q2   P—Q6
41. B—Kt4   Black Resigns.

9.

The Age of Botvinnik

WHILE Alekhine remained the official champion until his death in 1946, few felt that his strength was still what it had been. Political difficulties complicated the picture. Botvinnik with four great victories came forward more and more into the limelight and, when he took first prize at Groningen in 1946, Znosko-Borovsky publicly proclaimed him world champion.

In the years from 1939 to the present, chess supremacy gradually passed into the hands of the Russians. We have noticed time and again how chess has a way of settling in one country. In the earlier part of this century it was central Europe. Later it moved to America, and more recently to the U. S. S. R. What country will be next?

The political situation has also affected chess. Just as the political world is divided in two, the chess world is as well. Since 1948 players from behind the Iron Curtain have had virtually no contact with those from other countries, and it looks as though the situation will not change for some time. Some have even suggested two world champions—Botvinnik and one for the Western world!

Mikhail Botvinnik

Botvinnik stands for the spirit of combat in chess. Of the great masters of the past, in temperament and style he is closest to Lasker, who always emphasized that chess is a struggle from first to last.

Mikhail Botvinnik was born in 1911 in St. Petersburg, now Leningrad. He learned the moves at thirteen, which is rather late for a great master, but immediately demonstrated remarkable ability for the game. The first success of his career came in 1925, when he beat Capablanca in a simultaneous exhibition. Capa rightly predicted at that time that the boy would go far.

In 1927 Botvinnik scored his first national success—he qualified for the finals of the U. S. S. R. Championship, tied for fifth prize with Makogonov and acquired the title of master. All this at sixteen was unheard of.

The Soviet government had developed an active chess program, and the growth of the new generation was watched with great interest.

In spite of his chess prowess, Botvinnik stuck to his academic work, and became an electrical engineer, a profession in which his accomplishments are also said to be noteworthy, though not comparable with what he has done in chess. At the Nottingham tournament of 1936, Botvinnik said of Vidmar, "I wish I could do what he's done in electrical engineering," and Vidmar said of Botvinnik, "I wish I could do what he's done in chess."

He played in local Leningrad tournaments, and won everything with monotonous regularity. Then in 1931 came his big chance—the U. S. S. R. championship. After many ups and downs Botvinnik finished first—champion of his country at the age of twenty. Such a feat heralded the birth of a new world champion, but as usual people spoke of "luck" and the like, forgetting Capablanca's profound observation that the good player is always lucky.

In the ensuing years Botvinnik gradually worked his way up to a position among the world's top masters. In the U. S. S. R. championships he generally won without too much difficulty, though each time he was faced by a new and more dangerous competitor. In international competition his greatest successes came at Moscow, 1935, and Nottingham, 1936, in both of which tournaments he tied for first place.

When the war broke out, in 1939, and put a stop to international chess activity, Botvinnik was considered to be on a par with his major rivals, Alekhine, Capablanca, Euwe, Keres, Reshevsky and Fine. What happened in the ensuing years was that Botvinnik became somewhat stronger, while his opponents either retired or became weaker. Alekhine and Capablanca died, Euwe and Keres declined slightly, Reshevsky and Fine were inactive. Botvinnik impressed everybody by the magnificence of his play in four big tournaments—the Absolute Championship of the U. S. S. R. in 1941, the U. S. S. R. Championships in 1944 and 1945, and Groningen in 1946. The critics were impressed not merely by the fact that he won, but by the quality of his play.

Finally—in 1948—came the long-awaited world championship tournament. The world's five leading players were present; Fine had to decline because of his professional obligations. Botvinnik finished first by a comfortable margin. In his first test since winning the title, the match against Bronstein in 1951, Botvinnik drew after a shaky start. His play, however, was not too convincing.

Botvinnik's style is a hard one to grasp at first sight. But a closer study reveals a very consistent thread—he always seeks out the most complicated positions. If a move leads to a good fight he is for it. For this reason he sticks to certain favorite openings, which he knows to perfection. A curious feature of his style is that he often plays better with Black than with White; this is because he avoids easy drawing lines with Black and accepts involved defensive positions which other masters sidestep.

It was in a simultaneous exhibition against Capablanca that Botvinnik first came to public attention. Thirteen years later he scored an historic tournament victory against Capa which ranks among the greatest master-pieces of the game.

BOTVINNIK   CAPABLANCA

AVRO Tournament,
Holland, 1938
Nimzoindian Defense

1. P–Q4	Kt–KB3
2. P–QB4	P–K3
3. Kt–QB3	B–Kt5
4. P–K3	P–Q4
5. P–QR3 !	. . . .

An original idea, virtually un-known at that time, though it has since been analyzed a good deal. Botvinnik has a way, as here, of introducing new ideas and then discarding the variations when the novelty has worn off. He re-lies on the element of surprise much more than any of his rivals.

5.	B x Ktch
6. P x B	P–B4
7. BP x P	KP x P
8. B–Q3	O–O
9. Kt–K2	P–QKt3
10. O–O	B–R3
11. B x B	Kt x B

What has White to show for his initiative? At first glance his po-sition seems strategically bad, but he has a profound sacrificial theme in mind.

12. B–Kt2   . . . .

The alternative 12. Q–Q3 is more accurate; however, Botvin-nik is preparing a combination with the text.

| 12. . . . . | Q–Q2 |
| 13. P–QR4 | . . . . |

To stop . . . Q–R5 after White's Queen moves.

13. . . . .   KR–K1

Positionally inaccurate. Botvin-nik recommends instead 13. . . . P x P; 14. BP x P, KR–B1.

14. Q–Q3   P–B5

Capa accepts the challenge because he wishes to be admired for his courage.

15. Q—B2   Kt—Kt1
16. QR—K1 !   . . . .

Now the groundwork for the ensuing battle is laid: White sacrifices the QRP and allows Black to advance on the Q-side while he plans to break through in the center.

16. . . . .   Kt—B3

Missing a tactical opportunity: with 16. . . . Kt—R4; 17. B—B1, P—B4 ! he can offer much stronger resistance.

17. Kt—Kt3   Kt—QR4

Here again 17. . . . Kt—K5, and if 18. Kt—R1, P—B4; 19. P—B3, Kt—Q3, was better.

18. P—B3   Kt—Kt6
19. P—K4   Q x P
20. P—K5   Kt—Q2
21. Q—B2   P—Kt3
22. P—B4   P—B4

Forced.

23. P x P e.p.   Kt x BP
24. P—B5   . . . .

Capa has an extra Pawn, but the big question now is, can he hold off the attack?

24. . . . .   R x R
25. R x R   R—K1

To force more exchanges. On 25. . . . R—KB1; 26. Q—B4 !

leads to a win, e.g., 26. . . . Q—R7; 27. P x P !!, Q x B; 28. P—Kt7 !, K x P; 29. Kt—B5ch, K—R1; 30. Q—Q6, Kt—Q2; 31. Q x Kt, R—KKt1; 32. Q x QP.

26. R—K6 !!   R x R
27. P x R   K—Kt2

Actually it looks as though Black has weathered the worst, but there is much more to come!

28. Q—B4 !   . . . .

Threatening Kt—B5ch followed by Q—Kt5ch. Black does not have time to go after White's Bishop, for if 28. . . . Q—R7 ?; 29. Kt—B5ch, P x Kt; 30. Q—Kt5ch, K—B1; 31. Q x Ktch and mates in two moves.

28. . . . .   Q—K1
29. Q—K5   Q—K2

Allows a profound combination, but there was no alternative: if 29. . . . Kt—R4; 30. B—B1 !, Kt—B3; 31. B—R6ch !, K x B; 32. Q x Kt, Kt—K2; 33. P—R4 !, P—R4; 34. Kt—R5 !! wins.

30. B—R3 !!   Q x B

31. Kt—R5ch !!   P x Kt

Forced—if 31. . . . K—R3; 32. Kt x Kt wins, since Black has no perpetual check.

32. Q—Kt5ch   K—B1
33. Q x Ktch   K—Kt1
34. P—K7 !   . . . .

The Queen must remain at KB6 to avoid perpetual check. If first 34. Q—B7ch, K—R1; 35. P—K7, Q—B8ch; 36. K—B2, Q—Q7ch; 37. K—Kt3, Q x Pch; 38. K—R4, Q x Pch is sufficient for a draw.

34. . . . .   Q—B8ch
35. K—B2   Q—B7ch
36. K—Kt3   Q—Q6ch
37. K—R4   Q—K5ch
38. K x P   Q—K7ch
39. K—R4   Q—K5ch
40. P—Kt4   Q—K8ch
41. K—R5   Black Resigns.

The manner in which Botvinnik has so often managed to annihilate Keres is one of the mysteries of chess history. Here is one of his more devastating victories.

KERES   BOTVINNIK

U. S. S. R. Absolute Championship, 1941

Nimzoindian Defense

1. P—Q4   Kt—KB3
2. P—QB4   P—K3
3. Kt—QB3   B—Kt5
4. Q—B2   P—Q4
5. P x P   P x P

The alternative 5. . . . Q x P is theoretically stronger, but Botvinnik has something new in mind.

6. B—Kt5   . . . .

A two-edged move. With 6. P—QR3 White gets a solid, though minimal advantage. No doubt Botvinnik was playing psychologically, since he knows that Keres likes to complicate matters.

6. . . . .   P—KR3
7. B—R4   P—B4 !

New at the time, that is, new to Keres—not to Botvinnik. . . .

8. O—O—O ?   . . . .

An overanxious move which meets with a drastic refutation. The simple 8. P—K3 may be best, but 8. P x P is an excellent alternative, for if then 8. . . . P—KKt4; 9. B—Kt3, Kt—K5; 10. P—K3 with good chances.

8. . . . .   B x Kt !

In his game against Mikenas in the 1940 U. S. S. R. championship, Botvinnik played 8. . . . O—O ? and came out badly after 9. P x P, B x Kt; 10. Q x B. This innovation must have come as a surprise to Keres.

9. Q x B   . . . .

If first 9. B x Kt, B x Pch !

9. . . . .   P—KKt4
10. B—Kt3   P x P !
11. Q x P   Kt—B3
12. Q—QR4   B—B4

Black now has a formidable attack against the enemy King.

13. P—K3   . . . .

Loses quickly, but there was nothing really good.

| 13. . . . . | R—QB1 |
| 14. B—Q3 | Q—Q2 |

Releases the Knight—and wins.

15. K—Kt1	B x Bch
16. R x B	Q—B4
17. P—K4	. . . .

Desperation—if 17. Q—B2, Kt —Kt5.

17.	Kt x P
18. K—R1	O—O
19. R—Q1	. . . .

Or 19. Q—Q1, Kt—Kt5.

19.	P—Kt4 !
20. Q x KtP	Kt—Q5 !
21. Q—Q3	Kt—B7ch
22. K—Kt1	Kt—Kt5

White Resigns.

Nothing can be done against the discovered—double check threats.

Botvinnik has a number of pet variations which he handles with amazing skill. Here is a game which illustrates beautifully his mastery of the French Defense.

TOLUSH   BOTVINNIK

U. S. S. R. Championship,

1945
French Defense

1. P—K4	P—K3
2. P—Q4	P—Q4
3. Kt—QB3	B—Kt5

His preferred variation.

4. P—K5	P—QB4
5. P—QR3	B x Ktch
6. P x B	Kt—K2
7. Kt—B3	Q—R4

Botvinnik's continuation. His main idea is to play against the weak White Q-side Pawns, taking his chances on the K-side attack.

| 8. B—Q2 | P—B5 ! |
| 9. P—QR4 !? | . . . . |

A challenge which is accepted. 9. B—K2 is safer, though Black then gets his Queen to R5 and blocks White's Bishop.

| 9. . . . . | Kt—Q2 !! |

Announcing that he is willing to go after the QRP immediately! It takes a Botvinnik to get away with such a daring idea.

10. B—K2 . . . .

But this is too tame. Since he is going to lose a Pawn anyhow, he should play for the attack. Two interesting possibilities are 10. P—Kt3 and 10. Kt—Kt5 !

10. . . . . Kt—QKt3 !
11. O—O Kt x P !

Only two pieces developed— and he goes Pawn-hunting!

12. Kt—R4 Kt—KKt3 !
13. Kt x Kt RP x Kt

In spite of his lack of development Black already has a won game.

14. R—K1 B—Q2
15. B—KB1 . . . .

White is at a loss for good ideas . . . and the annotator is also.

15. . . . . P—QKt4
16. Q—B3 . . . .

Beginning the long-winded maneuver to free the Bishop.

16. . . . . R—QKt1
17. KR—Kt1 Q—B2
18. B—B1 P—R4 !

Botvinnik, with profound insight, sees that castling would be a serious mistake—the Rook is much more effective on the Rook file.

19. B—R3 R—Kt3 !

Preparing a sacrifice.

20. Q—Kt3 Q—Q1
21. B—Q6 ? . . . .

Underestimating the force of the sacrifice. The best try was passive play with 21. P—R3.

21. . . . . R x B !!

The most remarkable feature of this combination is that its purpose is purely positional—to liberate Black's game.

22. P x R B—B3 !
23. P—R3 K—Q2 !
24. R—K1 Q—R5 !
25. Q—K5 Q—B3
26. Q—Kt3 R—R5 !

To force the exchange of Queens.

27. R—K3 . . . .

To reply to 27. . . . . Q—B5 ? with R—B3.

27. . . . . R—B5
28. B—K2 Q—R5

At last possible.

29. B—B3 . . . .

It is not readily apparent what Black has accomplished: if the Queens are exchanged his Rook will be forced back unfavorably.

29. . . . .   P–Kt5 !

Suddenly this breakthrough turns out to be decisive.

30. Q x Q   R x Q
31. P–Kt3   . . . .

He has a chance to rid himself of the KtP by 31. P x P, P x P; 32. R–Kt1, but after 32. . . . R x QP Black's Rook enters too strongly.

Grigoriev

Botvinnik–TO PLAY

31. . . . .   R–R1
32. P x P   P x P
33. R–Kt1   R–QKt1
34. P–R4   R–Kt2
35. K–R2   K x P
36. P–Kt4   Kt–B6

Now we see what Black has accomplished. He has two Pawns for the exchange, and the Q-side Pawns may be expected to triumph.

37. R–QR1   Kt–Kt4 !
38. R–Q1   R–R2

After Black's Rook gets to the seventh rank it is all over.

39. P–R5   P–Kt4
40. K–Kt2   R–R7
41. B–K2 and White Resigns.

A magnificent game, remarkable for its profound long-range positional combinations.

Here are some more gems from the Botvinnik storehouse.

Match: Leningrad-Moscow, 1927

1. R x P !   P x R
2. P–Q6   Q–Q1
3. P x Kt   Q x R
4. Q x Rch   Kt–Kt1
5. P–B8 = Q   Black Resigns.

Botvinnik—TO PLAY

Stolberg

U. S. S. R. Championship, 1940

| 1. . . . . | R x Pch !! |
| 2. P x R | P—Q5 ! |

White Resigns.

For he cannot stop Q—Q4ch.

Botvinnik—TO PLAY

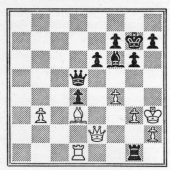

Lilienthal

Leningrad-Moscow, 1941

1.	R—Kt7 !
2. Q—K4	R x KRPch
3. K x R	Q—R4ch
4. K—Kt2	Q x R, winning another Pawn and the game.

Botvinnik—TO PLAY

H. Steiner

Groningen, 1946

| 1. . . . . | R—R5 |
| 2. Kt—B1 | B—Kt4 |

White Resigns.

For B—B5 cannot be prevented.

Yudovich

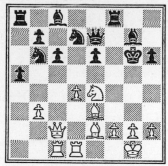

Botvinnik — TO PLAY

U. S. S. R. Championship, 1933

1. B—R5ch !!   Black Resigns.

For if 1. . . . K x B; 2. Kt—Kt3ch, K—any; 3. Q—K4ch.

Vassily Smyslov

Of the younger Soviet masters the first to achieve national and international prominence was Vassily Smyslov. For several years—from 1944 to 1948—he was Botvinnik's closest rival; more recently he has been outdistanced by Bronstein and possibly Boleslavsky. While Smyslov has scored no great successes which capture the imagination, he has been a consistent high prize winner. His style is typical of the eclecticism and striving for complications so often seen in the Soviet players. Here is an outstanding game.

SMYSLOV   KOTOV
Moscow, 1943
Sicilian Defense

1. P—K4   P—QB4
2. Kt—QB3   . . . .

Usually considered inferior, but Smyslov has made this his pet variation and does quite well with it.

2. . . . .   Kt—QB3
3. P—KKt3   P—KKt3
4. B—Kt2   B—Kt2
5. P—Q3   P—Q3

Here the old idea for White was to prepare a K-side attack by

KKt—K2, P—KB4, P—KR3, P—KKt4, etc. Experience has shown that Black can then equalize with a Q-side advance. Smyslov introduces a new wrinkle.

6. Kt—B3 !   P—K3

The main idea of White's sixth move is to reply to . . . Kt—Q5 with QKt—K2 !, which mobilizes his forces more quickly than Black's.

7. B—Kt5   KKt—K2
8. Q—Q2   P—KR3

Preferable to the risky O—O. Kotov gradually drifts into a lost position, but how—nobody knows. That is the essence of Smyslov's artistry.

9. B—K3   . . . .

To play P—Q4.

9. . . . .   P—K4
10. O—O   B—K3
11. Kt—K1   Q—Q2

Perhaps to castle on the Q-side.

12. P—QR3 !   . . . .

So that if Black does castle long, he can react with the immediate P—QKt4.

12. . . . .   B—R6

Better is . . . P—Kt3 and . . . P—Q4.

13. P—B4   Kt—Q5
14. R—Kt1   P x P
15. B x P   B x B
16. Q x B !   O—O

Black has freed himself somewhat, but Smyslov now shows that he has exposed himself to a formidable attack.

17. P—KKt4 !   QR—Q1
18. K—R1   Kt—K3
19. B—Q2   P—Q4

Normally this break equalizes for Black, but White manages to preserve the pressure.

20. Kt—B3   P—Q5

Consolidates too early; 20. . . . P—B4 was preferable.

21. Kt—K2   Kt—B3
22. Q—R3   K—R2
23. Kt—Kt3   P—B3

Kotov thinks he has solidified his position, but he is in for quite a surprise.

24. Kt—B5 !!   P x Kt
25. KtP x P   Kt—B2
26. R—Kt1   . . . .

With various neat ideas, e.g., 27. R x B ch !

26. . . . .   Kt—K1
27. R—Kt6   R—B2
28. QR—Kt1   . . . .

Smyslov's judgment is confirmed: the RP cannot be held, and the attack crashes through.

28. . . . .   K–Kt1
29. R x RP   K–B1
30. R–R7   . . . .

Threatening B–R6.

30. . . . .   K–K2
31. Q–R5 !   . . . .

No rest. Again B–R6 is threatened.

31. . . . .   K–Q3
32. B–B4ch   Kt–K4
33. B x Ktch   P x B

Again Black threatens to solidify with . . . Kt–B3.

34. P–B6 !!   . . . .

A beautiful thrust which keeps the attack alive.

34. . . . .   Kt x P
35. Q x Pch   K–B3
36. R(R7) x B   . . . .

The point. If 36. . . . R x R; 37. Q x Ktch.

36. . . . .   K–Kt4
37. Kt x Pch !   . . . .

No longer essential, but a few more sacrifices add to the charm of the game.

37. . . . .   K–Kt3
38. P–Kt4 !   R–QB1
39. R x R   Q x R
40. Q–Q6ch   R–B3

Reluctant to resign.

41. Kt x R   Kt x P
42. P x Pch   . . . .

And not 42. P x Kt ??, Q–B6ch ! with a perpetual.

42. . . . .   Black Resigns.

In the chess of the future, book knowledge will be increasingly important. Today already great masters are helpless against elaborately prepared variations. Here is a famous game in which Reshevsky comes to grief.

SMYSLOV   RESHEVSKY

Radio Match:
U. S. S. R.–U. S. A., 1945
Ruy Lopez

1. P–K4   P–K4
2. Kt–KB3   Kt–QB3
3. B–Kt5   P–QR3
4. B–R4   Kt–B3
5. O–O   Kt x P
6. P–Q4   P–QKt4
7. B–Kt3   P–Q4
8. P x P   B–K3
9. P–B3   B–QB4

The alternative . . . B–K2 is safer.

10. QKt–Q2   O–O
11. B–B2   P–B4
12. Kt–Kt3   B–Kt3
13. KKt–Q4   Kt x Kt

14. Kt x Kt   . . . .
14. . . . .   B x Kt

All "book" in Reshevsky's mind, but he discovers that Smyslov has a later edition.

15. P x B   P—B5
16. P—B3   Kt—Kt6

Still with a feeling of safety, because this had always been considered a sound sacrifice. On 16. . . . Kt—Kt4; 17. P—KR4, Kt—B2; 18. B x P, Q x P; 19. Q—Q2 White has the better of it.

17. P x Kt !   . . . .

First surprise; Reshevsky thought that the piece was untakable.

17. . . . .   P x P

18. Q—Q3 !   . . . .

The decisive rebuttal, which had been extensively analyzed by the Soviet masters.

18. . . . .   B—B4

On the alternative 18. . . . Q—R5; 19. Q x Pch, Q x Q; 20. B x Qch, Q x B; 21. B—Kt5 White wins the endgame.

19. Q x B   R x Q
20. B x R   Q—R5

21. B—R3   Q x Pch
22. K—R1   Q x KP
23. B—Q2   . . . .

At this point the American team radioed for time consumed by the Soviets. Reshevsky, who had taken an hour and a half, discovered to his consternation that Smyslov had taken exactly one minute! Then he knew what he was up against. The whole variation had been published in the June, 1945 issue of the official Soviet chess magazine!

23. . . . .   Q x P

Reshevsky had to figure everything out over-the-board, and it is just too much for mortal man. A better move is 23. . . . P—B4, but even then, analysis has shown, 24. QR—K1 !, Q x P; 25. B—B4 should win for White.

24. B—B4   P—B4
25. B—K6ch   K—R1
26. B x QP   . . . .

After this the rest is comparatively simple.

26. . . . .   R—Q1
27. QR—Q1   P—B5

28. B x KtP	P—B6
29. B—K5	P—Kt5

The alternative 29. . . . Q—K7 is neatly refuted by 30. B x P !, for if 30. . . . R x B; 31. QR—K1 ! and wins.

30. B—QKt3	R—Q7
31. P—B4	P—KR4

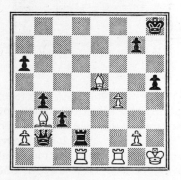

32. R—QKt1	R—KB7

A desperate stab. If 32. . . . Q—R6; 33. QR—K1, and P—B5 decides.

33. KR—K1	Q—Q7
34. QR—Q1	Q—Kt7
35. R—Q8ch	K—R2
36. B—Kt8ch	K—Kt3
37. R—Q6ch	K—B4
38. B—K6ch	K—Kt3
39. B—Q5 dis ch	K—R2
40. B—K4ch	K—Kt1
41. B—Kt6 !	Black Resigns.

Miguel Najdorf

The Polish master, Miguel Najdorf, attracted little attention outside of his own country until the team tournament at Buenos Aires in 1939. During that tournament, the war broke out and Najdorf, together with many other strong European masters, elected to remain in Argentina. Since then he has gone on from one success to another, and has won a top prize in almost every tournament in which he has played.

In contrast with a number of his colleagues, Najdorf is characterized by an exuberant self-confidence. * "I am going to be world champion," he declared in an interview with a Spanish newspaper in 1947, and since then he has made every effort to reach that goal, though without final success. The quotes from this interview are very revealing.

"My profession does not permit me to devote to chess all the attention that it merits and needs; but if I were to be invited to compete for the World Championship I would dedicate three months to the study of theory, abstaining from displays and casual games, hoping in this way to fill the vacuum in my knowledge of the openings.

"I am thirty-six years old and at the height of my powers. At first I was a 'brilliant' player, loving sacrifices."

Bit by bit he realized that a master cannot have too definite a style, that he must be the "complete player." He felt that he had achieved this

* This interview is also quoted in my book *The World's A Chessboard*.

highest ambition. Najdorf had applied his greatest energy to learning how to win won games—in almost all of the grandmasters he had observed numerous failures in this aspect of the struggle.

"I believe that I am inferior to none of the players who are to participate in the next World Championship . . . Botvinnik, Fine, Keres, Reshevsky, Euwe. None of these have a better record than I. I have played much less than they have, admittedly, but I am satisfied with my results."

Najdorf disclosed that he had rarely had occasion to play a move other than the one which struck him as best at first sight, in fact that his essential decisions came to him in master tournaments as quickly as if he were giving a simultaneous display. This filled him with confidence.

"I believe that I have the least book knowledge of all the masters; all are my superiors in theory. But as Kmoch and Tartakower (my teacher) have said, it is in the middle game and endgame that a good chessplayer reveals himself."

Najdorf has not yet made good his boast about being world champion; in fact he could not hold his own too well in the qualifying tournament at Budapest in 1950. But there is a remarkable persistence in the man. He has improved steadily at an age when most masters decline, and he may yet achieve his ambition.

In native ability for the game Najdorf is probably anybody's equal. In quick chess he is superb, and in blindfold chess incredibly phenomenal; he holds the world's record of 45 games played in Brazil in 1947. What he still lacks is the patience to build up a solid positional game; once he acquires that he may reach the top.

Najdorf first attracted world-wide attention in 1935 when he won a game which has been called the "Polish Immortal."

GLUCKSBERG   NAJDORF

Warsaw, 1935

Dutch Defense

1. P–Q4	P–KB4
2. P–QB4	Kt–KB3
3. Kt–QB3	P–K3
4. Kt–B3	P–Q4
5. P–K3?	....

Positionally weak; 5. P–KKt3 is to be preferred.

5.	P–B3
6. B–Q3	B–Q3
7. O–O	O–O
8. Kt–K2	QKt–Q2

9. Kt–Kt5?   ....

White just maneuvers and makes mistakes.

| 9. .... | B x Pch ! |
| 10. K–R1 | .... |

On 10. K x B, Kt–Kt5ch regains the piece.

10.	Kt–Kt5 !
11. P–B4	Q–K1
12. P–KKt3	Q–R4
13. K–Kt2	B–Kt8 !!
14. Kt x B	Q–R7ch
15. K–B3	....

It is not clear yet what Black has for the piece; it soon will be.

| 15. .... | P–K4 !!! |

The decisive break.

16. QP x P	QKt x Pch
17. P x Kt	Kt x Pch
18. K–B4	Kt–Kt3ch
19. K–B3	P–B5 !

Threatening . . . Q x P mate.

| 20. KP x P | .... |

20.	B–Kt5ch !!
21. K x B	Kt–K4ch !!
22. P x Kt	P–R4 mate !!

For sheer wealth of imagination this game is hard to equal.

In his first encounter with Botvinnik, Najdorf did splendidly. The game was played in the last round, when Botvinnik was assured of first prize regardless of the outcome; but the result must have given Najdorf much personal satisfaction anyhow.

NAJDORF   BOTVINNIK
Groningen, 1946
Nimzoindian Defense

| 1. P–Q4 | P–K3 |
| 2. P–QB4 | .... |

He declines the invitation to a French Defense.

| 2. .... | Kt–KB3 |

And he declines the invitation to a Dutch Defense.

3. Kt–QB3	B–Kt5
4. Q–B2	P–Q4
5. P x P	P x P
6. P–QR3	....

Avoiding Botvinnik's favorite line: 6. B–Kt5, P–KR3.

| 6. .... | B x Ktch |
| 7. P x B ! | .... |

A surprise which works out well.

7.	P–B4
8. Kt–B3	Q–R4
9. Kt–Q2 !	B–Q2
10. Kt–Kt3	Q–R5
11. Q–Kt2	....

White has the two Bishops and much positional pressure in the center.

| 11. . . . . | Kt—R3 |
| 12. P—K3 | P—B5 |

A dangerous decision. *12. . . .
R—B1* and eventually *. . . P x P*
was better.

13. Kt—Q2	O—O
14. B—K2	P—QKt4
15. B—Q1	Q—R4
16. B—B2	KR—K1
17. O—O	QR—Kt1
18. Kt—B3 !	. . . .

A subtle idea, which is stronger
than the routine *P—B3* and
P—K4.

18.	Q—B2
19. Kt—K5	B—K3
20. P—B3	. . . .

The respective strategies are
now clear—Black will advance on
the Q-side, White will attack on
the K-side.

20.	Kt—B4
21. B—Q2	Kt—R5
22. Q—Kt1 !	. . . .

Preparing to transfer the Queen
to the K-side.

22.	R—Kt3
23. Q—K1	Kt—Q2
24. Q—R4	. . . .

White's attack is in full swing.
Botvinnik has been forced into
the role of a passive defender, one
which he thoroughly dislikes.

24.	Kt—B1
25. P—K4	P—B3
26. Kt—Kt4	Kt—Kt3
27. Q—R5	. . . .

Pinning the Knight!

27.	Q—B2
28. QR—K1	R(Kt3)—Kt1
29. Kt—K3 !	Kt—K2

The difficulties mount. If in-
stead *29. . . . Kt—B5; 30. Q x
Qch, B x Q; 31. Kt x BP, Kt x
KtP; 32. K x Kt, QP x Kt; 33.
R—QKt1* wins the ending.

| 30. Q—R4 | P—B4 ? |

A definite mistake; *30. . . .
Kt—Kt3* offered better chances.

| 31. P—Kt4 ! | P—B5 |

There is no longer any defense.
If *31. . . . BP x KP; 32. P x P,
Kt—Kt3; 33. Q—R5* wins easily.

32. P x P !	Kt–Kt3
33. P x B	R x P
34. B x Kt(Kt6)	....

The rest is easy.

34.	P x B
35. Kt–Kt2	QR–K1
36. R x R	R x R
37. Kt x P	R–KB3
38. Q–Kt5	Kt x P
39. B x Kt	R x Kt
40. K–Kt2	Black Resigns.

Najdorf has never repeated his Polish Immortal, but sometimes he plays games where the opponent does not know what hit him. Here is one.

KRAMER   **NAJDORF**

New York, 1948–49
Gruenfeld Defense

1. P–Q4	Kt–KB3
2. P–QB4	P–KKt3
3. Kt–QB3	P–Q4
4. Q–Kt3	P x P
5. Q x BP	B–Kt2
6. Kt–B3	O–O
7. P–K4	....

The natural move, against which Najdorf has a prepared variation.

7.	Kt–R3 !
8. B–K2	P–B4
9. O–O ?	....

A decisive mistake. 9. P–Q5 is about the only playable move.

| 9. .... | P x P |
| 10. R–Q1 | .... |

If 10. Kt x P, Kt x P !

| 10. .... | P–K4 !! |

The brilliant refutation.

11. Kt x KP	Kt–Q2 !
12. Kt x Kt	B x Kt
13. Kt–Q5	R–B1
14. Q–Kt3	Kt–B4
15. Q–R3	R–K1 !

After a series of forced moves White finds himself faced by an overwhelming attack.

16. P–B3	P–B4 !
17. Q x P	P x P
18. P x P	Kt x P
19. B–B3	B–QB3
20. Kt–Kt4	....

| 20. .... | Kt–B7 !! |

A bolt from the Argentine.

21. Kt x B   . . . .

There is nothing better. If 21.
K x Kt, Q–R5ch; 22. K–B1, B–
Kt4ch and wins.

21. . . . . .   Kt x R !!

The point. Black's Queen may
not be captured because of the
mating threat.

22. B–Q2   P x Kt
23. R x K̃t   P–Q6

Black is the exchange ahead and
his attack continues.

24. Q–R6   Q–Q5ch
25. K̃–R1   Q x P

26. Q–B4ch   . . . .

Or 26. Q x P, QR–Q1.

26. . . . .   K–R1
27. P–KR3   P–B4
28. P–QR4   Q–Q5
29. Q x Q   B x Q
30. B–KKt4   R–B2
31. B–QR5   R–B2
32. B–K̃t6   R–B7 !

So that if 33. R x P, R–K8ch
and B–K4ch.

33. P–R5   P–Q7
34. K–R2   R–K̃8
35. K–Kt3   R x R
White Resigns.

Here is the finish from a recent Najdorf brilliancy.

Kramer

Najdorf—TO PLAY

Amsterdam International
Tournament, 1950

1. R–K6 !!   B x B
2. R x Q   P x R
3. Kt–Kt4   B–QB3
4. Kt–K5   B x K̃t
5. Q x Bch   K–Kt1
6. P–QR4   R–K1
7. Q–Q4   P–QKt4
8. P–R5 !   R–K̃3
9. P–B4   P–R3
10. K–B2   K–R2
11. P–KKt4   P–B3
**12. Q–Kt6   Black exceeded the
time-limit.**

Laszlo Szabo

Throughout the chess ages Hungary has continued to produce outstanding chess masters. Her latest product is Laszlo Szabo, who has been recognized since 1939 as one of the leading contenders for the world crown. His style is primarily on the aggressive order; his games are full of bold undertakings which lead to very pretty play. Here is a fine win of his from the first great post-war tournament.

SZABO   KOTOV

Groningen, 1946
Queen's Gambit Declined

1. P—Q4	Kt—KB3
2. P—QB4	P—K3
3. Kt—KB3	P—Q4
4. Kt—B3	P—B4
5. P—K3	....

An apparently quiet line which is not so silent as it appears.

| 5. .... | Kt—B3 |
| 6. P—QR3 | B—K2 |

Black does better to play P x BP first.

7. P x BP	B x P
8. P—QKt4	B—Kt3
9. B—Kt2	O—O
10. B—K2	....

10. P x P was more accurate.

| 10. .... | P x P |
| 11. B x P | Q—K2 |

The exchange of Queens is not so favorable for Black: his King is badly placed for the endgame.

12. O—O	P—QR3
13. Q—B2	B—B2
14. Kt—KKt5 !	....

A bold conception, which lends a most original twist to the game.

The idea is that on 14. . . . . P—KR3 ??; 15. Kt—Q5 !! wins, for if 15. . . . . P x Kt(Q4); 16. B x Kt.

| 14. . . . . | B x Pch !? |

The annotators have given this move a question mark, but it is difficult to suggest better. If 14. . . . P—KKt3; 15. P—B4 ! continues the attack. 14. . . . . Kt—K4 looks best.

| 15. K—R1 ! | .... |

Of course not 15. K x B, Kt—Kt5ch.

| 15. . . . . | P—R3 ? |

But this loses quickly. The best defense was 15. . . . . B—K4; 16. P—B4, B x Kt; 17. B x B, P—KKt3 with a complicated position.

16. Kt–Q5 !! . . . .

Decisive.

16.	P x Kt(Q4)
17. B x Kt	B–B4
18. Q x B	P–KKt3
19. Q x Pch	. . . .

An unnecessary refinement. After 19. B x Q, P x Q; 20. B x R, White is a Rook and a piece ahead; some of it goes back, but he still wins hands down.

19.	P x Q
20. B x Pch	R–B2
21. B x Q	P x Kt
22. K x B	Kt x B
23. B x Rch	K x B
24. QR–B1	. . . .

With the exchange and a Pawn to the good the win is easy.

24.	Kt–B3
25. KR–Q1	K–K3
26. R–B5	R–R1ch

He has scored a check anyhow.

27. K–Kt3	R–R4
28. R(Q1)–Q5	R–R1
29. R x P	Black Resigns.

As we have seen, Szabo excels in complicated positions. Here is another sample of his art.

SZABO   BOOK

Saltsjobaden, 1948
Catalan Opening

1. Kt–KB3	P–Q4
2. P–KKt3	Kt–KB3
3. B–Kt2	P–K3

Not the best defensive plan, but good enough.

4. O–O	B–K2
5. P–B4	O–O
6. P–Q4	P–B3

6. . . . P–B4 was the simplest way to equalize.

| 7. Kt–B3 | P–QKt3 |
| 8. Kt–K5 | B–R3 |

Patented by Book, says the Dutch note, which adds that he has never lost a game with it. There's always a first time . . . (rest of sentence censored).

9. P x P	BP x P
10. B–B4	KKt–Q2
11. R–B1	. . . .

Playing it safe. White had a brilliant speculative alternative available in 11. Kt x QP !, P x Kt; 12. Kt x BP !!, R x Kt; 13. B x P, which seems to give him an advantage in most variations, e.g., 13. . . . Kt–KB3; 14. B x R, QKt–Q2; 15. B–Kt2 with Rook and three Pawns for the two pieces. But Black can reply 13. . . . Kt–QB3; 14. B x Kt, Kt–B3; 15. B x R, Q x B with excellent prospects for a counterattack.

11.	Kt x Kt
12. B x Kt	P—QKt4 ?

Consistent—and bad. 12. . . . Kt—Q2 is essential to reduce White's advantage to a mini-mum.

13. P—K4 !   . . . .

A routine application of ele-mentary principles. From here on, Black does not get time to breathe.

13.	P—Kt5
14. Kt—K2	Q—R4

A desperate search. The trouble is that . . . B—Kt2 is refuted by 15. R—B7.

15. P x P	P x P

16. Kt—B4 !   . . . .

Of course! The fireworks begin.

16.	B x R
17. Q—Kt4	P—Kt3

Forced; for, if 17. . . . P—B3, there is a beautiful finish with 18. B x Pch, K—R1; 19. Kt—Kt6ch, P x Kt; 20. Q—R4 mate.

18. B x P   . . . .

Threatening 19. Kt x P and mate next.

18. . . . . .   B—Q6

The only chance. On 18. . . . Kt—Q2; 19. Q x Kt wins simply enough.

19. B x R	B—KB4
20. Q—K2	B—Kt4

Black has lost a Pawn and his game is hopelessly cramped.

21. P—KR4	B x Kt
22. B x B	Kt—Q2
23. B—B3	B—K3

Hoping against hope. On 23. . . . Q x P; 24. P—Q5 is too strong.

24. B—Q6 !   Black Resigns.

For White wins the exchange. On 24. . . . R—Q1; 25. B—B7 decides; on 24. . . . R—K1; 25. P—Q5 and it is all over.

Finally here is a splendid finish from another Szabo game.

Milner-Barry

Szabo—TO PLAY

Hastings, 1938–39

1. Q–B3 !!   . . . .

Threatening Q x KtP mate.

1. . . . .   Q–Kt3

If 1. . . . Q–KB3; 2. Kt–K7ch !

2. QR–K1 !!   K–B1

Loses, but there was no move. If 2. . . . R–B1; 3. Q x R !

3. Q–B5ch !!!   Black Resigns.

A highly original combination.

Isaac Boleslavsky

Another of the younger Soviet masters who has been a potential challenge to Botvinnik is Isaac Boleslavsky. But again, as with Smyslov, Boleslavsky's star shone for a few years, and the great hopes that had been pinned on him were not fulfilled. Today evidently the heyday of a chess master is short indeed, shorter than ever before.

Here is one of Boleslavsky's great victories, one of the most beautiful games in this collection.

KOTOV   BOLESLAVSKY
Moscow, 1945
Queen's Pawn Game

1. P–Q4   Kt–KB3
2. B–Kt5   . . . .

A little-used variation, also worth little.

2. . . . .   Kt–K5
3. B–B4   P–Q3
4. P–KB3   Kt–KB3
5. P–K4   P–KKt3
6. Q–Q2   QKt–Q2
7. B–KR6   . . . .

Ordinarily good, this move is a great loss of time.

7. . . . .   B x B
8. Q x B   P–B4 !
9. P–B3   Q–Kt3
10. Q–Q2   . . . .

A fatal retreat.

10. . . . .   P x P
11. P x P   . . . .

Black is now better developed, and initiates an attack of dazzling brilliancy.

11.	P–K4 !
12. Kt–QR3	P–Q4 !
13. P x KP	Kt(Q2) x P
14. B–Kt5ch	. . . .

Hoping for 14. . . . B–Q2; 15. B x Bch and 16. Kt–K2, which would free him slightly.

| 14. . . . . | K–B1 ! |

For 15. Q–R6ch, K–Kt1 leads to another blind alley for the White Queen.

15. P x P	K–Kt2
16. Kt–K2	P–QR3
17. B–B4	. . . .

If 17. B–R4, B–B4 and . . . QR–Q1.

| 17. . . . . | R–K1 |

Black's attack is now fully launched.

18. R–Q1	B–R6 !!
19. K–B1	Kt x BP !
20. Q–B4	. . . .

Or 20. Q–B3, R–K6.

| 20. . . . . | Kt–Kt5 ! |

Too many Black pieces crowd in!

21. Q x Kt(B3)	Kt–K6ch
22. K–K1	B x P
23. Q–B2	B x R
24. R–Q3	Q–Kt5ch
25. R–Q2	QR–B1

Or 25. . . . Kt x B. The finish is easy.

26. B–Kt3	B x P !
27. B x B	Kt x B
28. Q–Q4ch	Q x Q
29. R x Q	Kt–B3

Anything else also wins.

White Resigns.

Arturito Pomar

During World War II no new adult masters appeared. But a child was born—another of the rare wonder-children in Caissa's history. He is the Spaniard Arturito Pomar, who played in the Spanish championship at ten and became a full-fledged master at thirteen.

Pomar was born at Palma, Majorca, on September 1, 1931. He learned the moves from his father at the age of five, and was winning all their games within a few months. For a number of years after that his progress was not spectacular, until at the age of ten he became sub-champion of the Balearic Isles. The champion, Dr. Ticoulat, was unable to play in the Spanish championship, and, because of this lucky accident, Arturito was admitted instead. In the preliminaries he did quite well, but in the finals he scored only three points—finishing last. At that, to score three points in a national championship at ten years of age is in itself an incredible feat.

By that time he had become known, and lionized. He spoke over Radio Madrid, was filmed, and the president of the Spanish Chess Federation presented him with a magnificent board. A group of Madrid enthusiasts gave him a bicycle and the Spanish Ministry of Education resolved to grant him a scholarship to assist in his schooling.

The press ran an interesting interview with his mother. "Arturito is a prodigy," she said, "in anything connected with calculation and concentration." But apart from this he had the normal mentality for children of his age. "When he wins, his delight is infinite; when he loses, he is just as disconsolate as any little boy who breaks a toy. One of his greatest pleasures is in children's books, comics . . . he also loves his bicycle; he makes me promise that when he wins, he shall be allowed an hour's ride on this diabolical machine; and when he loses, I have to let him ride it to console himself."

After the Spanish Championship his family moved to Spain proper, and Arturito regularly gave simultaneous exhibitions and placed in national tournaments. Soon he got to be Spain's leading player.

Pomar's first trial in a tournament outside his own country was at London in 1946. He finished tied for sixth in his section. Since then he has played in other tournaments without much success. Thus unlike the other boy wonders he has not matured to world-championship caliber, though he may yet do so.

The first serious performance which attracted world-wide attention was a draw with Alekhine, his teacher, at Gijon in 1944. And what a game it was! Many a grandmaster could be proud of it. How a boy of thirteen could have acquired such extensive opening knowledge, such a profound grasp of position play, and such a quick appreciation of tactical possibilities passes human understanding, but Arturito possessed these qualities.

ALEKHINE   **POMAR**

Gijon, 1944

Ruy Lopez

1. P—K4   P—K4
2. Kt—KB3   Kt—QB3
3. B—Kt5   P—QR3
4. B—R4   Kt—B3
5. O—O   P—Q3

One of Alekhine's favorites. Could he be playing psychological chess at thirteen ??

6. P—B3 B—Kt5

An original twist which shows how deep his understanding of the openings is.

7. P—Q4 P—QKt4
8. B—Kt3 B—K2
9. B—K3 O—O
10. QKt—Q2 R—K1

The maneuvering shows how thoroughly familiar he is with positional chess. Black's objective is to compel White to lock the center.

11. P—KR3 B—R4
12. P—Q5 Kt—R4
13. B—B2 . . . .

13. . . . . R—QB1 ?

Waste of time. 13. . . . P—B4 should have been played at once. In spite of this error, Arturito manages to hold his own.

14. P—QR4 P—B4
15. P x P P x P
16. P—KKt4 B—Kt3
17. Kt—R4 ! Kt—Q2 !

Rising to the occasion. On 17. . . . B x P ?; 18. Kt x B, Kt x Kt;

19. B x Kt, B x Kt; 20. P—Kt5 ! gives White a crushing attack.

18. Kt—B5 B x Kt
19. KtP x B . . . .

Clearly indicating his intentions —attack along the KKt file.

19. . . . . B—Kt4
20. Q—K2 P—B5 !

The usual counterattack on the Q-side. One continues to marvel —how does he know so much?

21. K—R1 R—R1
22. R—KKt1 B x B
23. Q x B Q—B3
24. R—Kt4 K—R1

Not entirely necessary; he could also have allowed the exchange of the two Rooks for the Queen by 24. . . . Kt—Kt2. But it is understandable that he would play it safe against Alekhine.

25. QR—KKt1 R—KKt1
26. Kt—B3 Kt—Kt2
27. R—R4 . . . .

27. . . . . R—R3 ?

Hereabouts he becomes too cautious. 27. . . . R—R7 was preferable.

28. Q–Kt5	Kt–Q1 !
29. Q–R5	Kt–B1
30. Kt–R2	P–Kt3 !
31. Q–R6	Q–Kt2
32. Kt–Kt4	P–B3 !

Defending himself with great calm.

33. P x P   . . . .

The threat was . . . P–Kt4.

33.	Q x P
34. Q–K3	Q–Kt4 !
35. R–R6	Q x Q
36. P x Q	Kt–Q2 !

Defends the Pawn indirectly. On 37. Kt x BP, R x Rch; 38. K x R, Kt–B2 ! saves the day.

37. R–KB1   R–R7

Content to draw against the great Alekhine.

38. Kt x BP	Kt x Kt
39. R(R6) x Kt	R x P
40. B–Q1	R(Kt1)–Kt7
41. B–B3	R–KKt6
42. B–Kt4	R(Kt6)–Kt7
43. R–R1 !?	. . . .

Alekhine dislikes drawing—and as usual he almost manages to lose.

43.	R–R7ch
44. K–Kt1	R(R7)–Kt7ch
45. K–B1	. . . .

Still trying to win.

45. . . . .   R–KR7

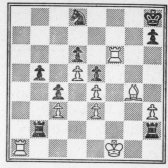

46. K–K1 ?   . . . .

He would rather lose than draw.

46. . . . .   P–Kt5 ?

Missing a great chance. 46. . . . Kt–Kt2, threatening . . . Kt–B4–Q6 and mate, wins at once. E.g., 47. R–R7, R–R8ch; 48. R–B1, R–Kt8ch decides.

47. P x P	P–B6
48. R–QB1	P–R4 !
49. B–Q1	K–Kt2
50. R–B1	P–B7
51. B–K2	Kt–B2
52. K–Q2	R x KtP
53. R x P	Kt–Kt4
54. R–QB7ch	K–Kt3
55. K–B3	R–R5
56. B–Kt5 ?	. . . .

After one try to get a win out of a drawn position—a try which should have lost—Alekhine goes in for another which should also lose! 56. K–Kt3 was necessary.

56.	Kt x Pch
57. K–Kt3	R(R5)–R7 !
58. R–Kt1ch	K–R3
59. R–Kt1	R(QR7)–Q7
60. B–Q7 !	. . . .

A last hope.

60. . . . .   R x QP
61. K—B4   . . . .

61. . . . .   R—B7ch ?

Missing his second and last chance.   61. . . . R(Q4)—Q7

wins, since Black's QP can safely advance.

62. K x R   R x R
63. K x Kt   R x B
64. P—R4   P—Q4ch

Forces the draw, but a win was no longer possible.

65. K x P   R—K2ch
66. K—B5   R x P
67. R—Kt6ch   K—R2
68. R—Q6   R—K5
69. R—Q7ch   K—R3
70. R—Q6ch   K—R2
71. R—Q7ch   K—R3

Drawn.

Svetovar Gligorich

Wars have a way of warping men's minds, and it is no wonder that when they are over it takes a long time for new chess blood to appear. After the first World War, there was only a handful of grandmasters produced, and of them, only Euwe and Botvinnik eventually reached the world championship class. It was not until 1930, twelve years after the Armistice, that a whole flock of top-notch young masters came on the scene. How long it will be after World War II nobody of course can tell. So far only one new name of promise has appeared on the scene, the Yugoslav Gligorich. While he is undoubtedly a player of great talent, he must still develop a good deal before he can be considered a serious challenger for the world title. Here is a good sample of his play.

GLIGORICH   YANOFSKY

Saltsjobaden, 1948
French Defense

1. P—K4   P—K3
2. P—Q4   P—Q4
3. Kt—QB3   Kt—KB3
4. B—Kt5   B—K2
5. P—K5   KKt—Q2
6. P—KR4 !   . . . .

Alekhine's attack.

6. . . . .   P—QB4

A risky reply, but Black has nothing really safe. 6. . . . P—KB3 is now considered best, though it leads to great complications.

7. B x B   K x B

Forced, for if 7. . . . Q x B; 8. Kt–Kt5.

8. P–B4   Q–Kt3

A new try. The older 8. . . . Kt –QB3 is also felt to be in White's favor.

9. Kt–B3 !   . . . .

A venturesome sacrifice: on 9. . . . Q x P White intends 10. Kt –QKt5.

9. . . . .   Kt–QB3

This is one case where the refusal of a sacrifice is worse than acceptance. After the text Black is slowly choked to death.

10. Kt–QR4 !	Q–R4ch
11. P–B3	P x P
12. P–QKt4	Q–B2
13. Kt x P	P–QR3
14. R–R3 !	. . . .

An ingenious method of getting the Rook into the game.

14.	Kt–Kt3
15. Kt–B5	B–Q2
16. P–R4	QR–KKt1

A strange place for the Rook, but what else can he do?

17. P–QR5	Kt–B1
18. R–K3	Kt(B1)–R2
19. Kt–B3	. . . .

Black is left without maneuvering space.

19.	P–KKt3
20. Q–Q2	B–B1
21. Q–KB2	P–R4

Both sides are maneuvering for the most favorable position. What White is up to will soon become clear.

22. Q–Kt3	K–K1
23. K–B2	Kt–K2
24. B–Q3	B–Q2
25. K–Kt1	B–Kt4
26. B x Bch	Kt x B
27. R–Q3	Kt–R2
28. R(R1)–Q1	Kt(R2)–B3
29. Q–B2	K–B1
30. Kt–Kt5	Q–B1

An elegant sacrifice which de-
stroys the Black set-up.

34. . . . .   P x R
35. P–K6 !   P–B3
36. Kt–B7   Kt–K2

He is hoping for 37. Kt x R, R x
Kt with some stabilization.

37. Q–Q4 !   . . . .

Instead he decides to try for the
mate: the threat is Kt–Q7.

The preliminaries are over, and
White now proceeds to the attack.

37. . . . .   Kt–B3
38. Q x P   R–Q1
39. Kt–Q7 !   K–Kt3

31. P–B4 !   K–Kt2
32. P x P   Kt x QP
33. P–B5 !!   KtP x P
34. R x Kt !!   . . . .

Not 39. . . . Kt–K2; 40. Q
–Q4.

40. R–KB1   Kt–K2
41. Q–Q4   Black Resigns.

David Bronstein

The youngest grandmaster on the chess firmament is the Russian,
David Bronstein. He was born in Belaya Tserkov on February 19, 1924,
and his rise to fame has been meteoric. He first attracted attention in 1944
when he beat Botvinnik in the Soviet championship; to beat Botvinnik is
always an achievement. After some hesitancy he began winning everything in sight—the Moscow City Championship, 1946, Saltsjobaden,
1948, U. S. S. R. Championship, 1949, Budapest Challengers' Tournament, 1950 and many others. Finally in 1951 came his great chance—a
title match against Botvinnik. The experts familiar with his play predicted
a tough struggle and they proved to be right—the match ended in a hard
fought tie after twenty-four games.

After his magnificent achievements of 1948–1951 Bronstein deserves to
be ranked second to Botvinnik, though how he would do against the
Americans Fine and Reshevsky must remain an open question. His style
is typical of the bold tactics adopted by the Soviet masters, with one especially original twist—his attacks come right out of the openings, which
he has studied more profoundly than his colleagues. Here is a case in point,
a game which almost won him the world's championship.

BOTVINNIK   BRONSTEIN

17th Match Game,
Moscow, 1951
Nimzoindian Defense

1. P–Q4	Kt–KB3
2. P–QB4	P–K3
3. Kt–QB3	B–Kt5
4. P–K3	. . . .

Currently in vogue.

4. . . . .   P–QKt3

A standard reply.

5. Kt–K2   B–R3 !

A new and vital idea which takes all the sting out of White's opening set-up.

| 6. P–QR3 | B–K2 ! |
| 7. Kt–Kt3 | P–Q4 ! |

The point; Black already has the initiative.

8. P x P   . . . .

This exchange leads to nothing. Yet after 8. P–Kt3, P–B4 Black also has the better of it.

8.	B x B
9. Kt x B	P x P
10. Kt–Kt3	Q–Q2

White's Bishop is hemmed in; in such positions he has the worst of it. It is astounding to note how completely Botvinnik has been outplayed.

11. Q–B3   . . . .

Intending both Kt–B5 and P–K4 when opportune.

11. . . . .   Kt–B3

If 11. . . . P–KKt3; 12. P–K4 is strong.

12. O–O   . . . .

He cannot continue as he wishes. On 12. P–K4, Kt x QP is devastating, while 12. Kt–B5, B–B1 ! is followed by . . . P–KKt3. However, had he realized the seriousness of his situation he might have played for the draw here with 12. Kt–B5, B–B1; 13. Kt–Kt3 !

12.	P–KKt3
13. B–Q2	O–O
14. Kt(B3)–K2	. . . .

Hereabouts Botvinnik operates with no definite plan. A good try was P–QKt4 followed by QR–B1 and pressure on the QB file.

14. . . . .   P–KR4 !

Meanwhile Bronstein knows exactly what he wants and goes after it.

| 15. KR–QB1 | P–R5 |
| 16. Kt–B1 | Kt–K5 |

17. Kt—B4   P—QR4 !
18. R—B2   B—Q1 !

White's attack against the QBP has been effectively stopped.

19. B—K1   Kt—K2

20. Q—K2?   . . . .

After inaccurate maneuvering he makes a serious mistake from which he never recovers. The best chance was 20. Kt—Q2, to force the exchange of Black's Knight. After the text his position goes from worse to worser.

20. . . . .   Kt—Q3
21. P—B3   P—KKt4
22. Kt—Q3   Q—K3
23. P—R4   Kt—Kt3
24. P—R3   P—KB4
25. B—B3   B—B3
26. R—K1   R(R1)—K1
27. Q—Q1   . . . .

White can do little more than mark time.

27. . . . .   R—B2
28. P—QKt3   R(B2)—K2
29. B—Kt2   P—B5 !

A beautiful conception. If in reply 30. P x P, Q x R !!; 31. Kt x Q, R x Kt; 32. Q—Q2, Kt x P, with too many threats all over the board.

30. Kt—K5   B x Kt
31. P x B   Kt—B2
32. P x P   Kt x BP
33. Kt—R2   P—B4 !

Decisive: the Bishop is blocked out of the game.

34. Kt—Kt4   . . . .

If at once 34. B—B1, Kt x KP ! wins.

34. . . . .   P—Q5

35. Kt—B6ch ??   . . . .

The fatal blunder. Although he should probably lose in the long run, there was some hope in 35. B—B1.

35. . . . .   Q x Kt !!
White Resigns.

For if 36. P x Q, R x Rch.

Even against a great theoretician like Levenfisch, Bronstein can display superior opening knowledge. And with what effect!

BRONSTEIN   LEVENFISCH
U. S. S. R. Championship,
1947
Queen's Gambit Declined

1. P—Q4   P—Q4
2. Kt—KB3   Kt—KB3
3. P—B4   P—B3

4. P–K3	P–K3
5. B–Q3	P x P
6. B x BP	QKt–Q2
7. Kt–B3	P–QKt4
8. B–Q3	P–QR3
9. P–K4	P–B4
10. P–K5	P x P

So far all according to Fine, but here White springs a new one.

11. Kt–K4	....

The main idea is if 11. . . . Kt x Kt; 12. B x Kt, R –QKt1; 13. Q x P, B–B4; 14. Q–Q2, but Black need not fear this variation.

11.	Kt–Q4
12. O–O	B–Kt2 ?

Bronstein has taken his eminent opponent by surprise. The text is a mistake; instead 12. . . . B–K2 was correct and good enough for equality.

13. B–Kt5	Q–Kt1
14. P–QR4 !	Kt x P
15. Kt x Kt	Q x Kt
16. P x P	P–QR4

17. P–B4 !   . . . .

Initiating a devastating attack.

17.	Q–Kt1
18. P–B5	Q–K4
19. P–Kt6 !	. . . .

Threatening Q–R4ch.

19.	B–Q3
20. Kt x Bch	Q x Kt
21. P x P	P–B3

Desperate already. On 21. . . . Q x KP White has his choice of winning procedures, of which perhaps the simplest is 22. R–K1, e.g., 22. . . . Kt–K6; 23. B –Kt5ch, K–B1; 24. Q x P, Q–Q4; 25. Q x Q, Kt x Q; 26. R x P !

22. Q–R5ch	K–Q1
23. B–R4	Q x KP
24. QR–K1	Kt–K6
25. Q–QB5	. . . .

This just about finishes Black off; the remainder is "kid stuff."

25.	Q–Q4
26. Q–B7ch	K–K1
27. Q x P !	R–KB1

Avoiding a pretty variation. If 27. . . . R–KKt1; 28. B–Kt5ch !!

28. B–Kt5ch !   . . . .

Anyhow!

28.	B—B3
29. B x Bch	Q x B
30. B x P	R—B2
31. Q—Kt8ch	R—B1
32. Q—Kt5	K—Q2
33. R—B2	. . . .

An inaccuracy; 33. Q—Kt7ch wins more quickly.

33.	Q x P
34. Q—Kt7ch	K—B3
35. B x P	. . . .

Now the Knight goes.

| 35. . . . . | R x R |
| 36. B x Kt ! | . . . . |

Not 36. B x Q, R x Pch !

36.	Q x P
37. R—B1ch	K—Kt4
38. Q—Kt7ch	K—R5
39. R—B4ch	K—R6
40. B—B1	Black Resigns.

Bronstein's games are usually a fight from start to finish. Here is one of his greatest.

KOTTNAUER   BRONSTEIN

Match: Moscow-Prague,

1946

King's Indian Defense

1. Kt—KB3	Kt—KB3
2. P—B4	P—Q3
3. P—KKt3	P—KKt3
4. B—Kt2	B—Kt2
5. O—O	QKt—Q2
6. P—Q4	P—K4
7. Kt—B3	O—O
8. P—Q5	. . . .

Releases the tension in the center too soon. 8. P—K4 is preferable.

8.	P—QR4
9. P—K4	Kt—B4
10. Kt—K1	Kt(B3)—Q2
11. B—K3	P—B4
12. Q—Q2	P—Kt3

The lines are drawn as usual in this position: White will push on the Q-side, Black on the K-side. The $64 question is: Who will get there first?

13. Kt—B2	B—QR3
14. Kt—R3	Kt—B3
15. P—B3	Q—K2
16. P x P	. . . .

A poor idea.

16.	P x P
17. QR—K1	P—R4
18. Kt(R3)—Kt5	Kt—R2
19. B—R3	QR—K1
20. Q—QB2	B—B1
21. Kt—R7	B—Q2
22. Kt—B6	Q—B2
23. P—Kt3	. . . .

At last he is ready for the Q-side advance.

23. . . . .   B x Kt !

Surprising—and strong.

24. P x B   Kt—K3

To play . . . P—B5 with effect.

25. Kt—Q5   Kt—Q1
26. P—R3   Kt x P
27. P—QKt4   P x P
28. P x P   Kt—Q1
29. R—R1   . . . .

White has strong pressure for the Pawn.

29. . . . .   P—B5 !

30. R—R7 !!   . . . .

The fun begins. If 30. . . . . P x B ?? 31. R x P and Black's Queen is lost.

30. . . . .   Kt—Kt4 !
31. B—B8 !   Kt(Q1)—K3
32. B x Kt   Kt x B
33. B x KtP   R—R1
34. R x R   R x R
35. B—B2   P x P
36. B x P   Kt—Q5
37. Q—KKt2   P—B3
38. Kt—Kt6   R—R3
39. P—B5   . . . .
39. . . . .   R—R7

The game is virtually decided with this infiltration.

40. Q—R3   P—Q4 !
41. K—R1   R—R6
42. P—B4 !   . . . .

The defense is brilliant, which enhances the merits of Bronstein's achievement.

42. . . . .   P—K5

On 42. . . . P x P White has 43. Q—B8ch.

43. Kt—B8   P—K6
44. Kt—Q6   Q—Kt3
45. P—Kt5 !   Kt x P
46. P—B5 !   Q—Kt5
47. Q x Q   P x Q
48. Kt x Kt   P x Kt

A wild position, with Pawns queening on all sides. The endgame must still be handled with precision.

49. P—KB6   B—B1

A bit more precise was 49. . . . . P—K7; 50. R—K1, B x P; 51. R x P, R—QB6.

50. P—B7ch   K—R2
51. P—B6   P—Kt5

The winning problem is by no means easy. If 51. . . . R—B6; 52. P—B7, P—Q5; 53. B—K5 with a probable draw.

52. R—B1   R—R1
53. P—B7   R—B1
54. R—Q1   P—Kt6 !
55. R x P   . . . .

Somewhat better was 55. K—Kt2, though 55. . . . P—Kt7 wins in any case.

55.	. . . .	P—K7
56.	R—QKt5	R x P
57.	R x P	R—B8ch
58.	K—Kt2	. . . .

Kotov

Now we have reached a problem-like position. If 58. . . . . P—K8 = Q; 59. B x Q, R x B; 60. P—R3 exchanges Black's last Pawn and draws. But . . .

58. . . . . . B—B4 !!!
White Resigns.

On 59. P—R3, R—Kt8ch; 60. K—R2, R x B wins, and on 59. B—B2, B x B; 60. P—B8 = Q, R—Kt8ch; 61. K x B, P—K8 = Q mate.

Here are some more samples of Bronstein's gems.

Moscow City Championship, 1946

Bronstein—TO PLAY

1. B—R6 !! Black Resigns.

If *1*. . . . Kt x Q; 2. B x Pch, K—Kt1; 3. B x Ktch, B—Kt4; 4. R x B mate.

Bronstein—TO PLAY

Saltsjobaden, 1948

Stoltz

1.	. . . .	Q—K7
2.	Kt(2)—B1	B x Kt !
3.	Q x Q	B x Q winning, since Black has gained a piece.

Goldenov   Kiev, 1944

Bronstein—TO PLAY

1. R—B8 !!!   Black Resigns.

Mate cannot be averted!
If *1.* . . . B x R; 2. Q x Q mate.
If *1.* . . . R x R; 2. R x R followed by mate.

Contemporary American Masters

Since 1931, when the United States team took first prize in the international team tournament at Prague, American chess masters have been in the forefront of world chess interest. Although the results of the matches with the U. S. S. R. in 1945 and 1946 were a disappointment, it is regrettable that the Soviet team did not visit New York, where the scores might have been quite different. In any event, next to the U. S. S. R., the United States easily has more top-notch masters than any other country, and may quite conceivably produce another world champion in the next ten or twenty years.

Arnold Denker

After Kashdan, Reshevsky and Fine, the first American master to enter international competition abroad was Arnold Denker. Denker won the U. S. Championship in 1944, and held the title for two years. His style is bold and forceful; he invariably plays for a winning attack. This has led to some brilliant achievements, though it has hampered his all-round development. In the following historic game, which clinched the title for him, we see him at his best.

DENKER   FINE

New York, 1944 U. S. Championship

Nimzoindian Defense

1. P—Q4	Kt—KB3	4. P—K3	P—QKt3
2. P—QB4	P—K3	5. B—Q3	B—Kt2
3. Kt—QB3	B—Kt5	6. Kt—B3	Kt—K5

7. O–O !   . . . .

An ingenious Pawn sacrifice, difficult to meet in over-the-board play.

7. . . . .   Kt x Kt

Black can safely decline the Pawn with 7. . . . B x Kt; 8. P x B, P–KB4, but he was playing to win.

8. P x Kt   B x P
9. R–Kt1   B–R4

Not 9. . . . O–O ?; 10. Q–B2.

10. B–R3   P–Q3
11. P–B5 !   O–O
12. P x QP   P x P
13. P–K4   R–K1
14. P–K5   P x P
15. Kt x P   . . . .

White's threats are already beginning to mount. The most immediate is 16. B x Pch followed by Q–R5ch.

15. . . . .   Q–Kt4 ?

The decisive mistake. After 15. . . . P–Kt3 Black's defensive resources are adequate.

16. P–Kt3   P–Kt3

Black is in hot water. On the more obvious 16. . . . Kt–B3 ?; both 17. P–R4 ! or 17. Kt x P ! wins.

17. Q–R4 !   Q–Q1

The only hope.

18. KR–B1   P–QKt4

A desperate try. On other moves Black is lost. The prettiest variation is 18. . . . Kt–R3; 19. Q x B !, P x Q; 20. R x B with a winning attack.

19. B x QKtP   Q–Q4
20. P–B3   B–Kt3

Hoping for 21. B x R, Q x Kt.

21. R–B5 !!   B x R ?

Loses immediately. There was still a lot of play left after 21. . . . Q x RP !; 22. B x R, Q x Rch; 23. R–B1, Q–B4; 24. B x Pch, K–Kt2.

22. B x B   R–KB1
23. B–B4 !   . . . .

Winning a piece.

23. . . . .   B–B3
24. B x Q   B x Q
25. B x QRP   Black Resigns.

Herman Steiner

Hungarian-born Herman Steiner has long been one of the most popular and colorful figures in American chess. Since 1932 he has settled in Los Angeles, where his chess club has attracted many of the celebrities of movieland. In 1948 he won the U. S. Championship, and has held it now for three years.

Steiner has an eclectic style. He is at his best in an aggressive defense, as in the following game.

KASHDAN   STEINER
New York, 1942
Ruy Lopez

1. P—K4	P—K4
2. Kt—KB3	Kt—QB3
3. B—Kt5	P—QR3
4. B—R4	Kt—B3
5. O—O	P—QKt4
6. B—Kt3	B—K2
7. P—QR4	R—QKt1

Black is heading for a prepared variation.

8. P x P	P x P
9. Q—K2	O—O
10. P—B3	P—Q4 !

A familiar idea in an unfamiliar setting. The Pawn cannot be accepted because White is exposed to too strong an attack, e.g., 11. P x P, Kt x P; 12. Kt x P, Kt—B5; 13. Q—K4, Kt x Kt; 14. P—Q4, Kt x P !, devastating White's position.

11. P—Q3	P—Q5

With a cute idea. . . .

12. P x P ?	. . . .

. . . . Which White does not see. 12. QKt—Q2 ! was correct

and good enough to keep the initiative at any rate.

12.	B—KKt5

The point. At the cost of an insignificant Pawn Black disrupts White's position.

13. P—Q5	. . . .

Accepting the challenge, since the alternative 13. P x P is most certainly worse.

13.	Kt—Q5
14. Q—Q1	Kt—R4 !
15. B—K3	. . . .

The pin is choking him, and there is no time to be lost in getting rid of it. On 15. QKt—Q2, Kt—B5 should win.

15.	Kt x Ktch
16. P x Kt	B—KR6
17. R—K1	B—QKt5

To gain a tempo and clear the road to the K-side for the Queen.

18. Kt—B3	. . . .

18. . . . . Kt–B5

The continuation of the attack by Black involves getting to the K-side "fustest with the mostest" wood. With the text he eventually wins the exchange but, as is often the case in an attack, material gain reduces speed and affords the defender counterchances. However, there is nothing better, for on 18. . . . Q–R5; 19. K–R1 provides an adequate defense.

19. B x Kt P x B
20. K–R1 R–Kt3

Getting thar fustest. . . .

21. R–KKt1 B x Kt
22. P x B Q–R5
23. R–Kt2 !! . . . .

He remains cool under fire. By giving up the exchange he hopes to take the sting out of Black's attack.

23. . . . . R–KR3

Too uncertain. As a rule, the capture of material stops an attack and transforms the problem into one of technique. Here Steiner must have been convinced that the rule held and accordingly preferred to postpone the gain of the exchange. Yet analysis reveals that 23. . . . B x Rch would not have slowed Black down appreciably and would have concluded more effectively than the text. After 23. . . . B x Rch; 24. K x B, R–Kt3ch; 25. K–B1, Q x RP; 26. K–K2, R–Kt7; 27. Q–B1, White's position can be pried open with 27. . . . P–Kt4 !

24. Q–KKt1 B x Rch
25. Q x B R–KKt3
26. Q–B1 Q–R4 !
27. B–Q1 . . . .

Forced, for if 27. Q–K2, R–KR3 mates.

27. . . . . R–B1 ?

Losing a vital tempo. 27. . . . P–QB3 at once was essential.

28. R–R5 ! P–QB3
29. P x P R(Kt3) x P
30. P–B4 ! R–B4
31. P–Q4 R–Kt4
32. P–B5 P–R3
33. R x P R–R1

Threatening . . . R–R8 followed by . . . R x B ! or . . . Q x BPch, or even . . . Q–R6 !

34. R–Kt1 R–R3
35. P–Q5 R(R3)–Kt3

36. P—B6 ?? . . . .

A blunder in a difficult position. With 36. B—K2 ! he could still have drawn, even though the Queen goes. The main variation runs 36. B—K2, Q—R5; 37. P—

R3, R—R4; 38. K—R2, R—Kt6 !; 39. P x R !, Q x KtPch; 40. K—R1, R x Pch; 41. Q x R, Q x Qch; 42. K—Kt1, and now Black is stopped because of White's powerful passed Pawns. The best he can do is draw by perpetual check.

36. . . . . Q—R6 !!

For if 37. Q x Q, R—Kt8 mate. Now it is all over.

37. B—K2	R—Kt7
38. Q—Kt1	R x Qch
39. R x R	R x Rch
40. K x R	Q—B1
41. B—Kt5	Q—B2

White Resigns.

Israel A. Horowitz

Al Horowitz is known not only for his over-the-board exploits, but also for his magazine, the *Chess Review*, which has been the leading American chess journal since its inception in 1933. Horowitz has played on a number of American teams, and has been one of the leading American masters since the 1920's. Here is his most famous game, which was awarded a special prize.

HOROWITZ	FLOHR

Radio Match:
U. S. A.–U. S. S. R., 1945
Caro-Kann Defense

1. P—K4	P—QB3
2. P—Q4	P—Q4
3. Kt—QB3	P x P
4. Kt x P	Kt—B3
5. Kt x Ktch	KtP x Kt

The alternative 5. . . . KP x Kt has always been considered safer, but some new attacking lines have been developed against it.

6. Kt—K2 ! . . . .

An excellent idea. White's purpose is to deprive Black's QB of good squares, and that purpose is soon accurately realized.

6.	B—B4
7. Kt—Kt3	B—Kt3
8. P—KR4	P—KR3
9. P—R5	B—R2
10. P—QB3	Q—Kt3

Playing for some counterattack on the Queen side.

11. B—QB4 ! . . . .

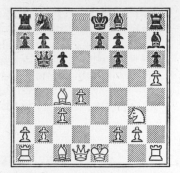

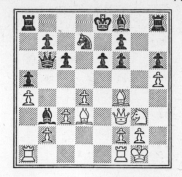

While Black's pieces are disjointed, White develops normally and soon has some major threats.

11. . . . .   Kt–Q2

Planning to play . . . P–K3 and castle on the Queen side.

12. P–R4 !   . . . .

To create a weakness there and thus prevent Black's King from finding a safe haven.

12. . . . .   P–R4

Stops P–R5, but White has achieved what he wanted, since it is now dangerous for Black to castle long.

13. Q–B3   P–K3
14. O–O   B–B7

Hoping to get this Bishop into the game more effectively.

15. B–B4 !   . . . .

The KtP is artificially defended: if *15. . . . Q x KtP ??; 16. R–R2* wins a piece.

15. . . . .   B–Kt6
16. B–Q3   . . . .

16. . . . .   P–K4

This move has been questioned, but certainly Black is at a loss for a good continuation. On *16. . . . B–K2; 17. Q–K3 !, O–O–O; 18. Kt–B5 !* is disastrous.

17. B–K3   B–Q4
18. B–K4   . . . .

Consistently playing for the attack. *18. Q–K2* was a good alternative.

18. . . . .   Q–Kt6
19. P x P   P x P
20. QR–Q1   B x B
21. Q x B   Q–K3
22. R–Q2   Kt–B3
23. Q–B3   R–KKt1
24. KR–Q1   . . . .

Black is in a tight spot. He cannot castle, he can scarcely develop.

24. . . . .   R–Kt5

Allows a decisive combination, but while many have criticized this move nobody has suggested anything better.

25. Kt–B5 !   . . . .

What? Seems to lose a piece. . . .

25. . . . .   P—K5

Where does the Queen go?

26. B—Kt6 !!!   . . . .

She doesn't, is the answer. Instead of winning a piece Black loses the exchange. For if 26. . . . B—K2; 27. Q x R ! followed by 28. Kt—Kt7ch.

26. . . . .   R x Pch
27. Q x R   Q x Kt
28. R—Q8ch   R x R

29. R x Rch   K—K2
30. Q—Kt3 !   . . . .

White must still play with precision against his wily opponent.

30. . . . .   Kt—Q2
31. B—B7   Q—Q4
32. P—QB4 !   . . . .

Forcing a decision. On 32. . . . Q—Q5 there follows 33. P—B5 ! and B x P, etc.

32. . . . .   Q—KKt4
33. Q x Qch   P x Q
34. R—R8   . . . .

From here on in it's simple.

34. . . . .   K—K3
35. B x P   P—KB4
36. B—B3   P—B5
37. P—R5   P—Kt5
38. P—Kt4   P—B6
39. B—Q2   K—B2
40. R—R7   P—Kt6
41. R x P   Black Resigns.

Arthur W. Dake

In the summer of 1930 a young sailor from Oregon appeared at the Manhattan Chess Club in New York. Usually such visitors from the "hinterlands" are greeted with disdain by snobbish New Yorkers, and Dake was no exception. How could a mere sailor from Oregon who had just learned the moves a year before be any match for the great nabobs of the metropolis? Dake took everyone by surprise. Within a few months he convinced everybody that he was right near the top, if not as good as Kashdan, then considered America's strongest player.

For several years Dake continued to impress the chess world with his natural genius for the game. At one time he held the championship of both the Marshall and the Manhattan Chess Clubs, probably the two strongest chess clubs in the world then. Then his play began to fall off somewhat. The newcomers, Fine and Reshevsky, came along and outclassed him. Unable to sustain himself as a professional chess master, Dake returned to his native Portland. Since 1936 he has rarely taken part in serious competition, though he has always remained among the top ten in the country. Dake had a natural gift for the game which has rarely been equalled. In the following game we see him defeat the great Alekhine at the height of his powers.

DAKE	ALEKHINE

Pasadena, 1932
Caro-Kann Defense

1. P–K4	P–QB3
2. P–Q4	P–Q4
3. P x P	P x P
4. P–QB4	....

A variation which Alekhine popularized.

4.	Kt–KB3
5. Kt–QB3	Kt–B3
6. Kt–B3	B–K3

A peculiar place for the Bishop, but Black wishes to force a clarification.

7. P–B5	P–KKt3
8. B–QKt5	B–Kt2
9. Kt–K5	Q–B1
10. Q–R4	B–Q2
11. O–O	O–O

As a result of the opening White controls considerably more terrain than Black, but that is still a far cry from a win against an Alekhine.

12. B–KB4	P–QR3
13. B x Kt	P x B

In such positions the two Bishops are a handicap.

14. KR–K1	Kt–R4
15. B–Q2	....

Threatening Kt x QP !

15.	R–R2
16. R–K2	B–K1
17. QR–K1	P–B4 !?

To secure a square for his Knight at K5. Typically Alekhine —he prefers to try to get himself out of his difficulties by a sacrifice.

18. Kt–B3	Kt–B3

On . . . Q–Q1; 19. Kt–KKt5 is too hard to meet.

19. R x P	R x R
20. R x R	P–B5

Another desperate try.

21. B x P	....

Dake remains cool against his famous opponent; he rightly sees that there is really nothing to be feared.

21.	Kt–K5
22. B–K5	B–R3
23. Kt x Kt	P x Kt
24. Kt–Kt5 !	Q–B4

On 24. . . . B x Kt; 25. R–Kt7ch is decisive.

25. Q–Kt3ch	B–B2
26. Kt x B	R x Kt

27. R x R   Q x R
28. Q—Kt8ch   Q—B1
29. P—Q5 !!   . . . .

The quickest: after 29. Q x Qch ?, K x Q; Black's King gets to Q4 and the ending is not so easy to win any more.

29. . . . .   P—K6 !
30. P—B4 !   Q x Q
31. B x Q   K—B2

Black must give up another

Pawn, for after 31. . . . . P x P; 32. P—B6 queens.

32. P x P   K—K1
33. P—QKt4   P—Kt4
34. P—Kt3   P x P
35. P x P   K—Q1
36. P—QR4   K—B1
37. B—Q6   B—Kt2
38. K—B1   Black Resigns.

To beat Alekhine was always a notable feat.

George Kramer

After the productive years of 1930–33 no new names of importance appeared in American chess until the war ended. The first youngster to become prominent was George Kramer, who won the New York State Championship at sixteen. Here is a victory of his which is one of the most brilliant games in this book.

KRAMER   DREXEL

New York, 1946
U. S. Championship
Reti Opening

1. Kt—KB3   P—Q4
2. P—B4   P—Q5

One of many good replies.

3. P—K3   P—QB4
4. P—QKt4   P x KP ?

But this is weak. 4. . . . P—B3 is called for.

5. BP x P   P x P
6. B—K2   Kt—KB3
7. O—O   Kt—B3
8. B—Kt2   P—K3
9. P—Q4   B—K2
10. QKt—Q2   . . . .

As compensation for his Pawn White is extremely well developed and has a powerful Pawn center—more than enough.

10. . . . .   Kt—Kt5 ?

Perchance you wonder at this play—well, wonder on. . . .

11. Q—Kt3   P—B4

Consistent. His main aim is to break the strength of P—K4. He does not succeed.

12. P—K4 !   P x P
13. Kt x P   O—O

All of White's pieces are now poised for the attack; Kramer presses his advantage home in a manner which any grandmaster could be proud of.

14. Q—Q3 !   . . . .

Threatening P—Q5—Q6 at an opportune moment, and preparing to shift his KB.

14. . . . .   Kt—B3
15. Kt—Kt3   Q—Kt3

Hoping to play . . . P—K4. . . .

16. K—R1   . . . .

. . . which is promptly stopped.

16. . . . .   Q—R4

It would be pointless to criticize Black's defense; anything else would have turned out equally badly. We ought rather to be grateful that he played in such a way as to stimulate Kramer's imaginative powers.

17. B—Q1 !   B—Q2
18. P—Q5 !   P x P
19. P x P   Kt—Kt1

Sad necessity. 19. . . . Kt x P is neatly refuted by the in-between move 20. B—B2 !, P—KKt3; 21. B—Kt3, B—K3; 22. Q—K4, B—B2; 23. Kt—K5, Kt—B3; 24. Kt x B !!, Kt x Q; 25. Kt—R6 mate!

20. B—B2   Q—Kt4

Where there are moves there is hope. The obvious 20. . . . B—Kt4 is best met by 21. Q—K3, B x R; 22. Q x B, B—B5; 23. Kt—K5, B x QP; 24. Kt—B5, B—B2; 25. B—Kt3, with a mating attack.

21. Q—Q4   Q—B4
22. Q—Q2   K—R1
23. QR—Q1   Kt—R3
24. Kt—K5 !   . . . .

Threatening R x Kt.

24. . . . .   B—Kt4

25. Kt—B5 !!   . . . .

The first of a series of dazzling combinations.

25. . . . .   B x R
26. Q—Kt5 !   . . . .

To begin with, a slight threat of mate.

26. . . . .   Kt—R4

26. . . . R—KKt1 is smothered by 27. Kt—B7 mate.

27. Kt—Kt6ch !!   . . . .

From now on every White move is a check.

27. . . . .   P x Kt

Or 27. . . . K–Kt1; 28. Kt x Bch.

28. B x Pch !!   . . . .

The real point, which White had to foresee on his twenty-fifth move. On 28. Q x P, B x Pch ! gives Black a breathing spell.

28. . . . .   K–R2

Or 28. . . . K–Kt1; 29. Kt–R6ch, K x B; 30. Q x Pch and mate next.

29. Q–R6ch   K–Kt1
30. Kt x Bch   Q x Kt

31. Q–R8ch   K–B2
32. R x Bch   Kt–B3

It looks as though Black, who is a Rook ahead, is escaping.

33. B x Pch !!!   . . . .

The last sacrifice, and the deciding one.

33. . . . .   K x B
34. Q–R6ch   K–B2
35. R x Ktch   K–K1
36. R x Rch   K–Q2
37. Q–K6ch !   . . . .

Black was threatening mate!

37. . . . .   Q x Q
38. P x Qch   K x P
39. R x R   Black Resigns.

Larry Evans

At the international team tournament in Yugoslavia, 1950, the high scorer for the American team was the eighteen-year-old Larry Evans, who won 90% of his games, the best result in the tournament. Evans' results in American tournaments are most impressive, though he has still to make his mark in individual international tournaments.

Evans has already outstripped all the other young hopefuls, and at nineteen has established himself as one of the leading American masters. In 1951 he won the United States championship ahead of Reshevsky and a number of others; he is the youngest ever to have won the title. Since the advent of Reshevsky and Fine in the early thirties no more promising master has appeared on the American scene, and time will tell whether he will yet surpass those two to become another American world champion.

Here is Evans' best game in the 1951 Championship.

EVANS   SANTASIERE

New York, 1951

Nimzoindian Defense

1. P–Q4	Kt–KB3
2. P–QB4	P–K3
3. Kt–QB3	B–Kt5
4. P–K3	P–QKt3
5. Kt–K2	Kt–K5

A weak rejoinder. 5. . . . B–R3 ! is best.

6. P–B3	Kt x Kt
7. P x Kt	B–K2
8. Kt–Kt3	Kt–B3
9. P–K4	B–R3
10. B–Q3	Kt–R4
11. Q–K2	O–O
12. O–O	P–Q4

Again a poor idea. 12. . . .

P–QB4 was best.

13. BP x P	B x B
14. Q x B	P x P
15. Kt–B5	. . . .

To lure the Rook away from the KB file.

15.	R–K1
16. P–K5	P–B4
17. P–KB4	Q–Q2
18. R–B3 !	. . . .

White's attack commences.

18.	B–B1
19. R–R3	. . . .

Threatening Kt–K7ch, which forces Black's reply.

19.	P–Kt3
20. Kt–K3	P x P
21. P x P	QR–B1

22. P–B5	Kt–B5
23. Kt–Kt4	B–Kt2

24. R x P !!	. . . .

A beautiful combination.

24.	K x R
25. Q–R3ch	K–Kt1
26. P–B6	Q x Kt

Desperation. Relatively best was 26. . . . Q–R5; 27. P x B, Q–Q8ch; 28. K–B2, Q x Pch; 29. B–K3, Q–Kt7ch; 30. K–Kt3, P–B4 !; 31. Q–R8ch, K–B2; 32. Q–R7 ! though White still wins.

27. Q x Q	B x P
28. P x B	R–K8ch

He had hoped to get some counterplay with this, but the hope is illusory.

29. K–B2	QR–K1
30. P–KR4	R(K1)–K5
31. Q–Kt5	R(K5)–K7ch
32. K–Kt3	Kt–Q3
33. K–R2	Kt–K5
34. Q x P	Kt x P
35. Q–Q8ch	Kt–K1
36. B–Kt2	R x R

37. B x R	P—B3
38. P—Q5	R—K5
39. P—Q6	R x Pch
40. K—Kt3	R—K5
41. P—Q7	Black Resigns.

Here is one of his most brilliant efforts, played when he was only fifteen.

EVANS   PILNICK

Marshall Chess Club Championship, 1947–48
French Defense

1. P—K4	P—K3
2. P—Q4	P—Q4
3. Kt—QB3	Kt—KB3
4. B—KKt5	B—K2
5. B x Kt	B x B
6. P—K5	B—K2
7. Q—Kt4	. . . .

An enterprising, but risky sortie.

7.	O—O
8. O—O—O	P—QB4
9. P—KR4	P x P
10. QKt—K2	Kt—B3
11. P—KB4	Q—R4

Playing for the counterattack, which leads to a wild and woolly game.

12. K—Kt1	P—Q6 !

13. P x P	B—Q2
14. R—R3	QR—B1

Somewhat reckless. 14. . . . . P—B4 first seems in order.

15. R—Kt3	P—KKt3
16. P—Q4	P—QKt4
17. P—R5	Kt—Kt5

The prelude to a hair-raising finish.

18. P—QR3	Kt—B3
19. P x P	BP x P
20. Kt—QB3 !	P—Kt5
21. B—Q3 !	B—K1
22. Kt—B3 !!	P x P ?

Missing his best bet: 22. . . . . R—B4 ! But for over-the-board play the combinations are almost beyond calculation.

23. Q x KPch !   B—B2

24. B x KKtP !!!   P x P

Such nonchalance! Yet the alternative 24. . . . . B x Q; 25. B x RP dbl ch is no better, e.g., 25. . . . K—R1; 26. R—R1 !, R x P ! 27. B—Q3 dis ch, B—R5; 28. Kt x B, B—Kt5; 29. Kt—Kt6ch, K—Kt2; 30, Kt x R with a winning attack.

25. B x RP dis ch	K–R1	27. K–B2	P–Kt8 = Qch
26. Q–R6	Q–R8ch	28. R x Q	Kt–Kt5ch

Black now has only a few spite
checks left.

29. K–Q1   Black Resigns.

Arthur Bisguier

Another youngster appeared on the American scene shortly after the conclusion of World War II. Arthur Bisguier has already achieved the rating of international master for winning the international tournament at Southsea, England, in 1950. He has also held the championship of the strong Manhattan Chess Club in New York twice, and has been "Open" champion of the U. S. A. The following is a forceful victory against another Manhattan Club junior.

BISGUIER   D. BYRNE

New York, 1945
Ruy Lopez

1. P–K4	P–K4
2. Kt–KB3	Kt–QB3
3. B–Kt5	P–QR3
4. B–R4	Kt–B3
5. O–O	B–K2
6. Q–K2	....

The Worrall Attack.

6.	P–QKt4
7. B–Kt3	O–O
8. P–B3	P–Q4
9. P–Q3	....

9. ....   P x P?

Logical is 9. ... P–Q5, and

if 10. P x P, B–KKt5 ! After 11. P–Q5, Kt–Q5 Black's compensation is certainly adequate.

10. P x P   P–R3

Extremely cautious.

11. R–Q1	B–Q3
12. QKt–Q2	B–Q2

Fishing for an idea. Since the pin is so annoying, he might just as well have gotten out of it at once with 12. ... Q–K1.

13. Kt–B1   R–K1

Better 13. ... Kt–K2.

14. Kt–Kt3	Kt–K2
15. Kt–R4	P–Kt4

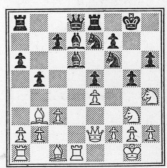

16. Kt–R5 !   . . . .

The fun begins.

16. . . . .   Kt–R2

Obviously 16. . . . Kt x Kt; 17.
Q x Kt is hopeless.

17. Q–B3   R–KB1
18. Kt–B6ch   K–R1

Forced, for if . . . Kt x Kt ??;
19. Q x Kt decides.

19. Kt x Kt   K x Kt
20. Q–R5 !   Kt–Kt3 ?

Up to this point Byrne had
atoned for some of his earlier
mistakes by very accurate defense, but here he misses the best
chance. Correct was 20. . . . P–
KB3 ! threatening not . . . P x
Kt, but . . . Q–K1. The best
after 20. . . . P–KB3 ! seems to
be 21. B–B2, Q–K1; 22. Q x Q,
QR x Q; 23. Kt–B5, Kt x Kt; 24.
P x Kt with a minimal plus.

21. Kt–B5   B x Kt
22. P x B   Kt–R1
23. R–Q3   Q–B3
24. R–R3   B–K2

Or 24. . . . K–Kt2 ?; 25. B x
KtP ! wins.

25. B–B2   . . . .

Threatening 26. B x P.

25. . . . .   R–KKt1

How does White continue?

26. P–R4 !   P–QKt5
27. B–K3   QR–Q1
28. B–K4   P x P

. . . K–Kt2 would have offered
temporary relief.

29. P x P   P–B4

. . . R–Kt1 was more to the
point.

30. R–Kt1   R–Q2

Not 30. . . . R–QKt1; 31. R x
R, R x R; 32. B x KtP.

31. K–B1 !   K–Kt2
32. P–R5   B–Q1
33. R–Kt8 !   Q–Q3

There was no good defense. If
33. . . . P–B5; 34. B x P !, P x
B; 35. Q–R7ch, K–B1; 36. R–
R6, Q–Kt2; 37. Q x Qch, K x Q;
38. R x P, P–B3; 39. R(R6)–
R8, Kt–B2; 40. P–R6 with a
winning endgame.

34. B x BP !   . . . .

Concludes nicely. Neither
Bishop nor Rook can be taken
because of the mate at KR6.

31.	Q–Q8ch
35. Q x Q	R x Qch
36. K–K2	R–QR8
37. B–Kt6 !	B x B
38. R x Rch	. . . .

Anything wins.

| 38. . . . . | K x R |
| 39. P x B | R–R7ch |

40. K–Q1	R–Kt7
41. P–Kt7	P–B3
42. K–B1	R–Kt3
43. P–QB4	Kt–B2
44. P–B5	R–Kt5
45. B–Q5	Black Resigns.

R–QKt3 or the advance of the Pawns will decide.

Hail the Unknown

Full many a chess master is born to blush unseen. Occasionally we come across games which bear the unmistakable stamp of real creative genius, yet the player has never been heard of. In honor of all the unsung heroes of the chessboard we present one such game.

ADAMS   TORRE

New Orleans, 1925
Philidor's Defense

1. P–K4	P–K4
2. Kt–KB3	P–Q3
3. P–Q4	P x P

Inferior to 3. . . . Kt–KB3.

4. Q x P	Kt–QB3
5. B–QKt5	B–Q2
6. B x Kt	B x B
7. Kt–B3	. . . .

By transposition a variation of the Ruy Lopez favorable for White has been reached.

7.	Kt–B3
8. O–O	B–K2
9. Kt–Q5	B x Kt
10. P x B	O–O
11. B–Kt5	P–B3 ?

Better 11. . . . Kt–Q2.

| 12. P–B4 | P x P |
| 13. P x P | R–K1 |

14. KR–K1	P–QR4
15. R–K2	R–QB1
16. QR–K1	Q–Q2

Black seems to be working his way out of his difficulties, but White rises to the occasion.

| 17. B x Kt ! | B x B |
| 18. Q–KKt4 !! | . . . . |

With threats of mate or loss of the Queen.

| 18. . . . . | Q–Kt4 |
| 19. Q–QB4 !!! | Q–Q2 |

Again the Queen cannot be taken because of mate.

21. P—QR4 !! Q x RP
22. R—K4 !!! Q—Kt4

20. Q—B7 !!! Q—Kt4

And still the Queen cannot be taken.

23. Q x KtP !!! Black Resigns.

A combination unique in the annals of chess.

Retrospect and Prospect

Chess has been in existence for almost two thousand years, yet as an art it began only a little over a hundred years ago. In that period several thousand masters have made their appearance, played their games and gone their way. Of these several thousand only a handful have achieved immortality. Why? Always this question arises—what makes a great chess master?

If we look over the masters described in this book, several striking facts emerge. First of all, the chess master may come from any country and any stock. Pillsbury came from middle-class Boston, Torre from a poor Mexican family, Sultan Khan from an Indian plantation. Chess supremacy on the whole has shifted from one country to another. First the greatest masters were found in Italy. Successively it became Spain, France, England, Germany, the U. S. A. and the U. S. S. R. It seems to parallel the rise of these countries as world powers. Yet where the individual genius will come from is totally unpredictable. The Cuban Capablanca, the Dutchman Euwe, the Estonian Keres, to mention only a few, all came from environments which never before and never since have produced a master of even remotely comparable strength. Although the chess strength of the U. S. S. R. as a whole is today greater than that of any other nation, where the next geniuses will come from is still anybody's guess. It is in fact surprising that Soviet Russia has produced so few native grandmasters who are near the stature of a Botvinnik.

The chess master begins young. As we turn the pages, we find increasing youth the rule. In the nineteenth century many of the great names were unknown before their thirties; today every prominent grandmaster alive has scored some notable success in his late teens, or at the most early twenties. One could almost safely say that if a chess player has not reached the national championship class before he is twenty-one he will never become world champion, and probably will never even become a grandmaster.

Genius for chess seems to be specific. Some of the great masters, like Staunton and Vidmar, have been eminent in other fields; they are the exception, not the rule. What this genius consists of we do not as yet know. That need hardly dismay us, for we know little about genius in general.

Several characteristic differences stand out, however, between the world champions and most of their challengers. World champions last longer. At his best Rubinstein was probably as good—if not better—than Lasker, but his best lasted only about five years. And why do world champions last longer? This question we can answer. They maintain themselves because they continue to grow with the growth of chess, and because they are many-sided, not one-sided. Lasker at sixty-five could master the intricacies of post-hypermodern chess sufficiently to finish third in a tournament as strong as Moscow, 1935. On the contrary, a lesser master like Bogoljubow could not grasp the new ideas which came up when he was in his forties and was bowled over by the rising generation. If we compare Lasker and Blackburne, or Capablanca and Marshall, we cannot say that the world champions had more innate ability. Blackburne's genius was extraordinary; perhaps, if such things can be measured, superior to Lasker's. But he was one-sided. He had one approach to the game—to attack—to sacrifice—to be brilliant. The positional subtleties of a Steinitz were beyond him, and once he could not attack he could not adapt himself to the situation. The world champion has always been—and must be—a past master of every phase of the game.

And finally, world champions take years to develop. As chess becomes more complex, it will no doubt take longer. But even as we know it today, the champion must be at the game from five to ten years before he has reached his true height. My own experience, I think, is typical: five years after I had learned the moves I was a master; it took me another five years to reach the grandmaster class.

Putting it all together, we can predict what the world champion of the future will be like. He may come from any country in the civilized world. He will be young; before he is twenty-one he will have done something of major importance, though the age at which he wins the title depends on historical accidents. It will take him at least ten years after he learns the moves to reach the world championship class. And he will be a many-sided genius, fully at home in every branch of the game.

Who will it be?